The Children's Literature Dictionary

DEFINITIONS, RESOURCES, AND LEARNING ACTIVITIES

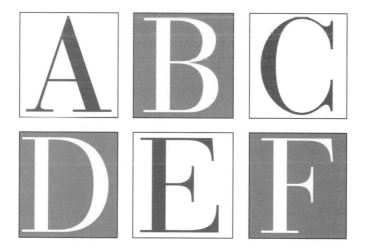

BY **KATHY H. LATROBE, CAROLYN S. BRODIE, AND MAUREEN WHITE**

D0366199

NEAL-SCHUMAN PUBLISHERS, INC.
NEW YORK   LONDON

Published by Neal-Schuman Publishers, Inc.
100 Varick Street
New York, NY 10013

Printed and bound in the United States of America

Library of Congress Cataloging-in-Publication Data

Latrobe, Kathy Howard.
    The children's literature dictionary : definitions, resources, and learning
activities / Kathy Labrobe, Carolyn S. Brodie, Maureen White.
      p. cm.
    ISBN 1-55570-424-7
    1. Children's literature—Dictionaries. 2. Literature—Terminology—
Dictionaries. 3. CriticismTerminology—Dictionaries.
  I. Brodie, Carolyn S., 1958– II. White, Maureen. III. Title.

PN1008.5 .L38 2001
809'.89282'03—dc21

                      2001044434

Dedicated to

V. J.
Jim
Dan

Contents

Preface

The Children's Literature Dictionary: Definitions, Resources, and Learning Activities is both a reference handbook and a source of innovative teaching activities for adults who plan and deliver literature programs for young people. The dictionary provides a complete yet concise examination of 325 terms relevant to the critical and applied considerations of children's literature. Each entry examines a separate term by defining it using examples. Entries for those terms frequently taught to children include recommended activities that will reinforce children's understanding and retention of its meaning and significance in literature. Moreover, when specific denotations for terms are not within a child's development range, the learning activities can still lead them conceptually into the structure and conventions of literature. Definitions include relevant information on the term's origin, history, and inclusion in related professional resources. Each term is illustrated with clear examples from quality children's literature and by relating the term's basic concepts to suggested literature activities for young people in school and public libraries and classrooms.

The following sample from *The Children's Literature Dictionary: Definitions, Resources, and Learning Activities* illustrates how a typical entry is composed:

Antagonist: Typically, the character in direct opposition to the protagonist or hero. However, antagonists can be a group of people, a setting, or the protagonist against himself. The antagonist is not necessarily a villain but is always in opposition (*e.g.*, Mr. McGregor in Beatrix Potter's *The Tale of Peter Rabbit*). However, older readers of Robert Cormier's *The Chocolate War* will find an antagonist who is a villain, the force of evil in opposition to Jerry, the protagonist. And, younger readers will recognize Voldemort as the antagonist in J.K. Rowling's *Harry Potter and the Sorcerer's Stone*. A group (Nazis) is the antagonist in the 1986 Batchelder winner, *Rose Blanche* by Roberto Innocenti in which Nazi soldiers are responsible for the starvation and death of Rose's Jewish friends and classmates. For Brian in *Hatchet* by Gary Paulsen, the northern wilderness is his antagonist when he must survive with only a small hatchet as his only tool. Illustrating the antagonist as oneself are the protagonists in Katherine Paterson's award-winning books, *The Great Gilly Hopkins*, *Jacob Have I Loved*, *Preacher's Boy*, and *Lyddie*. Young people may be introduced to the terminology of antagonist and protagonist as stories are read aloud. They may also enjoy playing a game where one young person after another names a protagonist from stories in the library and challenges others in the group to name the antagonist. They should defend their judgments when differences of opinion occur.

Professionals can prepare lessons and programs using this literature dictionary to facilitate the natural introduction or reinforcement of literary concepts as they arise in the makeup of a story and by matching a term with the appropriate developmental level of the child. Librarians and teachers who work with young people hope students will develop as critical readers through activities that encourage exploration and comprehension of the concepts and principles implicit in the terms. It's a wonderful moment when students first consider the repetitive structure typical of folktales, grasp the use of simile in a poem, or see language come alive in bold, new ways by exploring the metaphor inherent in many riddles.

The authors developed this work by building on a basic philosophy that enjoying quality folklore, picture books, fairy tales, and other genres often leads to a lifelong love of reading. Teaching children to think carefully about what they read from a young age not only aids comprehension but also may enhance critical thinking skills. These enhanced abilities encourage an awareness and appreciation of the artistic structures that increase pleasure and understanding. The prepared professional—supplied with easy-to-understand definitions, examples, and activities to illustrate the ideas and elements that make literature great—will make a difference for young readers.

AUDIENCE

The intended audience for *The Children's Literature Dictionary: Definitions, Resources, and Learning Activities* includes developers of children's and young adult collections, university students in children's literature classes, reviewers of books for young people, and librarians and teachers who plan literature programs that encourage young people to gain pleasure and understanding from books and stories. The students that these professionals teach will be the audience to ultimately benefit from this dictionary. In an age that often measures intelligence by standardized tests, knowing useful, literary terms could only increase the skill level of test takers. The dictionary indirectly aims to nurture an audience of special young people. For these students, discovering and understanding the definitions in this dictionary will encourage them to respond thoughtfully and imaginatively to the literature in their lives.

DEVELOPING THE DICTIONARY

To cull the best material for this dictionary from all the possible sources was a rewarding but daunting task. First the authors compiled a list of potentially relevant terms. Next they identified the terms by examining traditional literary dictionaries and handbooks. They searched the indices of textbooks in children's and young adult literature. They made lists as they read professional books for teachers and librarians as well as children's and young adult book reviews. Finally, they requested suggestions and recommendations from colleagues. The authors developed the entries by researching each term and its history, identifying illustrative works within the literature for young people, and devising ways to engage young people with the term's meaning in action.

SCOPE

The terms addressed in *The Children's Literature Dictionary* are a selected set that librarians and teachers encounter in reviews and criticism of books for young people (through age 14), literature programming and activity guides, literature handbooks and glossaries, and texts for children's and young adult literature. Factors that shaped the selection of the final list included the frequency of occurrence in professional resources, recommendations of practicing teachers and librarians, experts in the field, and the consensus of the authors. The selection process, both objective and subjective, resulted in the inclusion of 325 terms related to critical considerations in literature, illustrations, and programming activities.

Believing children's literature is a part of all literature, the authors approached the terms from the perspective that definitions and concepts should not shift or change in meaning for young people as they progress from one reading stage to another—that is, the terms should be relevant for lifelong reading. Therefore, words like *comedy* or *epic* are defined as they would be applied in traditional literary criticism. This treatment assumes that young people, without being able to identify a term, can be aware of some aspects implicit in the term and that, as they become more experienced readers, they will be more conscious of the term's usage and meaning. This scope of treatment is relevant to the needs of teachers and librarians who, understanding the developmental needs of young readers, guide their literature collections and programming.

The authors cite specific titles of children's literature to illustrate terms or concepts and to identify widely accessible works that are respected by professionals and that appeal to young people. The selected references to children's literature, professional resources, and Web sites were reviewed to include publications, editions, and award citations current for the time of the dictionary's publication. Web sites were chosen for their accuracy and stability.

This dictionary addresses the terms as the building blocks, or basic elements, of story as considered critically in literature programming for young people. Advantages to this term approach are efficient access and an easier ability to compare and contrast terms, such as *Comedy* and *Wit and Humor* or *Ballad* and *Narrative Poetry*. As a reference resource, it offers definitions and explanations of the terms, identifies children's and professional works, and suggests relevant activities for young people. However, it will be most useful to readers who have an awareness of the general frameworks of literary, artistic, and educational theories. With those frameworks, the terms, as building blocks, gain unity of purpose. Basic to such frameworks is the belief that an early love for story, enhanced over the years by an understanding of its form and structure, is the intrinsic motivation for lifelong reading.

ORGANIZATION AND USE

The book's alphabetical organization of the terms facilitates access to information when the reader is considering a specific term. That organizational structure is supported with many *See* and *See also* references within the dictionary entries. The dictionary boasts many useful resources (see pages 181 through 188), including a complete bibliography of the materials consulted in the preparation of the dictionary. All of the individual terms are arranged in a cross-referenced index of the entries arranged by subject—from activities to words and wordplay. Another way to discover all the literary terms cited is by utilizing the comprehensive cross-referenced title/author/term index and the subsequent author/title index. These indexes also furnish the publisher and publication date of each individual work cited throughout the dictionary.

The Children's Literature Dictionary: Definitions, Resources, and Learning Activities is dedicated to the wondrous work accomplished by the inspired adults who introduce young people to literature and may perhaps engage students into a lifelong love of reading. The authors thank all the students, teachers, librarians, and colleagues who generously offered them suggestions and advice.

Abridgement: A compressed story or retelling that shortens the text but retains major plot events. Children's books are generally short enough not to be abridged; however, publishers do abridge and market adult classics to audiences of young people. Historians consider the earliest example of an adult classic abridged for children to have been Jonathan Swift's *Gulliver's Travels* in the year following its publication. A contemporary version of Gulliver's Travels is *Gulliver in Lilliput*, retold by Margaret Hodges. Considerations on whether to include the condensation of an adult classic in a children's collection are: Will the retelling provide background and an interesting introduction to the classic, or will it spoil the classic story? And, will a young person believe that he or she has actually read the complete work? Often condensations are produced inexpensively from works no longer protected by copyright and by authors who do not invest in the imagery and figurative language of the original. Therefore, their quality is typically less than the other books in the library that have been written and reviewed with the developmental level of the child in mind.

In order for young people to understand the difference between an original story and an abridgement, they may engage in the activity of condensing a story. After hearing Patricia McKissack's *Flossie and the Fox* read aloud, they may rewrite the story as a class or in small groups using chart-sized Post-it notes. Encourage children to list each of the major concepts in the story. Compare the original with the condensed versions. Were all major events included? If someone retold the story from your framework, would it still retain the "heart" of the story? Did anyone capture phrases rich in imagery? What does the retelling reveal about the character?

Abstract Art: Nonrepresentational art; that is, art that does not resemble the real world. Because abstract art emphasizes form and not content, there has been a debate on whether it is appropriate for illustrations in children's books. In 1965 Roger Duvoisin wrote, "pure abstract painters, that is painters who have completely eliminated the subject in conceiving their paintings, have never illustrated books. Illustrative art and abstract art are too opposed to each other" (Duvoisin, 1965: 22–23). Other critics argue that all painting is abstract. And, still others would argue that abstract illustrations can support a story, citing examples like those in Kurt Vonnegut's *Sun Moon Star* and Leonard Weisgard's illustrations in Margaret Wise Brown's *The Noisy Book*. Both works demonstrate the idea that abstract art is an intellectual process that translates specific objects into universal shapes. The quality of universality holds potential for abstract illustrations to reach many more audiences in a global and multicultural environment.

Young people may experiment with abstract art by taking a favorite picture book illustration and translating it to universal colored shapes (*e.g.*, circles, triangles, squares) that create a mood but that do not represent real world objects.

Acetate: A transparent, translucent, or semi-transparent sheet of plastic which is sometimes used as a page in a children's book or as an overlay of an illustration. Acetate is also available as opaque sheets in a variety of colors. Sometimes acetate is used as a book jacket.

In Eric Carle's *Dreamsnow* clear acetate pages are inserted and covered with snowflakes and a white blanket of snow on a page preceding each illustration of a dreaming farmer and his animals. When an acetate page is turned, the reader discovers the type of animal that lies beneath the snow.

A series of information books titled "See through History" includes acetate pages which cover the outside of a building or house as in Sarah Howarth's *The Middle Ages*. When turning the acetate page (described in the book as "see-through scenes"), the reader looks inside a water mill, a castle, a monastery, and a shop. Additional books in the series with the same feature include *The Aztecs, Ancient Egypt, Ancient Greece, Ancient Rome*, and *The Renaissance*.

Young people may create hidden illustrations similar to those in *Dreamsnow* by applying opaque paint to a piece of clear transparency film. This film will serve as the overlay for a "hidden" illustration on a page underneath. Students may write an original story or poem which provides background information and hints to what might be hidden. An example might be a painted desert scene on the film which is covering a camel.

Acrostic: A puzzle within a poem that uses the first, middle, or final letter of each line to spell a word by reading the letters vertically. Acrostics may also be found in prose by reading in order the first letter of each paragraph or sentence.

Another type of acrostic is abecedarius, a literary form, typically in verse, in which the first letters of the lines or stanzas form the alphabet. Although in its most precise form each word in a line begins with the same letter, this added challenge is rarely accomplished. Examples of this form of acrostic include: Alice and Martin Provensen's *A Peaceable Kingdom: The Shaker Abecedarius;* Steven Schnur's *Spring: An Alphabet Acrostic;* or Schnur's *Autumn: An Alphabet Acrostic,* which includes acrostic poems related to fall subjects, such as acorns, bats, and corn. An example of an acrostic from *Autumn: An Alphabet Acrostic* is the use of *P, U, M, P, K, I,* and *N* for the initial letters in a seven-line poem describing a market square on a cold November day.

Young people may use the letters in their own name to create an acrostic poem by writing the letters of their name downward and then beginning each line of the poem with the initial letters. Following is an example:

> J ust when you think
> I am a good boy
> M y true self comes out!

Children may additionally be challenged to discover the pattern of the abecedarius form. A further activity could include encouraging a group of children jointly to produce and illustrate an abecedarius from a favorite alphabet book.

Acrylic: A permanent, plastic-based, modern synthetic paint which is usually water soluble, though certain types are oil compatible and may be used with turpentine or a spirit solvent. Acrylics dry quickly when applied thinly to surfaces and within a matter of hours when applied in a thick coat. They can be obtained in either paint tubes or jars can be mixed according to individual needs and used to achieve a variety of effects from washes similar to watercolors to a thick opaque, textured surface of very bright color.

Three Caldecott Honor books that have been painted with acrylics are Dav Pilkey's *The Paperboy;* Faith Ringgold's *Tar Beach;* and David Shannon's *No, David!* Young people may recreate their favorite scene from one of the picture books using acrylic paints.

Adaptation: The rewriting of a work from one form to another; or, the recast work. Examples of adaptations are folktales, literary tales, excerpts from novels that have been rewritten into the picture book format, novels that have been developed into films, and works or excerpts of works that have been developed into readers theater scripts. A rewritten work is not usually considered to be an adaptation if its author is also the author of the original.

Young people may explore the concept by developing their own adaptations or by comparing and contrasting an adaptation with its original. For example, young people could compare the original and video adaptations of Louise Fitzhugh's *Harriet, the Spy,* Maurice Sendak's *Where the Wild Things Are,* or Beverly Cleary's *The Mouse and the Motorcycle.*

Adventure Story: A fiction genre that generally plots an individual against nature and features action as the key conflict element in the story. Readers are intrigued by these stories because they are compelled to find out what happens next as characters struggle to control their sometimes uncontrollable situation. Readers often note the development or growth of characters because the adventure usually changes them in some way. Sometimes a secondary plot that reinforces the individual-against-nature conflict is included.

One of the best known adventure stories for young people is Gary Paulsen's *Hatchet.* With only a hatchet, thirteen-year-old Brian Robeson fights to survive alone in the Canadian wilderness after a tragic plane crash. Brian's challenge is both physical and personal as he struggles with both nature and himself during his ordeal. Other noted adventure stories include Scott O'Dell's *Island of the Blue Dolphins*; Jean Craighead George's *Julie of the Wolves*; Will Hobbs' *Downriver*; and Sharon Creech's *The Wanderer.*

Adventure stories for younger audiences include those similar to William Steig's *Abel's Island,* which follows the trials of Abel, a mouse. After being swept away in a torrential stream of water, he makes the best of a year while stranded on an island far away from his home. Young people will enjoy hearing adventure stories read aloud. After hearing the first chapter of an adventure book, such as *Hatchet,* they may predict events to come, either telling or writing their predictions. A popular variation of the adventure story genre is the *Choose Your Own Adventure* paperback series (Bantam) for readers ages 9–12. Young people may read aloud selections from these stories and make decisions about how they would handle a particular situation. In Vince Lahey's *River of No Return* readers choose the route for a whitewater rafting trip on Montana's Anacasta River.

Aesthetic Scanning: Capturing an image with the use of an electronic device such as a scanner to create a digital representation of an image. After the image has been scanned and is displayed on the computer screen, it can be altered, manipulated, and stored on the computer. Nina Crews' *You Are Here* is a children's book created with full-color photo collages, using Adobe Photoshop. The story follows two young girls named Mariah and Joy who can't go out In the rain to play, so they go on an imaginary trip indoors in miniature. See *Computer-generated Graphics*. Young people may enjoy applying Adobe Photoshop software to scanned images to create their own illustrations.

Afterward: A brief author's statement appended to a literary work. The statement describes the author's feelings, creative inspiration, and responses to the work's issues. A Newbery Medal book with an afterward is Lois Lowry's *Number the Stars*. There Lowry explains some of the novel's fictional elements; for example, "Annemarie Johansen is a child of my imagination though she grew there from the stories told to me by my friend Annelise Platt, to whom this book is dedicated, who was herself a child in Copenhagen during the long years of the German occupation" (Lowry, 1989: 133). Lowry also explains the novel's factual elements, such as the Danes' destruction of their own navy and the Resistance movement's use of cocaine-soaked handkerchiefs to numb the dogs' senses of smell. When reading aloud this historical novel to young people, a teacher/librarian may pause before the afterward and challenge young people to speculate which aspects of the story were imagined by Lois Lowry and which were based on history.

Airbrush or **Air brush:** A painting tool used to finely spray paint, dye, ink, or a protective coating onto a surface by using a mechanized air compressor. (Also describes the act of applying the medium.) Application of the paint or other medium can be graded for deepening color. Commercial artists often use the airbrush. Young people may be familiar with airbrush painting on t-shirts. This method of painting can be simulated by computer programs such as *Adobe Photoshop*.

Donald Crews has illustrated a number of children's books which feature illustrations using the airbrush method. The fine spray of the airbrush can be used to show movement as in Crews' 1979 Caldecott Honor book *Freight Train*, which is comprised of preseparated art and airbrush with transparent dyes. Other examples of Crews' use of the airbrush can be seen in *Sail Away*; *Flying*; and *This Is the Sunflower* (written by Lola Schaefer).

Young people may see Donald Crews demonstrate the use of an airbrush by viewing *Trumpet Video Visits Donald Crews*. If an airbrush can be borrowed from a high school art department or rented from an art supply store, young people may try their own hand at creating artwork through this medium or watch an artist demonstrate the technique. Trying to identify illustrations created with the airbrush method, young people may also look through other picture books, such as Verna Aardema's Caldecott Award-winning *Why Mosquitoes Buzz in People's Ears*, illustrated by Leo and Diane Dillon, and *Two of Everything*, retold and illustrated by Lily Toy Hong.

Allegory: Any form or genre of narrative fiction in which the characters, setting, and events take on underlying meanings different from the surface story; that is, a work that brings to mind another story. The term allegory has its roots in the Greek word *allos*, which means other. An allegory is much like a symbol; however, unlike allegory, symbol is not a continuous technique that controls the entire work. Once a reader determines that a work is an allegory, the possible interpretations for the work are limited. Thus, critics note that allegorical analysis both obscures and explains. John Bunyan's *Pilgrim's Progress* is a classic allegorical story of a man's quest and adventures in search of a city, which translates as a person's struggle on this earth to reach a safe haven or salvation. George Orwell's *Animal Farm* is an allegory of the Bolshevik Revolution and the era of Stalin that followed. Orwell's allegory demonstrates the use of animals as the personification of greed, envy, and other human attributes.

An example from children's literature is C. S. Lewis' *Chronicles of Narnia*, adventure stories that are allegorical in nature. In the first book in the series, *The Lion, the Witch, and the Wardrobe,* the stage is set for the battle of the forces of good and evil, God and the devil. Allegorically the Lion stands for Christ; the White Witch, the devil; and young Edmund, a person whose desires cause him to make wrong decisions that are harmful to all. The Lion, Aslan, gives his life to save Edmund and is later raised from the dead. Young people with access to biographical information about C. S. Lewis could explore and discuss the ways his religious principles are reflected in the *Chronicles of Narnia.*

Alliteration: A language pattern that frequently repeats the initial consonant sounds at the beginnings of words, in nearby sentences of a story, or in the lines of a poem. Alliteration often establishes the mood of a work. Alphabet books sometimes use alliterative lists in Odette and Bruce Johnson's *Apples, Alligators and also Alphabets,* which, for example, for the letter "O" includes a sea scene of an otter on the ocean in an oilskin rowing oars and looking for oysters. Anita Lobel's *Alison's Zinnia* also follows an alliterative presentation style. The book begins with

"Alison acquired an Amaryllis for Beryl," which is followed on the next page with "Beryl bought a Begonia for Chrystal." The book concludes with "Zena zeroed in on a Zinnia for Alison," coming full circle to reflect the title of the book.

Other picture books with alliteration in the text include Pamela Edwards' *Some Smug Slug* and Ann Jonas' *Watch William Walk*. Dr. Seuss used alliteration in the classic *How the Grinch Stole Christmas*. Identified also as tongue twisters, *The Sheep in a Shop*, written by Nancy Shaw and illustrated by Margot Apple, and other *Sheep* books by Nancy Shaw, incorporate the use of the letter "S" in an alliterative fashion. Jack Prelutsky uses alliteration in some of the poems that he writes for young people. For example, in his *New Kid on the Block* are poems with alliterative titles: "We Heard Wally Wail," (p. 42) and "Suzanna Socked Me Sunday" (p. 121). Older readers will recognize the humor of J. K. Rowling's alliteration, especially with names, in the *Harry Potter Series*; and they can quickly find many examples, such as ". . . said Bagman brightly" in *Harry Potter and the Goblet of Fire* (Rowling, 2000: 349).

Young people may select a favorite consonant such as "C" or "P" or "T" and write a poem which features alliteration. Help in poetry writing can be found at *Poetry Writing* with Jack Prelutsky (*http://teacher.scholastic.com/writewit/poetwit/index.htm*). Young people may work through Prelutsky's poetry writing challenges and ultimately post their poem in the online student anthology. Or, they may take the consonant of their first name and create a descriptive alliterative phrase.

Allusion: An implied or indirect reference in a literary work that asks the reader to make an association with a familiar or famous person, historic event, place, or another piece of literature or a work of art. When using allusion, a writer implies that there is a common body of knowledge that the reader will know about and understand. Poets sometimes use allusion to create imagery.

The 1992 Caldecott Honor book, Faith Ringgold's *Tar Beach,* has many allusions central to African American culture such as the past history of slavery and the slaves' "flight" to freedom. Jon Scieszka's *The Frog Prince Continued*, illustrated by Steve Johnson, alludes to several other tales such as *Hansel and Gretel, Snow White,* and *Sleeping Beauty.* Young people may read these and other children's books and identify the elements of allusion in the story.

Alphabet Book or ABC Book: Picture books that present the twenty-six letters and their sequence by depicting one or more objects which begin with the letter being considered. These books are primarily designed to help children learn their letters via creative and colorful illustrations. Books that provide beginning readers with a fun and imaginative introduction to the alphabet include John Archambault and Bill Martin's *Chicka Chicka Boom Boom* and Lois Ehlert's *Eating the Alphabet*. Young people may also consider the artistic media in alphabet books that have received the designation as Caldecott Honor book: David Pelletier's *The Graphic Alphabet*, Stephen Johnson's *Alphabet City*, Suse MacDonald's *Alphabatics*, Arnold Lobel's *On Market Street*, Muriel Feelings' *Jambo Means Hello: Swahili Alphabet Book*, illustrated by Tom Feelings, and Margaret Musgrove's *Ashanti to Zulu*, illustrated by Leo and Diane Dillon.

Children may be interested in the presentation of the alphabet in other creative forms, including Laura Rankin's *The Handmade Alphabet*, which introduces the American Sign Language's manual alphabet; Roberto De Vicq De Cumptich's *Bembo's Zoo: An Animal ABC*, which uses the Bembo typeface to illustrate the spelling of an animal's name that begins with each letter of the alphabet; and David M. Schwartz's *G Is for Googol: A Math Alphabet Book*, illustrated by Marissa Moss, which presents math terminology in alphabetical order. Young people may enjoy alphabet books that have been transformed into other mediums, such as *Chicka Chicka Boom Boom*, available in both video and audio.

Considerations for the evaluation of an alphabet book may include: (1) appropriateness of the theme; (2) organization; (3) placement and size of letters; (4) number and use of objects to illustrate the letter; (5) use of large and/or small letters; (6) use of artistic medium; and (7) intended audience. The intention of some alphabet books is to provide information about a particular subject in a logical sequence (often naming objects that begin with the sequenced letters), such as Michael McCurdy's *The Sailor's Alphabet*, which features a nautical alphabet based on a sea chant from 1837 ("Oh, A is the anchor and that you all know/ B is the bowsprit that's over the bow"). The book's rhyming verse runs across the top of the pages, and each page depicts the object on the sailing ship through McCurdy's detailed etchings. Alphabet books for a more sophisticated audience include Graeme Base's *Animalia*, which has elaborate illustrations, and *The Butterfly Alphabet* by Kjell Sandved, which features photographs of butterflies in their natural habitats around the world.

After sharing a broad selection of thematic alphabet books, young people may use the criteria listed above to compare their favorites to each other. They may work as a group to choose a theme for their own alphabet book (*e.g.*, animals, food, a place, or historical time period or event). Their alphabet book could be bound as a group or class book or displayed around a room as individual poster pages. Older students might create a tactile alphabet book with felt and fabrics for a younger class in their school. A digital camera could also be used to photograph objects, and students could create an "alphabet book" on a classroom Web page. Ideas for ABC book selection and activities are presented in Cathie

Hilterbran Cooper's professional book, *ABC Books and Activities: From Preschool to High School.*

Anagram: A word or phrase made by transposing the letters of another word or phrase. Anagrams can be games or sophisticated figures of speech as, for example, in Samuel Butler's satirical classic *Erewhon* (a transposition of *nowhere*). Anagrams have also been used to conceal information and to develop pseudonyms. Theodore Geisel (Dr. Seuss) developed the pseudonym *LeSieg* as a backward spelling of his last name. Young people may be introduced to the concept of anagrams by inventing an anagram pseudonym for a favorite author or by creating or solving anagram word pairs (*e.g.*, letters and settlers). An example of a concrete poem that incorporates an anagram is:

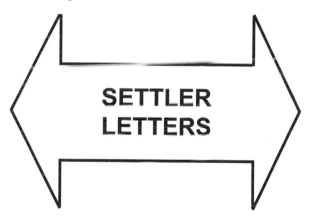

SETTLER
LETTERS

Young people may enjoy anagram wordplay in Jon Agee's *Elvis Lives*, or develop their own anagram creations with Michael Curl's *The Anagram Dictionary*, which contains 20,000 known anagrams. For a specialized type of anagram, see *Palindrome*.

Analogy: A comparison of similar things that otherwise are unlike, yet, when used together, make a connection that increases understanding. For example, the human heart is analogous to a pump, and a camera is like the human eye. Analogies are often written in the figurative language of poetry as similes (quiet as a mouse) and metaphors (it was mouse quiet).

Children can be introduced to the use of analogies through the reading of Valerie Worth's *All the Small Poems and Fourteen More*. Provide small groups with a copy of the book. A member of the group can read a poem with others in the group ready to identify the similes and metaphors. A small display may be prepared so that when children read stories and poems that contain analogies, they may write and post the analogies. For example, older children may note that the decision to drink from the spring and gain eternal life in *Tuck Everlasting* is analogous to the decision that society must make with regards to genetic altering of DNA to prolong life. Younger children might pick up on the analogy in Karen Ackerman's *Song and Dance Man*, illustrated by Stephen Gammell, in which grandfather's "tap shoes make soft, slippery sounds like rain on a tin roof."

Anapest: See *meter*.

Annotation: An explanatory statement. An annotated bibliography includes both bibliographical details and information about an entry's contents. Most fiction works contain their own summary annotation within the Library of Congress Cataloging in Publication (CIP) data.

The following classic guidelines offered by Helen Haines in *Living with Books* will assist young annotation writers; try to write the annotation as a single sentence of less than thirty-five words; do not give the ending away; avoid the second person; avoid adjectives; write in the active voice; provide information about the time and the place of the work; use action words; do not repeat the title; rarely begin an annotation with *A* or *The;* do not exaggerate the book's strengths; and check the written annotation by reading it aloud to identify awkward or repetitious wording.

Encouraging young people to write annotations about their favorite books not only strengthens their writing skills but also provides an avenue for sharing their reading and encouraging peers to read. They may post their annotations to a Web site.

Antagonist: Typically, the character in direct opposition to the protagonist or hero. However, antagonists can be a group of people, a setting, or the protagonist against himself. The antagonist is not necessarily a villain but is always in opposition (*e.g.*, Mr. McGregor in Beatrix Potter's *The Tale of Peter Rabbit*). However, older readers of Robert Cormier's *The Chocolate War* will find an antagonist who is a villain, the force of evil in opposition to Jerry, the protagonist. And, younger readers will recognize Voldemort as the antagonist in J. K. Rowling's *Harry Potter and the Sorcerer's Stone*. A group (Nazis) is the antagonist in the 1986

Batchelder winner, *Rose Blanche* by Roberto Innocenti in which Nazi soldiers are responsible for the starvation and death of Rose's Jewish friends and classmates. For Brian in *Hatchet* by Gary Paulsen, the northern wilderness is his antagonist when he must survive with a small hatchet as his only tool. Illustrating the antagonist as oneself are the protagonists in Katherine Paterson's award-winning books, *The Great Gilly Hopkins, Jacob Have I Loved, Preacher's Boy*, and *Lyddie*. Young people may be introduced to the terminology of antagonist and protagonist as stories are read aloud. They may also enjoy playing a game where one young person after another names a protagonist from stories in the library and challenges others in the group to name the antagonist. They should defend their judgments when differences of opinion occur.

Anthem: Any song of reverence, allegiance, praise, or gladness, typically one that has official recognition, such as "The Star-Spangled Banner" or "God Save the Queen." The word *anthem* shares its origin with *antiphon*, a hymn or psalm that was sung between priest and choir. In addition to singing or listening to anthems, young people can also be introduced to the concept of anthems through picture book editions of Francis Scott Key's *The Star-Spangled Banner*, illustrated by Peter Spier, or James Weldon Johnson's *Lift Every Voice and Sing*, illustrated with 1940s woodcuts by Elizabeth Catlett. For a history of the composition of "The Star-Spangled Banner" during the War of 1812, young people may read Steven Kroll's *By the Dawn's Early Light: The Story of the Star-Spangled Banner*, illustrated by Dan Andreasen.

Anthology: A collection of verse, short stories, plays, or literary excerpts from the works of various authors (known and unknown). The term originated from the Greek for *a gathering of flowers*. Anthology selections are made by an editor, and the collection is sometimes limited by genre, literary theme, or form. They are typically arranged by a table of contents and supported by indexes with author, title, and subject entries.

Poetry anthologies usually contain a wide range of works from both traditional and contemporary poets, and the variety in the selected poetry is often arranged by themes or subjects. The classic generalized anthology of children's poetry is May Hill Arbuthnot's *Time for Poetry*, which was later included in its entirety in *The Arbuthnot Anthology of Children's Literature*, 4th ed. Valuable generalized poetry anthologies for children's collections include: Beatrice Schenk de Regniers' *Sing a Song of Popcorn: Every Child's Favorite Book of Poems*; Jack Prelutsky's *The Random House Book of Poetry for Children: A Treasury of 572 Poems for Today's*

Child, illustrated by Arnold Lobel; and Helen Ferris' *Favorite Poems Old and New*. Examples of specialized anthologies, which feature poems by many poets on the same subject or theme, would include many of the edited or selected poetry books of Lee Bennett Hopkins, Nancy Larrick, and Jane Yolen. A recent specialized anthology is Naomi Shihab Nye's *Salting the Ocean: 100 Poems by Young Children*, a collection of 100 different poems by 100 different young poets. Usually, a gathering of works by one poet is known as a collection, such as Colin McNaughton's *Wish You Were Here and I Wasn't: A Book of Poems and Pictures for Globe-Trotters*.

Young people may explore other types of literary anthologies by format that include folktale collections such as Virginia Hamilton's *The People Could Fly: American Black Folktales* or mythology collections like *D'Aulaire's Book of Greek Myths* by Ingri and Edgar Parin D'Aulaire and legends such as Molly Perham's *King Arthur & the Legends of Camelot*. Nancy Van Laan's *With a Whoop and a Holler: A Bushel of Lore from Way Down South* is a specialized anthology by theme and includes rhymes, folktales, superstitions, and riddles.

Anthropomorphism: The giving of human motivations, activities, and motions to entities such as animals, inanimate objects, plants, mountains, and oceans. When writers use the technique in stories and poems, it is respected as personification, a traditional figure of speech. However, when writers apply anthropomorphism to works of nonfiction like Babette Cole's *Hair in Funny Places: A Book about Puberty* that presents Mr. and Mrs. Hormone as hairy monsters who wear wicked expressions and wield life-changing hypodermic needles, the effect can be misleading. Young people may be engaged in a discussion about what is actually known about inanimate objects or animals when they are given human attributes in information books. See *Personification*.

Apprenticeship Novel: See Bildungsroman.

Archetypal Criticism: An approach to analyzing, interpreting, and evaluating literature in which the critic focuses on a character type, a plot pattern, an image, or other literary element which occurs often enough in literature, myth, or folklore to be recognizable as part of what Carl Jung described as the "collective unconscious." Young people may be introduced to Jan deVries' identification of the characteristics of the archetypal hero from the translation of his original 1959 work *Heroic Song and Heroic Legend*: (1) a noble begetting, (2) an obscure birth, (3) a threatened youth, (4) youthful accomplishments that exceeds expectations, (5) acquisition of invulnerability, (6) fight with a monster or other extraordinary foe, (7) winning romantic love, (8) a journey to the underworld, (9) a victorious return to the home of the hero's youth, and (10) the death of hero.

Young people may discuss these characteristics of the archetypal hero in relation to the *Star Wars* film series, and they may search for them in fantasies such as J. K. Rowling's *Harry Potter Series* or Lloyd Alexander's *Prydain Series*. See *Archetype*.

Archetype: A universally recognizable element (*e.g.*, character, image, action, or structure) that recurs across all literature and life. Because these recognizable elements are not based upon experience, C. G. Jung hypothesized they were a kind of "collective unconscious" and described archetypes as "the secret to great art and its impact on us" (Campbell, 1976: 321). The word archetype is a derivation of two Greek words: *arche*, which means "original," and *typos*, which means form or model—hence, *original model*. An excellent resource on related archetypes is Marie-Luise von Franz's *Archetypal Patterns in Fairy Tales*.

A rich source of archetypes for young people is folktales. For example, one folktale archetype is the wicked stepmother found in such works as Rika Lesser's *Hansel and Gretel*, illustrated by Paul Zelinski, or Charles Perrault's *Cinderella*, illustrated by Marcia Brown. Another folktale archetype is that of the wolf as a villain. This archetypal villain is found in Wilhelm and Jacob Grimm's *Little Red Riding Hood*, retold and illustrated by Trina Schart Hyman, and Paul Galdone's *The Three Little Pigs*. The universal understanding of the wolf archetype supports the humor in Jon Scieszka's fractured tale, *The True Story of the Three Little Pigs*, illustrated by Lane Smith. Young people may explore a literary archetype, such as the wolf, by locating a variety of fiction and nonfiction books about wolves, and charting how many times wolves are portrayed positively and how many times they are portrayed negatively.

Arthurian Legends: Stories based on the legendary King Arthur and the Knights of the Round Table. Thomas Malory's *Morte d'Arthur* was probably based upon events that occurred in the fifth century, A.D., around a Welsh or Roman leader who fought Germanic invaders. The tales of this original hero grew in the oral tradition to include the stories of Arthur's queen Guinevere, Lancelot, and Arthur's illegitimate son, Mordred. The legend holds the promise that Arthur was taken to Avalon to be healed and will return when Britain needs him the most. Among award-winning children's books based upon the legend are Susan Cooper's *The Dark Is Rising Series* of which the first was *Over Sea Under Stone*; Selina Hastings' retelling of *Sir Gawain and the Loathly Lady*, illustrated by Juan Wijngaard; and *Arthur and the Sword*, retold and illustrated by Robert Sabuda. The Sabuda retelling offers young people a good introduction to Arthur. Young people who have also read Margaret Hodges' adaptation, *Saint George and the Dragon*, illustrated by Trina Schart Hyman, and Marcia Williams' *The Adventures of Robin Hood* may compare Arthur to two other British legendary figures, Saint George and Robin Hood.

Assonance: A poetry pattern consisting of the repetition of identical or similar vowel sound syllables stressed repeatedly within a single line or in a few lines of poetry; sometimes called "vowel rhyme" or "vocalic rhyme." It is different from rhyme because the consonants are not the same though the vowels match. A popular example is "Twinkle, Twinkle, Little Star" with assonance found in each of the following lines:

> Twinkle, twinkle, little star,
> How I wonder what you are!
> Up above the world so high,
> Like a diamond in the sky.
> —Anonymous

Young people may look for assonance in the following popular poetry books: Jack Prelutsky's *The New Kid on the Block*; Shel Silverstein's *Where the Sidewalk Ends*; and Shel Silverstein's *A Light in the Attic*. They may also write their own poetry that includes the repeated vowel pattern of hoop, gloom, moon, soon, toots, and boots or other vowel sound syllables of their choice.

Atmosphere: The aesthetic or emotional effect of a literary work or a part of a literary work. Generally, atmosphere is related to details of setting, and, like the plot device of foreshadowing, it directs a reader's expectations for events to come. When young people predict a story's future events from the details of setting, they are reading the work's atmosphere. Young children who examine the illustrations in the first pages of Maurice Sendak's *Where the Wild Things Are* will observe that there is a jungle-like quality to the end papers and to changes in Max's room and that Max is energetic (bounds down the stairs), plays roles (dresses in wolf suit), and creates imaginary monsters (displays his drawings on the wall), and they may predict what they think could happen. They may also consider Max's feelings when he is misbehaving or escaping into an imaginary world or returning to the place "where he is loved best of all." Older children may read Virginia Wolff's *Bat 6* and consider details (*e.g.*, the small town's focus on pre-World War II traditions, Aki's ruined home, Shazam's strange clothes as well as her hatred, and the Mikamis' neglected orchard) that communicate opposing feelings and foreshadow the novel's crisis.

Australian Children's Books of the Year Awards: A set of children's book awards administered by the Children's Book Council of Australia. The first award was presented in 1946 when there was only one category, and over the years four other categories have been added. The current five categories are: Early Childhood (2001), Young Readers (1982), Older Readers (1946), Picture Book of the Year (1952), and the Eve Pownall Award for Non-Fiction (1993). Young people may find information about Australian Children's Books of the Year Awards, the five categories, and lists of the award-winning books on the Web (*www.cbc.org.au/awards.html*); they may also find additional information on Australian awards in children's literature on the Web (*http://eddept.wa.edu.au/centoff/cmis/eval/fiction/awards/aw1.htm*).

Author: A writer or an individual who creates the text in a literary work. Although literary critics, such as Michel Foucault in "The Author as Producer," doubt the importance of the author on interpretations of text, it is accepted that young people who learn about the authors are motivated to read and to read with greater understanding. Excellent resources for information about authors are *Something About the Author* and its companion *Something About the Author: Autobiography Series.*

Authors may be introduced to young people through biographies, videotaped interviews, and personal appearances. To understand the work of an author and illustrator, young people may read Janet Stevens' *From Pictures to Words* in which she explains the management of literary elements (*e.g.*, plot, setting, and characterization). An excellent introduction to authors may be found on various sites, including the Web sites of David K. Brown (*www.calgary.ca/~dkbrown/*) and Kay Vandergrift (*www.scils.rutgers.edu/special/kay/author.html*).

Autobiography: An account of a person's life written by that person. In an autobiography the author should present a straightforward story of his or her life, which is introspective in nature, full of personal details to capture the reader's attention, and written with a specific purpose in mind.

A number of current authors and illustrators of children's books have recorded their life story to share influences that shaped their writing or illustrating, often presenting information on the background of specific works. Children may read a book by Betsy Byars, such as her *The Summer of the Swans*. Then, a teacher/librarian may read chapter seven, "The Write Stuff," from Byars' autobiography *The Moon and I*. After a class member has read the entire autobiography, that student may share with the class what he or she feels was Betsy Byars' purpose in writing the work. Others who read the autobiography may report on personal details that captured the reader's attention, influences on Byars' writing, and any facts or concepts that a biographer might not have included if writing a biography about her. Similar activities may follow the autobiographies of other writers, such as Beverly Cleary's *The Girl from Yamhill* and *On My Own Two Feet*; Sid Fleischman's *The Abracadabra Kid: A Writer's Life*; Jean Fritz's *Surprising Myself*; Lois Lowry's *Looking Back: A Book of Memories*; Bill Peet's *Bill Peet: An Autobiography*; Cynthia Rylant's *Best Wishes*; and Jerry Spinelli's *Knots in My Yo-Yo String*. A list of additional author and/or illustrator autobiographies and biographies can be found at Kay Vandergrift's Web site (*www.scils.rutgers.edu/special/kayauthorbios.html*).

Backdrop setting: See *Setting.*

Balance: The element of artistic composition that addresses the placement of visual weight within an illustration or painting. Formal balance is symmetrical; informal balance is asymmetrical. Young people may be introduced to the concept of balance by considering the analogy of a seesaw. A picture of two riders on an equally balanced seesaw, centered on a page with an imaginary line drawn vertically through the seesaw's fulcrum, is completely symmetrical. If the picture were of two riders, one in the air and one on the ground, the balance would be asymmetrical. However, in the rich visual environment of picture books, balance can be exploited in a variety of ways to communicate meaning. For example, balance can be defined horizontally, and the weight of visual objects can be controlled with color, shape, gesture, size, juxtaposition, and variety. The concept of symmetry could be introduced to young people by sharing illustrations from any picture book while reflecting halves of pages with a mirror in the manner of *Demi's Reflective Fables*, retold and illustrated by Demi. Young people may explore formal balance in Mary Lyn Ray's *Shaker Boy* and informal balance in Robert McCloskey's *Make Way for Ducklings.*

Ballad: A form of verse that tells a story. It is characterized by short stanzas, simple structure, minimal detail, a focus on a dramatic or adventurous episode, an uncomplicated and fast-paced meter, the use of dialogue to convey action, an impersonal nature, and repetition. One of the oldest forms of literature, the folk ballad developed in the oral traditions of almost all countries, and it usually was sung. The literary ballad (one originally composed by an author) is a form that remains popular. The ballad's characteristics (especially its fast-paced tempo, dialogue, and repetition) appeal to children.

Literary ballads that young people enjoy include Myra Cohn Livingston's *Keep On Singing: A Ballad of Marian Anderson*, illustrated by Samuel Byrd; Henry Wadsworth Longfellow's *Paul Revere's Ride*, illustrated by Ted Rand; and Ernest Thayer's *Casey at the Bat; A Ballad of the Republic Sung in the Year 1888*, a Caldecott Honor book illustrated by Christopher Bing.

In addition to singing popular ballads, young people could be encouraged to brainstorm a list of contemporary individuals who would make interesting subjects for a contemporary ballad, and for their favorite subjects, they could identify the events or activities that a ballad could emphasize.

Batchelder Award: See *Mildred Batchelder Award.*

Batik: A form of painting in which wax is placed in a design on a paper or fabric surface and, when the surface is dry, it is dipped into paint that does not adhere to the wax. The process can be repeated again and again with careful planning and removal of the wax after each dipping. Batik was developed by the Sumerians, improved to an art form by the Javanese, and was commercialized by the Indonesians.

Young people may find examples in several picture books. A master of the technique is Marie Hall Ets who won four Caldecott Honors for batik-illustrated works: *Just Me, Mr. Penny's Race Horse, Mr. T.W. Anthony Woo,* and *In the Forest.* Other picture book illustrators who have used batik are Edda Reinl in *The Three Little Pigs* and *The Little Snake;* Patricia MacCarthy in *The Horrendous Hullabaloo,* by Margaret Mahy; and Jan Ross in *Little Eagle Lots of Owls,* by Jim Edmiston. Young people may experiment with batik by using white wax crayons on paper to draw simple illustrations for a story and then dipping the drawings into black diluted tempera.

Battledore: A lesson book composed of three leaves of folded cardboard, including alphabets, numerals, and beginning reading material. Decorated with crude animal woodcuts and intended to instruct, battledores were used from about 1746–1770. They are believed to be a creation of Benjamin Collins.

Upper grade children may want to prepare folded three section battledores from one sheet of thin cardboard and include the alphabet in upper and lower case, numerals, and selected single words or combination of sounds. After decorating the battledores with small familiar animals, they may be presented to a first grade class as a medium of learning used over 200 years ago.

Beast Fable: An allegorical tale with animal characters that in prose or poetry conveys a cautionary message. Aesop is credited with recording the earliest fables, and Caxton published the first English version in 1484. Among collections of fables young people may browse and read are *Feathers and Tails: Animal Fables from Around the World*, retold by David Kherdian and illustrated by Caldecott Award-winning illustrator Nonny Hodgrogian; Arnold Lobel's *Caldecott Award-winning Fables*; Tom Paxton's *Aesop's Fables* and *Belling the Cat: And Other Aesop's Fables*; *The Best of Aesop*, retold by Margaret Clark; and John Bierhorst's *Doctor Coyote: A Native American Aesop's Fables*. After young people have read several fables, they may be encouraged to select a favorite one to dramatize in a small group. They may also create a display of proverbs that they have taken as quotes from fable morals or that they have created from the fables. See *Fable*.

Bestiary: A genre of literature which presents a moral by describing in either verse or prose the behavior of real or imaginary animals which have been given human characteristics. Many stereotypes of animals (*e.g.*, the lamb's gentleness and the fox's cunning) come from the early bestiaries. Although the genre was probably developed by Physiologus who lived in Greece in the second century, A.D., it was most popular in Europe (especially France) during the Middle Ages when it was used to present Christian teachings. Elizabeth Wilson's *Bibles and Bestiaries: A Guide to Illuminated Manuscripts* contains examples of bestiaries from the Middle Ages.

Because many modern works, such as *Watership Down* by Richard Adams, are thought to have developed from the bestiary, children's future understanding of literature may be enhanced by their developing an understanding of the genre. Excellent introductions to the bestiary are John Hunt's *Bestiary: An Illuminated Alphabet of Medieval Beasts* and John Gardner's *A Child's Bestiary*. The preface to Gardner's work poetically advises readers, "in the Middle Ages, such books were the rage" and that, if they cannot find a moral, they should "turn the page." *A Child's Bestiary* includes sixty-eight poems, and it offers the opportunity for each child in a group to choose a poem, create an original illustration for it, read it to the group, and perhaps research the accuracy or the factual basis of a particular animal's presentation.

Bibliography: A list of works about a particular subject or by a specific author. This list may be comprehensive in nature, or it may be a selective list of those materials that are deemed most important, most easily available, or most closely related to the topic. The term may also refer to the sources that were used by an author in preparing a work or additional sources the reader may consider. The bibliography may be annotated, in which case the items listed are each followed by a brief description or criticism.

Excellent sources for bibliographic form are Joseph Gibaldi and Herbert Lindenberger's *MLA Style Manual and Guide to Scholarly Publishing* (for an online guide, see *http://libweb.sonoma.edu/research/citation/mlastyle.html*) and *The Chicago Manual of Style*, edited by John Grossman (for an online guide, see *www.wisc.edu/writing/Handbook/DocChicago.html*). The following examples of bibliographic entries are from pages 516 and 518 in *The Chicago Manual of Style*:

> Anscombe, G. E. M. "Modern Moral Philosophy." *Philosophy* 33 (May 1958): 1–19.
> Austen, Jane. *The Novels of Jane Austen*. Edited by R. W. Chapman. 5 vols. 3rd ed. London: Oxford University Press, 1932–34.
> Auden, W. H. "Notes on the Comic." In *Comedy: Meaning and Form*, edited by Robert Corrigan, 61–72. San Francisco: Chandler, 1965.

These examples should be adapted to the appropriate developmental level when the concepts are introduced to young people.

Bibliographies may be introduced to young people by sharing with the group a bibliography such as that found in Russell Freedman's *The Wright Brothers* in which Freedman annotates three recent books in "For Further Reading." Teachers may wish to make a transparency of these three listed works. Young people may consider why Freedman thought it worthwhile to note these works. Why did he choose to annotate the bibliography? What information was included in each entry?

Young people may go to the media center or public library and use the catalog to prepare a bibliography of books by favorite author or on a selected subject. Young people may use Freedman's bibliographic form without annotations. If they wish, they may create a bibliographic bookmark to share with their friends.

Big Book: Books published with a paperback binding and in an oversized format. They are almost always adaptations of popular children's books previously published in a traditional format. Primarily used by teachers and librarians of preschool and primary students, big books are sometimes referred to as an "enlarged text." These oversized books allow groups of children to see and respond to a story, and some include a teacher's guide. Numerous longtime favorite picture books have been released in this larger format including Robert McClosky's *Make Way for Ducklings*; Charles G. Shaw's *It Looked Like Spilt Milk*; Leo Lionni's *Frederick*; and Donald Crews' *Freight Train*.

All types of genres have been released in an oversized format. For example, Lois Ehlert's *Eating the Alphabet: Fruits and Vegetables from A to Z* is an alphabet book; Ann Morris' *Bread Bread Bread*, photographs by Ken Heyman is an informational book; Janet Stevens' *Three Billy Goats Gruff* is a folktale; and Maurice Sendak's *Chicken Soup with Rice* is a rhymed story.

Big books come in a variety of sizes. Leo Lionni's *A Busy Year*, a story about Willie and Winnie as they love their tree through all four seasons, is 22 inches high and only 9 1/2 inches wide. Denise Fleming's *In the Tall, Tall Grass* is a perfect square, 18 inches by 18 inches. Peggy Rathmann's wordless book *Good Night Gorilla* is 15 1/2 inches high and 18 1/2 inches wide.

Young people may enjoy comparing the size of illustrations and text in a regular book and a big book; taking turns reading a selection of big books that are set upon an easel; and creating their own illustrated stories using large sheets of craft paper for the pages and colored poster board for the covering. Robin Davis' *Big Books for Little Readers* provides many ideas on using Big Books to enhance reading experiences and provides many related literature activity ideas, including about 50 patterns for classroom use. Davis' resource also includes a selective bibliography and provides a list of Big Book publishing resources.

Bildungsroman: A novel about the education and character development of a young protagonist who is moving from inexperience to maturity. The novel usually involves a crisis that directs the focus of the protagonist and causes the individual to come to terms with his or her identity and role. *Bildungsroman* is also known as *apprenticeship novel, Erziehungsroman* (novel about education), and *Entwicklungsgeschichte* (a story about development). Classic adult works in this category include Charles Dickens' *David Copperfield* and *Great Expectations*. Katherine Paterson's *Jacob Have I Loved* is an example within contemporary fiction for young people. As an activity, young people reading such a novel may explore the unity of plot and character and the potential use of a crisis to focus the protagonist on choices of identity and role.

Binding: The outer covering of a volume of printed pages. The binding may be a hard cardboard cover, paperback, wood, vinyl, or other material. Some books are bound with glue and others are sewn. When purchasing books for children, the outside covering is a factor that determines the book's durability. Sewn, hard-back books are the most durable. Books for very young children are bound in sturdy cardboard and are known as "board books."

Aliki's *How a Book Is Made* includes a description of how new books are folded, gathered, sewn, trimmed, and bound. Michele Edwards' *Dora's Book* relates the story of Dora who writes and illustrates her own book and then asks her friend Tom to help with the publishing and binding. This children's book features an easy-to-understand explanation of the hand-binding process. An excellent pro-fessional title which details the step-by-step process of making and binding one's own book is Paul Johnson's *A Book of One's Own: Developing Literacy through Making Books*. Young people may try different types of materials to bind their own book, using cloth, vinyl, cardboard, and others.

Biographical Criticism: Basing the interpretation of a literary work upon the author's life. Biographical criticism is related to *expressive criticism*, focusing on the individuality of the artist, and to *psychological criticism*, emphasizing the author's psyche. *New Criticism*, which promoted the consideration of the work itself, considered the approach a fallacy; and too heavy a reliance upon the author's life in interpreting a literary work is known as *biographical* or *genetic fallacy*. How-ever, there is a long tradition of interpreting literary works in light of the author's life (*e.g.*, by considering Charles Dickens' early deprivations or Samuel Taylor Coleridge's political idealism). Critics within children's literature also apply bio-graphical criticism, noting for example, that Theodore Geisel began his career as a political cartoonist and satirist; Katherine Paterson was the daughter of mis-sionaries to China and holds an advanced degree in theology; Jean Fritz lived much of her childhood in China; and Cynthia Rylant has childhood ties to Appala-chia.

Young people may be introduced to authors' lives through videos, such as *Get-ting to Know Gerald McDermott*; biographies (*e.g.*, Ruth McDonald's *Dr. Seuss*); and autobiographies (*e.g.*, Sid Fleischman's *The Abracadabra Kid: A Writer's Life* or Beverly Cleary's *A Girl from Yamhill: A Memoir* and *My Own Two Feet: A Memoir*). A resource that identifies works about children's authors is Kay Vandergrift's Web site: *www.scils.rutgers.edu/special/kay/author.html*. Young people may be involved in the concept of biographical criticism by reading Cynthia Rylant's *Best Wishes* and *But I'll Be Back Again* and considering how her books, such as *When I Was Young in the Mountains* and *Appalachia: Voices of Sleeping Birds*, reflect her life. See *Criticism* and *Psychological Criticism*.

Biography: A book that shares the well-researched account of a real person's life. Biographies are usually written about someone who has made important historic contributions, made significant achievements in a particular area, or has led an inspirational or influential life.

Biographies for children may be categorized in several areas. Authentic biographies provide accurate details through careful research that incorporates information from written documents, eyewitness accounts, or video/audio recordings. Authors of authentic biographies especially value the use of primary sources. A fictionalized biography is based on research and accurate documentation but may include some recreated episodes or conversation based on fact. Biographical fiction may include original conversation, reconstruction of events, and even fictional characters to add to the story. Criteria for selection of biographies include purpose, scope, treatment of the subject, accuracy of information, writing style, format, and intended audience. Well-known children's book biographers include David Adler; Leonard Everett Fisher; Russell Freedman; Jean Fritz; Kathleen Krull; Patricia and Fredrick McKissack; Milton Meltzer; and Diane Stanley.

Complete biographies are those that include information on a subject from birth to death such as Russell Freedman's 1988 Newbery Award winning *Lincoln: A Photobiography*. Partial biographies include an event in someone's life or offer an account of part of their life; examples include Alan Schroeder's *Minty: A Story of Young Harriet Tubman*, illustrated by Jerry Pinkney, which presents events from Harriet Tubman's childhood; and Golenbock's *Teammates,* which relates the story of Jackie Robinson, the first black player on a major league baseball team, and his friendship with PeeWee Reese.

Picture book biographies are intended for younger readers. This type of biography usually provides a general overview of the individual's life and is presented in the standard 32-page picture book format. Some examples include David Adler's *Lou Gehrig: The Luckiest Man*; Diane Stanley's *Cleopatra;* and Jeanette Winter's *My Name Is Georgia: A Portrait.*

Young people may read a biography and write a letter to the individual in response to some of the events in the story. Instead of a book report, additional extension ideas are writing a poem about the individual that includes numerous facts and events from the biography; creating a mural that highlights several events from the individual's life; or playing "charades" in a classroom setting by re-enacting a scene from the biography and allowing others to guess the identity of the individual. See also *Autobiography* and *Collected Biography.*

Block Printing: A technique for producing illustrations by cutting a design or picture into a block of wood, linoleum, or other substance; coating it with paint, ink, or dye; and then pressing the design onto paper, cloth, or other material. Also known as relief printing, the technique typically produces strong colors and primitive lines. See *Linoleum Block* (Printing), *Potato Printing*, and *Woodcut*.

Blurb: A brief, enthusiastic introduction to the contents or plot of a book, usually printed on the inside flap of a book's (dust) jacket. Because it is created by the publisher's staff to market the work, the approach is upbeat and often, after a brief overview of content, describes and praises the author's style or gives brief background about that person's work. The term is believed to have originated in Gelett Burgess' *Burgess Unabridged: A New Dictionary of Words You Have Always Needed* where he humorously considered a blurb to be a sound made by a publisher.

As an activity associated with the term, the teacher or librarian may read several blurbs from book jackets of titles familiar to the upper grade group. After a discussion of the lively nature of the blurbs, the young people may create an illustrated jacket for a favorite book and write a blurb that a publisher could have used to promote the work. When laminated, these new productions may be used to replace worn-out originals.

Board Book: A sturdy book of heavy, glossy cardboard, designed for young children. The simple text usually identifies familiar objects, animals, or activities. Illustrations are easily identifiable without a distracting background. Sizes of board books vary; however, books within a range of 5 3/4 by 5 3/4 inches to 8 1/2 by 9 1/4 inches are common.

Books that are published originally as board books often are better suited to the smaller format than works originally published as picture books. For example the balloons are cropped from illustrations in Peggy Rathmann's board book version of *Good Night, Gorilla*. Also, books that are published originally as board books tend to be more developmentally appropriate for the intended audience of birth to age two. Three such original productions are Patricial Hubbell's *Wrapping Paper Romp*, Thacher Hurd's *Zoom City*, and Joyce Carol Thomas' *You Are My Perfect Baby*. Picture books that have adapted successfully to board books are Margaret Wise Brown's *Good Night, Moon*, Bill Martin's *Brown Bear, Brown Bear*, and Sam McBranty's *Guess How Much I Love You*.

Board books can be shared with a preschooler by asking the child to name the content of each picture. After examining board books such as Helen Oxenbury's *Shopping Trip* or Rosemary Wells' *Max's Breakfast*, a primary class may select a topic such as farm, food, or toys, and each child may then illustrate one planned picture on four inch by six inch white cardboard. After the identifying text for each picture is added, the cardboard may be laminated, compiled into a book, and presented to a preschool class.

Book: A collection of written sheets (usually paper) bound together; a major division of a longer literary work. Two illustrated information books present the history of writing, writing surfaces, papermaking, printing, and bookbinding: Karen Brookfield's *Book* and *The History of Making Books*. *The History of Making Books* is in a spiral format that includes color overlays, cut-outs, and folded pages. Young people who have access to these histories could adapt a brief tale or fable to an earlier format of written communication, such as a scroll, folded paper, hornbook, or cloth.

Book Discussion. An exchange between individuals after listening to or reading a common book. Book discussions may range from a structured situation between a predetermined group of individuals in a library or classroom or in an informal situation after a story has been shared with a group. Sharing opinions about books allows individuals to share their feelings and interpret what they have read or heard. A book discussion leader can guide a formal or informal discussion in regard to the author's intent, characterizations in the story, and meaning of the story. Book discussions can be particularly important in a literature-based curriculum and as a part of a reading program. Examples of book discussion questions might include:

> What did you enjoy about the book?
> What is the major theme?
> Who was the main character; how did the author let the reader know about the character?

An excellent online resource about book discussion groups with young people is at the Multnomah County Public Library's Web site (Portland, OR). Where a set of suggested book discussion guidelines, "Resources for Book Group Leaders," is located on the Web (*www.multnomah.lib.or.us/lib/talk/resources.html*). The site also includes how to start a book group, universal book discussion questions, and common questions about book groups.

Additional book discussion guidelines, written by Ginny Moore Kruse and Kathleen T. Horning, are posted at the Cooperative Children's Book Center's (CCBC) Web site (*www.soemadison.wisc.edu/ccbcdiscguid.htm*). Each November through December the CCBC posts discussion lists for the major children's book awards of the Newbery, Caldecott, Coretta Scott King, and Printz awards. Young people may participate in a book discussion in their own library, following one of the sets posted by the CCBC. (The suggested discussion lists are selected by the CCBC staff and are not the official award book discussion lists, which are highly confidential.)

Additional helpful resources in organizing book discussions include Elizabeth Knowles and Martha Smith's *The Reading Connection: Bringing Parents, Teachers and Librarians Together* and Knowles and Smith's *More Reading Connections: Bringing Parents, Teachers and Librarians Together*.

Book on Tape: An adaptation of a book into audiocassette format by producing an audio recording of the book being read aloud. They are also known as recorded books and audiobooks. The production may use either an author who reads his/her own work or a professional reader or actor. Books on tape were originally designed to be used by individuals with visual impairments.

The American Library Association's Notable Children's Recordings lists (both most recent and from past years) can be found at *www.ala.org/alsc/ awards.html#notable*. These recordings lists include not only some of the finest children's books on tape available but also storytelling and music for children. Among the titles on the 2000 Notable Children's Recordings are Beverly Cleary's *Ramona's World*, read by actress Stockard Channing; Tomie dePaola's *Strega Nona*, read by Jim McDonough; Jack Gantos' *Joey Pigza Swallowed the Key*, narrated solely by the author; Patricia Polacco's *Meteor!* and *Thank You, Mr. Falker!*, both read by the author; Marjorie Priceman's *Zin! Zin! Zin! A Violin*, performed by Maureen Anderman as she introduces the ten instruments in the book; and Phillip Pullman's *The Golden Compass*, narrated by the author who was supported by a full cast of British actors. Jack Prelutsky performs his own poetry on several audiocassettes, including the recent *A Pizza the Size of the Sun*. Some books, especially children's picture storybooks, are sold packaged with the book-on-tape adaptation. Having both the book and the tape allows younger children to follow the words visually while listening to the story being read aloud.

A selection of recommended audiobooks for an older audience may be found at the American Library Association's Young Adult Audiobook Selections Web site (*www.ala.org/yalsa/booklists/audio/*). Among recent selections there are J. K. Rowling's *Harry Potter and the Sorcerer's Stone* and *Harry Potter and the Chamber of Secrets*, both read by Jim Dale; Gary Soto's *Jesse*, narrated by Robert Ramirez; and Kimberly Willis Holt's *My Louisiana Sky*, read by Judith Ivey.

Young people will enjoy exploring the books on tape collection in the school or public library and listening together as a class or in a small group. Parents may appreciate having books on tape for a long car ride. Some books on tape for upper elementary school students include Louis Sachar's *Holes*; Richard Peck's *A Long Way from Chicago,* and Christopher Paul Curtis' *Bud, Not Buddy.*

Book Review: A professional description that assesses a book's contents, literary quality, and potential audience. Older readers could be introduced to book reviews and book selection by teachers or librarians who choose a set of positive book reviews for books that would have value in the library collection and involve the young people reading the reviews and prioritizing their choices. Teachers and librarians could then discuss with the young people the factors that shaped their priorities. After the books they choose are added to the collection and young people have read them, they could further assess how well the review reflected their own judgments and evaluations. Young people may write reviews of their favorite books and submit them to Teen Hoopla at *www.ala.org/teenhoopla/ reviews/index.html.*

Book Size: Children's books come in all sizes. Large picture storybooks are often used as a read aloud for groups of children while smaller picture books are more suited for an individual child or a very small group.

Books about trees or skyscrapers are sometimes tall such as Janice May Udry's 1957 Caldecott Award-winner *A Tree Is Nice*, illustrated by Marc Simont, and Gail Gibbons' *Up Goes the Skyscraper.* Lois Ehlert's *Feathers for Lunch* is a tall book that features a cat reaching up to try and catch a bird for a lunchtime treat.

One classic small book series is that written by Beatrix Potter, who is most famous for *The Tale of Peter Rabbit.* The books in this series measure 4-1/2 × 5-1/2 inches. Maurice Sendak created the four volume miniature set called *The Nutshell Library,* which includes *Alligators All Around, Chicken Soup with Rice, One Was Johnny*, and *Pierre.* The four books each measure 1-3/4 × 4 × 2-3/4 inches.

Book size sometimes relates to what the book is about. Gail Gibbons' *Apples* is in the almost perfect square shape of a small apple crate measuring 10 inches × 10 inches. Michael O. Tunnell's *Mailing May*, illustrated by Ted Rand, is in the rectangle shape of a suitcase and illustrated as such on front and back.

Young people may examine a dozen library picture books in various sizes and determine if the book size is important to the story. See *Big Book.*

Booktalk: An oral presentation given by teachers, librarians, educators, and students to promote interest in books and motivation in reading or shared among teachers and librarians to inform collection development decisions. It is not a book report or critique of the book, rather an "advertisement" to interest an audience in a book. Any genre may be used in a booktalk.

For the promotion of reading, Joni Bodart has written over ten professional books on this subject; the first book was titled *Booktalk! Booktalking and School Visits for Young Adult Audiences*. *Booktalking with Joni Bodart* is a useful 28-minute video, designed for young adult school and public librarians. In the video Bodart draws on years of booktalking experience to outline the basic techniques and personal touches she uses when planning and delivering booktalks. Her basic advice for giving booktalks includes three important rules: (1) do not give a booktalk on a book you have not read; (2) do not give a booktalk on a book you do not like; and (3) do not tell the ending. Additional suggestions for booktalking include: show enthusiasm; keep the talk brief; feature a scene, a character, or a bit of the action; tell enough to entice the potential reader; compare the books with others; and booktalk a group of books that share a theme.

Patrick Jones includes a chapter on "Booktalking: Don't Tell, Sell" in *Connecting Young Adults and Libraries*, second edition, which lists numerous resources and provides useful hints, tips, and sample booktalks. Additional resources that include sample booktalks include Rebecca Thomas' *Primary Plots*, volumes 1 and 2, a booktalk guide for use with readers age 4–8; John Thomas Gillespie's *Middleplots 4: A Booktalk Guide for Use with Readers Ages 8–12*, 4th edition; *JuniorPlots 4: A Booktalk Guide for Use with Readers Ages 12–16*; and *Seniorplots: A Booktalk Guide for Use with Readers Ages 15–18*.

Young people may explore Nancy Keane's Web site "Booktalks-Quick and Simple" (*http://ms.concord.k12.nh.us/booktalks/*), which offers booktalking tips and numerous sample booktalks.

———

Boston Globe–Horn Book Awards: Awards given for excellence in children's literature. The awards have been co-sponsored since 1967 by The Boston Globe and The Horn Book, Inc. The awards are presented in three categories: Picture Book, Fiction, and Nonfiction. The judges may also name several honor books in each category. On occasion, a book will receive a special citation for its high quality and overall creative excellence. Eligible books must be published in the United States, though they may be written or illustrated by citizens of any country. Young people may find more information about these awards on the Web (*www.hbook.com/bghb.html*).

———

Bowdlerize: To sanitize or expurgate literature to rid it of anything offensive to a person. The word is a derivative of Thomas Bowdler (English, 1754–1825), who published a popular expurgated edition of Shakespeare in 1818. Some children's books have words that have been bowdlerized without indication of the adaptation. For example, books sold to children and parents at book fairs may be purged of "offensive" material or words and sold to children under the assumption that it is the same book as the original. Older children could compare various versions of Chaucer's tales for children to see which have been the most "bowdlerized," comparing, for example, Barbara Cohen's, *Canterbury Tales*, illustrated by Trina Schart Hyman, with *The Canterbury Tales*, retold by Geraldine McCaughrean. Which tales are included in each? Why might some tales be excluded from one version over another? Another activity may be to chart the common or different elements in a single tale, e.g., Barbara Cooneys, *Chanticleer and the Fox*, with other retellings of the story from "The Nun's Priest's Tale," including Fulton Roberts' *Chanticleer and the Fox: A Chaucerian Tale*. Likewise, young people may also make comparisons of various tales published by the Grimms.

Briticism: A word or characteristic peculiar to the English language spoken in Great Britain. For example, Mummy or Mum are commonly spoken in Great Britain; Mommy or Mom are United States equivalents. Other terms used in Great Britain but not the United States include da, telly, lift, lorry, water closet, pram, bonnet, queue, to let, and motor way. Book titles are often changed to accommodate one market or the other. For example, the British bestseller *Harry Potter and the Philosopher's Stone* had its title changed to *Harry Potter and the Sorcerer's Stone* for the U.S. audience. And, Eric Carle's *The Grouchy Ladybug* was changed to *The Bad-Tempered Ladybird* for British readers. Young people could compare and contrast other books published separately for American or British audiences, considering, for example, Janet and Allan Ahlberg's *The Jolly Postman* and Bernard Waber's *Ira Sleeps Over*.

CD-ROM: (Compact Disc—Read Only Memory) A disc measuring 4 3/4 inches in diameter which is used in the recording, storage, and retrieval of electronic information that cannot be changed or altered. CD-ROMs are read using a computer's specialized optical drive and each can hold the equivalent of 700 floppy discs or 600 megabytes. CD-ROMs are used prevalently in computer multimedia applications.

The Association for Library Service to Children (ALSC) denotes an award-winning list of children's computer software each year. The ALSC evaluation criteria looks for both content and technological applications. It additionally includes a specific guideline statement for preschool children, primary children, intermediate children, and junior high students. The detailed criteria statements are posted at *www.ala.org/alsc/notablesoftware_terms.html*. *Children's Software Revue* (Active Learning Associates) is a bimonthly print journal that includes professional articles and numerous reviews all related to electronic information.

A listing of the most recent Notable Children's Computer Software is located at *www.ala.org/alsc/nsoft01.html*. CD-ROMs include many different types of information. Notable CD-ROMs based on children's books have included: *Cat in the Hat*, *The American Girls Premiere*, and *The Magic School Bus Explores the World of Animals*. Notable information CD-ROMs have included: *My Amazing Human Body* and *The Digital Field Trip to the Rain Forest*. *Piano Discovery for Kids*, *Carmen San Diego Math Detective*, and *Dr. Seuss' Kindergarten* have all been ALSC Notable CD-ROMs that are all educational skills related. *Encarta Africana* and *Encarta Interactive World Atlas 2000* were both reference sources featured on the ALSC Notable list.

The journal's Web site is at *www.childrenssoftware.com*. Young people may print out the ALSC evaluation criteria for children's software and evaluate a CD-ROM in their own classroom or school library collection. They may also use some of the excellent CD-ROMs listed above.

Caldecott Medal: See *Randolph Caldecott Medal.*

Calligraphy: The art of producing elegant handwriting with ink and with specialized pens or brushes. Prior to the invention of the printing press over 500 years ago, books were individually handwritten on vellum or parchment and often embellished with elaborate penmanship.

Calligraphy is used by Trina Schart Hyman on the title page of the 1985 Caldecott Medal book *Saint George and the Dragon,* retold by Margaret Hodges, and by Lisbeth Zwerger for the text of O. Henry's *The Gift of the Magi.*

Young people may consult Fiona Campbell's *Calligraphy* for an introduction to a variety of lettering techniques. They may try their own hand at calligraphy with specially designed felt tip pens; and, as their expertise improves, they may progress to India ink and calligraphy pens.

Canadian Library Awards: Awards presented annually by the Canadian Library Association in three categories: Book of the Year for Children (1947), Amelia Frances Howard-Gibbon Illustrator's Award (1971), and Young Adult Canadian Book Award (1981). Young people may find information about these awards and lists of the award-winning books at *www.cla.ca/awards/bookaw.htm.*

Carnegie Medal: A medal, named after the American philanthropist Andrew Carnegie, presented annually since 1936 (except for 1942 and 1943) by the British Library Association to the author of a distinguished children's book written in English and first published in the United Kingdom. Young people may find information about the award and a list of the award winning books at *www.la-hq.org.uk/directory/medals_awards/medals_pastcar.html.*

Cartoon: Today, a drawing that is humorous or satirical. The word originated from the Italian word *cartone,* which means *a big sheet of paper,* and *cartoon* was a detailed preliminary drawing created on a large sheet of paper for the purpose of transferring the design to another surface, such as canvas, wall, tapestry, or stained glass. However, since the mid–1800s the term referred to a single illustration often published in a newspaper or magazine that served as a parody or witticism.

When applied to children's illustrated books, *cartoon art* refers to an artistic style of simple line drawings created with sparing use of line. The work of Dr. Seuss, William Steig, and James Stevenson are examples of illustrators who create comic art. Two artists whose comic art has earned the Caldecott Award are William Steig for *Sylvester and the Magic Pebble* and Peggy Rathmann for *Officer Buckle and Gloria*. Betsy Lewin won a 2001 Caldecott Honor for her cartoon illustrations in Doreen Cronin's *Click Clack Moo: Cows that Type*. Young people may see comic art reminiscent of the Katzenjammer Kids in Marc Rosenthal's illustrations in *The Absentminded Fellow*, written by Samuel Marshak. They may examine Judith St. George's 2001 Caldecott book *So You Want to Be President?*, illustrated by David Small, for examples of political cartooning.

Young people could compare several different picture books illustrated with comic art and identify the ways that facial features (*e.g.*, eyes, eyebrows, mouth) and gestures (shoulders, hands, head) are created to evoke specific emotions.

Casein Paint: An opaque water-based paint that is made with a milk protein (also known as casein). Casein is the basis of cheese, and it is used not only to make paint but also to make plastics, adhesives, and foods. When applied to paper or art board, casein paint dries quickly as a matte, brittle, waterproof surface. The addition of oil or gum makes the paint more flexible.

Examples of casein paintings in children's books include the 1958 Caldecott Award book, Robert McClosky's *Time of Wonder*; the 1965 Caldecott Honor book, Elaine Greenstein's *Mrs. Rose's Garden;* Elaine Greenstein's *Emily and The Crows*; and Lee Bennet Hopkins' *My America: A Poetry Atlas of the United States*, illustrated by Stephen Alcorn. Young people may compare the use of casein paint obtained from an art supply store to that of acrylic, tempera, and oil paints.

Cautionary Tale: A story that warns of consequences resulting from inappropriate actions. For example, a classic cautionary tale is *Little Red Riding Hood*, in which Red Riding Hood, despite her mother's warning, strays off the path, and the reader is certainly aware of the results of Red Riding Hood's actions. In Charles Perrault's version (the earliest recorded), the grandmother and Little Red Riding Hood are both eaten by the wolf and the moral is "Never trust a stranger . . . Wolves may lurk in every guise . . . " *Perrault's Fairy Tales*, illustrated by Gustave Doré.

Young people could compare Perrault's version with Trina Schart Hyman's Caldecott Honor book *Little Red Riding Hood,* a retelling of the tale as the Grimms recorded it, and Ed Young's Caldecott Medal-winner *Lon Po Po*. Issues young people could address for comparison of cautionary tales include the harshness of the punishment, the strictness of the warning, and the explicitness of the moral. Young people may also compare those versions to a contemporary parody, such as Lisa Campbell Ernst's, *Little Red Riding Hood: A Newfangled Prairie Tale*.

Censorship: Examination of books or other materials for the purposes of altering or suppressing the whole or parts thought to be objectionable or offensive. Censorship is the opposite of selection: censorship requires negative reasoning for why a book should be excluded; selection requires positive reasoning to justify a book's value to the collection. Children's and young adult books have been primarily banned because of language or sexual connotations. American Library Association's annual publication of *Banned Books: Resource Guide* provides up-to-date facts on the books being challenged, including their status in the reconsideration process. The guide also cites case law.

Young people may be surprised to learn that in 2000 the most banned book was *Harry Potter and the Sorcerer's Stone*. Newbery Award-winning authors, such as Katherine Paterson, often find themselves on the list over a few words or in the case of *Bridge to Terabithia*, the use of an imaginary kingdom. The American Library Association's Web site for banned books, *www.ala.org/bbooks/*, provides ideas and suggestions for the preparations for Banned Book Week, traditionally the last week in September.

Chalk: A type of soft white rock or similar substance that can be pressed together with colored pigments. Chalk, often a stick form similar to a crayon, is used for drawing or writing. Probably the best-known example of chalk used as the artistic medium in a children's picture book is John Steptoe's *Stevie,* which incorporates brightly colored chalks applied one on top of the other to create depth in the illustrations. Children's books that have included chalk as a part of mixed mediums used to create illustrations include the 1987 Caldecott Award book, Ann Grifilconi's *The Village of Round and Square Houses*, with the mixed media of chalk and colored pencil/wash, and Glen Rounds' *Wash Day on Noah's Ark*, in chalk with pen.

Young people may create their own illustrations using colored chalks obtained from an art supply store. They may also obtain sidewalk chalk from a discount retail store and create illustrations on concrete that will wash away with water or rain.

Chant: Historically, a prayer sung to express love of God. Christian chants borrowed elements of Greco-Roman religious songs and Jewish Synagogue chants. The chant in pure form contained no musical meter and made use of natural language, utilizing both the meanings of words as well as their rhythms. In the secular realm, chants have been used to set a rhythm for cooperative work or play. The link between the secular and the religious chant may have little to do with language and meter, and rather, may be attributed to reaching for a common goal that encourages coordinated participation whether the activity is praying or pulling an anchor. In the late twentieth century the chant has been rediscovered as a musical art form and many examples are available in CD or cassette format. An activity for young people could include a jump rope session using a favorite chant. Sources of some available chants include: *A Rocket in My Pocket: The Rhymes and Chants of Young Americans* compiled by Carl Withers and illustrated by Susanne Soba, *Anna Banana: 101 Jump-Rope Rhymes* by Joanna Cole, and *Songs for Survival: Songs and Chants from Tribal People Around the World* compiled by Nikki Siegen-Smith.

Chapbook: Printed material sold by traveling peddlers (chapmen) in England from the sixteenth to the nineteenth centuries. Chapbooks were marketed for children in the United States especially during the nineteenth century. Cheaply produced, a typical chapbook was about six by four inches and contained about 24 stitched pages, although some chapbooks were merely a single folded sheet. Subject matter included rhymes, riddles, abridged folk tales, and contemporary narratives, such as "Jack the Ripper." Often hand-painted with watercolor by child laborers, chapbooks set a precedent by bringing popular readable material to the masses. They were books that many young people could afford to purchase prior to the introduction of the dime novel. For a learning activity young people could make a chapbook, stitching together small sheets upon which they have printed and illustrated a shortened version of a favorite fairy tale, a contemporary event, or a small collection of riddles. Young people could simulate a chapbook's black and white woodcut illustrations by using potato or linoleum block prints.

Chapter Book: A book created for young readers (typically third graders) who are making the transition from easy readers to children's novels. Kathleen Horning in *From Cover to Cover* describes Ann Cameron's *The Stories that Julian Tells*, "A Stepping Stone" series book, as the prototype for chapter books. It has a large typeface; never more than fifteen lines per page; six episodic chapters with interesting, memorable events; simple sentences and vocabulary; ample white space;

justified right margins; and, for young readers, the look and feel of a chapter book. In addition to *The Stories that Julian Tells* transitional readers may choose to read Ann Cameron's other chapter books about Julian, *More Stories Julian Tells* and *Julian's Glorious Summer*.

Character: An imaginary being in a literary work. A *character* can be a realistic person, such as Bud in Christopher Paul Curtis' *Bud, Not Buddy*, a realistic animal, such as the bull terrier, the Labrador retriever, or the Siamese cat in Sheila Burnford's *The Incredible Journey*, a fantastic being, such as Taran's wizard guardian, Dallben, in Lloyd Alexander's *The High King*, a personified animal, such as Peter in Beatrix Potter's *The Tale of Peter Rabbit*, or an object, such as Willy, a wind-up mouse, in Leo Lionni's *Alexander and the Wind-Up Mouse*. Regardless of the imaginary origins of literary characters, their personal qualities and roles are limited by their functions in stories. The central character in a story is the *protagonist*, a typically admirable being who interacts with the sequences of the plot, both shaping and being shaped by the events. The *antagonist* is in conflict with the *protagonist*. Other character roles include *foil*, whose qualities contrast with those of the protagonist; *narrator*, who tells the story; and *stock character*, who represents universal traits (*e.g.*, stinginess); *stereotype*, who represents traits (typically negative) that have been attributed to a social or racial group (*e.g.*, the absent-minded professor), and *archetype*, a universal pattern or model for action (*e.g.*, the wicked witch). Characters can also be described as *round*, being fully developed; *flat*, being less developed; *dynamic*, changing significantly during the story; and *static*, unchanging. Youngest participants in story times can be introduced to the concepts of protagonist (*e.g.*, Hansel and Gretel or Little Red Riding Hood) and antagonist (*e.g.*, the witch or the wolf), and they can be led through thoughtful literature programs to distinguish between round or flat and static or dynamic characters and on to identify specialized character roles, such as narrator or foil. See specific terms in this description; see also *Characterization*.

Characterization: The artistic representation of the appearance and personality of an imaginary being in a literary work. A key issue in characterization is the level of complexity with which characters are portrayed. Well-developed characters, like real human beings, are multi-dimensional (*round*); that is, they have multiple qualities that are neither all negative nor all positive. The issue of complexity is one of privilege and responsibility for the author. Readers expect the main character to be well developed—to be believable, but an array of characters cannot be well developed in any one work. Therefore, the author must determine which characters will be round (and close to the conflict) or flat (and in the background). However, regardless of characters' levels of complexity, authors reveal them through dialogue (what they say and what others say about them), their actions, their appearance, their interior feelings and motivations, and through explicit narrative description. Young people can be led to discover how authors reveal characters by sharing with them a picture book with strong characterization, such as *Lilly's Purple Plastic Purse* by Kevin Henkes, and asking them to describe Lilly. Using a picture book to consider characterization allows young people to use not only verbal but also visual clues. They may note that Lilly loves school and can be happy, joyful, irrepressible, impatient, vengeful, miserable, disappointed, hurt, and angry (even furious). They may then be encouraged to explain how they know Lilly's characteristics—*e.g.*, by what she writes ("BIG FAT MEAN MR. STEALING TEACHER"), by what others say ("WOW!"), by what she does (plays with the purse in class), by what her parents do (they trust her to do the right thing), and by how the illustrations communicate facial expressions (eye brows with U-shaped dips for sadness and with hard slants for anger) and body language (Lilly stepping high in red boots or with her head down). Perspective and layout also reveal Lilly—she shrinks smaller and smaller when she realizes she has not behaved fairly. From such discussions young people can determine whether characters are round or flat and explain their rationale.

Charcoal: An artistic medium of dark or black absorbent carbon made by heating wood, bone or nutshells. Because charcoal is easy to erase and to smudge, it is an easy medium to work with in relation to changing or altering illustrations in progress. Charcoal has often been used as an underdrawing or to do preparatory studies for more formal pieces of artwork.

Pieces of charcoal or charcoal pencils have been used to create charcoal drawings in children's picture books. Chris Raschka used the medium to illustrate *Charlie Parker Played Be Bop* and the charcoal illustrations in Camille Yarbrough's *Cornrows* provide black and gray shadings for a visual explanation of the symbolic African hairstyle known as "cornrows." Thomas B. Allen used charcoal for Judith Hendershot's *In Coal Country* to portray coal dust on the endpapers of the book and to depict coal dust on the face of a miner returning home from his long, hard day at work. Ed Young combined charcoal and pastels to illustrate Nancy Larrick's anthology *Cats Are Cats*. Ian Falconer used charcoal and gouache for the illustrations of *Olivia*, a 2001 Caldecott Honor book about a feisty little pig who, whether getting ready for the day, enjoying the beach, or preparing for bedtime, has too much energy for her own good.

After examining charcoal artwork in picture books, young people may produce their own charcoal drawings. Artistic-quality charcoal can be obtained from an art supply store, or young people may use charcoal pieces gleaned from a cold fireplace. Using plastic gloves when handling charcoal pieces is a good idea.

Choral Speaking (Reading): A group's reading or reciting of literature, most often poetry. Poetry is to be read aloud, and choral reading is an entertaining way to encourage young people to read aloud together or in parts. Formal choral reading requires attention to key words, phrases, and accents as well as much practice to make the voices sound as one. However, there are informal and impromptu ways to encourage choral reading. Young children will enjoy reading the repetition and rhythmic structure in Bill Martin and John Archambault's *Chicka Chicka Boom Boom*. Paul Fleischman's 1989 Newbery Award book, *Joyful Noise: Poems for Two Voices,* and his other two collections, *I Am Phoenix: Poems for Two Voices* and *Big Talk: Poems for Four Voices,* offer the opportunities for multiple groups or voices to enjoy choral reading with a minimum of practice or preparation time. Other sources for choral reading are X. J. and Dorothy Kennedy's *Knock at a Star: A Child's Introduction to Poetry* and Georgia Heard's *Creatures of Earth, Sea, and Sky.*

Cinquain: Any stanza with five lines. However, Adelaide Crapsey (United States, 1878–1914), a poet and translator of Japanese poetry, is credited with inventing the cinquain as it is typically defined today: a poem of five lines that do not depend upon rhyme and that have a set number of syllables (respectively, 2, 4, 6, 8, 2). Another popularly accepted convention of the cinquain is that the first line has one word (title); the second line is two words which describe the title; the third line has three words that express an action of the title; the fourth line has four words that express a feeling of the title; and the fifth line is a synonym of the title or the title restated. Examples of Crapsey's poetry can be found on the Web at *www.britannica.com/*. Also, young people can find her cinquain "The Pearl" in Avis Harley's *Fly With Poetry: An ABC of Poetry.*

If a teacher or librarian leads a group of young people through the process of the group's writing a cinquain, they can develop an impromptu one, such as the following:

> Winter
> Mittened mornings
> Blowing, snowing, whirling
> Bundled coats at the school bus stop
> Winter.

The group can mount their cinquain on a bulletin board; other cinquains may be added by individuals who are inspired to write and contribute.

Classic: A literary work that has established itself as having enduring significance or worth and is still in print. G. Robert Carlsen in *Books and the Teenage Reader* acknowledged that it is a cliché to say a classic "has stood the test of time" and identified four characteristics of a classic: a significant theme, timeless symbols and images, well-designed structure, and a subtlety to be enjoyed repeatedly (Carlsen, 1980: 148–149). Identified as classics in children's literature are books such as E. B. White's *Charlotte's Web*, Mark Twain's *Tom Sawyer*, C. S. Lewis' *The Lion, the Witch and the Wardrobe*, Lewis Carroll's *Alice in Wonderland*, and Margaret Wise Brown's *Goodnight Moon*. Young people may consider what new classics will be added to the list. They may interview their parents to see what books they liked to read when they were young. Young people led to focus their discussions on one of Carlsen's characteristics, for example, theme or timelessness, may suggest books like Chris Van Allsburg's *Polar Express*. As a group, they could create a time capsule for a display of books they believe may become classics.

Clerihew: A light verse consisting of four lines that rhyme a,a,b,b. The form was invented by the English writer Edmund Clerihew Bentley (1875–1956). Typically the first line identifies a person, and the second line characterizes the individual. The third and fourth lines present the author's opinion. Using the form of the clerihew, David McCord in "Excerpts from 'Write Me Another Verse'," presented "The Clerihew," a poem that defines the "tricky form" of a clerihew.

The best clerihews can be witty and clever, and writing them sometimes has been a parlor game. Children who find the form engaging may be encouraged to create their own clerihews. Suggesting favorite authors for the subject may further assist children in that creative process. An example is:

> Beverly Cleary
> Is never weary.
> Her books are great
> And up-to-date.

Cliff-hanger: A suspenseful episode at the end of a chapter that has not been resolved. The formula fiction of the *Nancy Drew* and *Hardy Boys Series* made use of the technique to draw a reader through the book from one suspenseful incident to the next. It was common in the movie serials during the first half of the twentieth century, and it is still common in contemporary television serials. The cliff-hanger is a characteristic of the episodic plot, such as that in Lloyd Alexander's *Gypsy Rizka*. In contrast to the structure of *Gypsy Rizka* is the plot in Ruth White's *Belle Prater's Boy* in which chapters end quietly but progressively develop the story to a climax.

One popular series that has made highly effective use of the cliff-hanger is the *Harry Potter Series*. In *Harry and the Sorcerer's Stone* Harry leaves on the train for Hogwarts and wants to watch Hagrid until he was out of sight, " . . . but he blinked and Hagrid had gone." The reader wants to know why and how Hagrid disappeared and what will become of Harry. After young people have finished reading one of the Harry Potter books, they may chart how many chapters ended with a suspenseful sentence that left them wondering what would happen next.

Climax: The point in a progressive plot where the rising action reaches its greatest emotional intensity. The word *climax* is from the Greek word for *ladder*; hence, the origin implies the concept of rising to the highest point. A book for younger readers, Peggy Rathmann's *Officer Buckle and Gloria*, builds to the climax with safety talks given by Officer Buckle (secretly aided by the dog, Gloria). When Officer Buckle at last learns who is the real star of the show, the climax is reached. What will happen to the relationship between Gloria and Officer Buckle? Another example, Lois Lowry's *Number the Stars* reaches its greatest emotional intensity through events leading to the Jewish family's escape from Denmark by boat. Nazi soldiers and their vicious dogs block all routes. Will the dogs be able to find the family on the boat?

Young people may develop an understanding of climax by discussing the plot structure in the books they read. Youngest readers may practice identifying the climax by considering a small group of familiar books, such as Virginia Burton's *Mike Mulligan and His Steam Shovel*, E. B. White's *Charlotte's Web,* and Tomie dePaola's *Strega Nona: An Old Tale*. See *Plot*.

Closed Ending: A plot resolution that answers readers' expected questions. Most readers, and especially children, like a closed ending. Folktales provide simple examples of closed endings: the wolf runs away; the witch is shoved into the furnace; the giant is killed; and everyone lives happily ever after. However, novels have more involved resolutions that young people may plot with *Freytag's Pyramid*. (See *Progressive Plot*.) For example, the crisis in Ruth White's *Belle Prater's Boy* occurs when Gypsy is standing in front of her class and is confronted with the forgotten truth about her father's death. The reader finally understands how her loss is like Woodrow's whose mother had left him. However, it is a thirty-eight page resolution that produces a closed ending. Gypsy first must confront her anger and punish her father and herself. It is only after Gypsy, Woodrow, and Benny spend the night walking and talking that they accept their losses. At the end, Gypsy is planning a recital, and Woodrow is scheduled for eye surgery. The reader is satisfied that Gypsy and Woodrow will have a happier life.

Coincidence: The concurrence of events so that the advancement of the plot is determined or significantly influenced by chance. One coincidence may not destroy believability because the reader knows that coincidences do occur in real life. However, a number of chance events occurring without adequate foreshadowing to make them seem to be distinct possibilities will cause the reader to question the credibility of the plot.

After young people have read E. L. Konigsburg's *From the Mixed-Up Files of Mrs. Basil E. Frankweiler*, they may consider whether events or situations appeared to be coincidences. Young people may note that Mrs. Frankweiler's lawyer is also the children's grandfather, that Claudia finds the needed ticket, and that Jamie's class visits the museum. For these and other apparent coincidences, they may discuss possible foreshadowing that protects the credibility of the book.

Collage: A picture created entirely or in part from pieces of paper or other materials glued to a background. The technique was used by Cubists who attached pieces of newspapers to their paintings. Matisse used colored paper collage rather than painting during his last years. Caldecott awards for works in paper collage include Ezra Jack Keats' *Snowy Day*, Gerald McDermott's *Arrow to the Sun*, and David Diaz's *Smoky Night*, written by Eve Bunting. The use of a wide range of materials in collage illustrations can be found in Jeannie Baker's *Where the Forest Meets the Sea* or Lois Ehlert's *Red Leaf, Yellow Leaf*. Bryan Collier illustrated *Freedom River* by combining collage with watercolors.

After examining a work of collage by Ehlert, Baker, or another artist, young people may identify all incorporated materials they can recognize. Then, choosing a favorite picture book with painted illustrations, young people may reproduce one of the book's illustrations in collage. They may choose to create individual collages or work in groups to produce mural-size collages from materials they have collected.

Collected Biography: A work made up of brief life stories of several people who have a common element. Their common experiences may relate to any area of life—for example, occupation, physical abilities or disabilities, gender, age, avocation, or cultural identity. Collected biographies are usually organized into chapters with one individual per chapter or section. Two recent collections about famous women include Milton Meltzer's *Ten Queens: Portraits of Women of Power* and Andrea Davis Pinkney's *Let It Shine: The Stories of Ten Black Women Freedom Fighters*. Two popular collected biography series are Kathleen Krull's *Lives of . . . Series,* which includes *Extraordinary Women: Rulers, Rebels (And What the Neighbors Thought),* and Pat Cummings' *Talking with the Artists; Talking with the Artists,* Volume Two; and *Talking with the Artists,* Volume Three.

Young people may select some of their favorite individuals from history and think about what they have in common. Brief biographical sections could be written on each person for a unique collected biography. Young people might even compose a collected biography of important people in their own life. A classroom might work together on a collected biography to celebrate a holiday or historical event.

Colloquialism: Common speech not used in formal writing or speaking; slang. In Richard Peck's *A Long Way from Chicago* Joey Dowdel and his sister Mary Alice travel each August to spend a week with their grandmother. In the first chapter, Joey describes his first view of a dead body, "But I'd grown to the age of nine, and my sister Mary Alice was seven, and we'd yet to see a stiff" (Peck, 1998: 3). The reader understands the meaning, and at the same time the dialogue sets the stage for a time and a place. Encourage young people to find examples of colloquialisms in the dialogue of the stories they are reading. Colloquialism differs from dialect in that a dialect represents a distinct speech group within a language. See *Dialect*.

Color: The property of objects and light sources that can be described by the attributes of hue or tint (the color itself, for example, *blue*), intensity (strength or saturation), and value (lightness or darkness). Among picture books that directly address hue are Tana Hoban's *Colors Everywhere*, Lois Ehlert's *Color Farm* and *Color Zoo*, and Ann Jonas' *Color Dance*. Mary O'Neill's *Hailstones and Halibut Bones*, second edition, illustrated by John Wallner, introduces twelve hues, one in each of twelve poems, and presents older readers an opportunity to consider the connotations associated with color. *Hailstones and Halibut Bones* is also in video format. For a follow-up activity after sharing *Hailstones and Halibut Bones*, young people may work in small groups to create displays of objects organized around various hues. Intensity (describing the amount of hue) and value (describing the presence of black or white within a hue) further distinguish hues along two continua. Young people can strengthen their visual literacy skills by considering ways illustrators use intensity and value to communicate meaning. Uri Shulevitz's *Dawn* has watercolor illustrations that portray the approaching daylight as a dark blur that becomes bright and full color; Maurice Sendak's *Where the Wild Things Are* has darker illustrations as Max becomes more involved with his imaginary world; Audrey Wood's *The Napping House*, illustrated by Don Wood, has lighter, brighter illustrations as the various sleepers awake; Donald Crews lightens the hues and blurs the shapes to communicate speed in *Freight Train*; and Robert McCloskey uses darker hues to portray a storm and lighter ones to depict distance in *Time of Wonder*.

Color Separation: The process of separating the primary colors in a color picture for commercial art purposes or for picture book illustrations. After the colors are separated, a full-color book is printed from plates coated with yellow, blue (cyan), red (magenta), and black ink. The illustration on each plate is created with a special camera or a scanner that separates the colors. Sometimes artists make separate overlays for each of the four colors, and these are used to make the negatives or images in a process that is known as *preseparated art*.

Ruth Heller's *Color, Color, Color* and Aliki's *How a Book Is Made* (Aliki, 1986: 18–19) use four-color transparent overlays to demonstrate the four-color process. Aliki notes that "When the four colors are printed together, they combine to make up many more colors. Lighter shades of each color combine to make up still more colors." Young people may simulate the color separation process by creating artwork using sponges dipped in the four colors of yellow, blue, red, and black.

Comedy: Popularly, an amusing drama or other form of humorous entertainment; however, critically, one of the four modes or fundamental stories identified by Northrop Frye in *Anatomy of Criticism: Four Essays*. According to Frye, the comedy is a story of hope and renewal that moves from chaos to order, and comedies can vary from ironic to romantic. An example of a comedy is E. B. White's *Charlotte's Web*, which opens with a chaotic situation in which Wilbur is aided by Charlotte who creates a new and hopeful order at the conclusion. Young people can explore comedy as a fundamental story by considering how *Charlotte's Web*, Robin McKinley's *Spindle's End*, and *The 500 Hats of Bartholomew Cubbins* by Dr. Seuss are alike in presenting characters that move from chaos to order and from hope to renewal during the sequence of events. See *Wit and Humor*.

Comic Relief: A humorous element within a serious work. Comic relief serves the immediate function of relieving emotional tension. However, by contrast, it can sharpen the work's overall emotional impact.

Young people who read Jerry Spinelli's *Wringer* will discover a plot that is centered on the ritualized massacre of hundreds of pigeons at an annual fund-raising event. Yet, they will also find humor in the antics of a pet pigeon, Nipper, and in Palmer's efforts to hide and protect him. A discussion of the book could help readers see how the comic elements hold their interest while heightening the story's emotional impact by personalizing the slaughter of a single innocent bird that can think and win the care of a human being.

Comic Strip: A sequence of cartoons that relate a brief narrative through blocked images that may or may not include words. One of the most popular forms of mass communication in English tradition, the comic strip became a fixture in Sunday papers around 1900. Precursors to the modern comic strip include cartoons created by such illustrious names as Rembrandt, Leonardo DaVinci, Raphael, and Michelangelo. Young people can encounter the comic strip format in Maurice Sendak's *In the Night Kitchen*, Raymond Briggs' *The Snowman*, and Brian Pinkney's *Sparrowboy*.

Activities that allow young people to explore the format include clipping favorite comics to place on a bulletin board; cutting favorite comics apart and challenging peers to sequence the blocks; and using Ellison die cuts for illustrations to adapt to comic book format an episode from Arnold Lobel's *Frog and Toad Series* or Cynthia Rylant's *Henry and Mudge Series*.

Complication: An entangling of affairs early in the development of the plot of a narrative. Part of the rising action, complications follow the exposition of the initial situation and must be unraveled in the resolution at the end. Examples of early complications include Kit Tyler's new friendship with an accused witch in Elizabeth Speare's *The Witch of Blackbird Pond*; Leigh Botts' school assignment to write a letter to an author in Beverly Cleary's *Dear Mr. Henshaw*; and Marty's first seeing Judd's scared and scrawny beagle in Phyllis Naylor's *Shiloh*.

Young people may be encouraged to identify complicating factors in books read aloud or in novels that are the subjects of book discussion. See *Rising Action*.

Computer-generated Graphics: All types of images created by computers. Computer-generated graphics may be simple line drawings, lavish illustrations that resemble artistic paintings, or realistically detailed shaded pictures that simulate a photograph. These images may have been totally created by the computer or could be natural images that have been manipulated or enhanced through the use of computer software. The images may be created using some combination of input devices such as digitizers, scanners, and pattern recognition devices. And, an artist may utilize output devices such as plotters, displays, laser printers, and film recorders.

J. Otto Seibold used computer-generated, smooth airbrushed characters in *Olive, the Other Reindeer*, written by Vivian Walsh. Seibold's other titles include *Mr. Lunch Takes a Plane Ride*; *Mr. Lunch Borrows a Canoe*; *Monkey Business*; *Free Lunch*; and *Penguin Dreams*. Additional examples of computer-generated artwork in children's picture books include *Bright and Early Thursday Evening: A Tangled Tale* and *Jubal's Wish*, both written by Audrey Wood and illustrated by Don Wood, as well as Rachel Isadora's *ABC Pop* and *1 2 3 Pop!* and Janet Stevens and Susan Stevens' *Cook-a-Doodle-Doo!* Computer-generated graphics were used in David Pelletier's *The Graphic Alphabet*, a 1997 Caldecott Honor book, and in Christopher Bing's illustrations for Ernest Thayer's *Casey at the Bat: A Ballad of the Republic Sung in the Year 1888*, a 2001 Caldecott Honor book.

Young people may consult *www.audreywood.com/mac_site/jubal/jubal.html* to learn how Don Wood illustrated *Jubal's Wish*, or they may use any of a variety of computer software programs to produce their own computer-generated graphics that may be printed for display or contributed to a Web site.

Concept Book: A type of information book that explores the similarities and differences (*e.g.*, colors, opposites, or shapes) in a group of objects or actions in order to illuminate the larger concepts or contribute to the understanding of the item's varied aspects. In its broadest sense all information books that are designed to stimulate a child's cognitive development are concept books. Narrowly, they include those books which assist pre-school/primary children to comprehend relationships between objects, note essential elements, and anticipate the whole from one of its parts. Carolyn W. Lima and John A. Lima's *A to Zoo: Subject Access to Children's Picture Books*, fifth edition, provides an extensive list of general and specialized concept books.

Concept books are more meaningful to children if they are preceded or followed by first-hand experiences. Children will easily relate to Tana Hoban's *Circles, Triangles and Squares* because she uses familiar objects to build these concepts. After sharing the work children may be encouraged to locate in their classroom or schoolyard objects that could be labeled circles, triangles, and squares. This experience may be followed by an introduction to Lois Ehlert's *Color Zoo* in which heads of animals are represented by using a variety of shapes (for example, a heart shape as the basis for her stylized deer's head). Children will enjoy accepting Ehlert's invitation to "make some new ones for your zoo" and seeing their efforts displayed.

Concrete Poetry: A form of poetry in which the arrangement of the letters, the words, or the layout of the lines is such that the meaning is enhanced by the visual presentation. At times, only punctuation marks are used, as in "Showers, Clearing Later in the Day" from Eve Merriam's *A Sky Full of Poems*.

Among the collections of concrete poetry are Robert Froman's *Seeing Things*; J. Patrick Lewis' *Doodle Dandies*, illustrated by Lisa Desimini; Paul Janeczko's *A Poke in the Eye: A Collection of Concrete Poems*; and Jan Bransfield Graham's *Flicker Flash*, illustrated by Nancy Davis, as well as her *Splish, Splash*, illustrated by Steve Scott. After exploring and enjoying concrete poetry, children may wish to create an original concrete poem to be displayed on a "The Shape of Things" bulletin board.

Conflict: In fiction, the struggle between the main character and another force. There are four basic types of conflict: (1) *person against person* as, for example, in the struggle between Willy and Stone Fox in John Gardiner's *Stone Fox*, and between the miller's daughter and the little man in Paul Zelinsky's *Rumpelstiltskin*; (2) *person against society* as demonstrated by Kit Tyler's struggle against Puritans in Elizabeth Speare's *The Witch of Blackbird Pond* and by Annemarie's struggle against the Nazis in Lois Lowry's *Number the Stars*; (3) *person against nature* as in Jason's fight for survival in the Klondike in Will Hobbs' *Jason's Gold* and in Sam Gribley's struggle for survival in Jean George's *My Side of the Mountain*; and (4) *person against self* as demonstrated by Joel's conflict over guilt in Marion Dane Bauer's *On My Honor* and by Jess' struggle with loss in Katherine Paterson's *Bridge to Terabithia*.

For the books young people read, they may explore the relationship of character to conflict. That is, how do they see conflict reflecting and revealing the attributes of the main character?

Connotation: See *Denotation*.

Contemporary Realistic Fiction: Fiction that presents today's world through characters, plots, and settings that are imaginative but that represent the real world. Contemporary realistic fiction is one of the most popular genres of fiction for young people for a number of reasons: the setting is familiar and contemporary; characters encounter problems and challenges that are relevant to readers; readers can discover that others have coped with personal problems similar to theirs; and readers can experience cultures and backgrounds different from their own. Contemporary realistic fiction should be honest, portraying believable plots and characters, hopeful, and respectful of young people's abilities to draw conclusions and make judgments. When reading contemporary realistic fiction, young people should be able to enjoy a good story and to discover insights about themselves and others.

Examples of contemporary realistic fiction include Sharon Creech's *Walk Two Moons*; Audrey Couloumbis' *Getting Near to Baby*; Louis Sachar's *Holes*; Elaine Konigsburg's *The View from Saturday*; Kevin Henkes' *Sun and Spoon*; and three 2001 Newbery Honor books: Joan Bauer's *Hope Was Here,* Jack Gantos' *Joey Pigza Swallowed the Key,* and Kate Di Camillio's *Because of Winn-Dixie* as well as series books such as Lois Lowry's *Anastasia Series* and Phyllis Reynolds Naylor's *Alice Series* and *Shiloh Series.*

An activity for young people who are reading contemporary realistic fiction is that they evaluate works by appropriate criteria for the genre. They could also participate in a discussion group, applying some of the techniques of psychological criticism. That is, could this story happen to someone that they know? Could this story happen to them? See *Realistic Fiction.*

Convention: An established graphical or literary device, form, style, technique, or subject matter. Examples of literary conventions include exaggeration in tall tales, a predictable pattern of 17 syllables in the three lines (5, 7, 5) of the haiku; the use of figurative language in lyric poetry; repetition of events in folktales; and the familiar subjects and content of nursery rhymes. Examples of graphic conventions include voice and dream bubbles, blurred shapes to indicate speed, frames, and altered type to show shifts in point of view. A young child who responds to rhyme, humor, or rhythm, or who can predict the subjects, events, and outcomes common to a specific genre is developing critical abilities, including an awareness of literary conventions. See *Genre.*

Copyright: The exclusive legal right to reproduce, adapt, perform, display, or disseminate works of art, literature, music, or other creative endeavors. In the United

States the complicated issues of copyright are defined by the Copyright Act of 1976, and the Digital Millennium Copyright Act of 1998, as well as their numerous court interpretations. Ideally, copyright law balances the intellectual property rights of creators against the artistic and scientific advancement of society. The concept of fair use extends special rights to those engaged in scholarly activities. Young people may develop an awareness of the importance of copyright to authors and publishers by noting the copyright notices in the books they read and by acknowledging sources in their research.

Coretta Scott King Awards: A children's book award presented annually by the Coretta Scott King Task Force of the American Library Association's Social Responsibilities Round Table. Recipients, including honor awards, are authors and illustrators of African descent whose distinguished books promote an understanding of and appreciation for peace and world brotherhood. Young people may find information about the award and past award winners at *ala.org/srrt/csking*.

Counting Book: A type of concept picture book designed to teach young children to identify numbers, their shapes, their names, and to count. Counting books for younger children often emphasize the numbers zero to ten or one to ten. Criteria for their evaluation are that the text and illustrations are closely related and that objects are clearly identifiable and countable.

As with other concept books, counting books represent a wide range of approaches, complexities, themes, and formats. Illustrations in counting books range from the simple as in Denise Fleming's *Count* to the more complex as in Arthur Geisert's *Pigs from 1 to 1*, which requires finding the numbers and piglets on each page. Two books that count backwards from ten are Molly Bang's 1988 Caldecott Honor book *Ten, Nine, Eight* and Peggy Rathmann's *10 Minutes Till Bedtime*. Young children learn a nursery rhyme and also learn to count when reading Keith Baker's *Big Fat Hen*.

Counting books often correspond with a particular theme or subject such as Maggie Smith's *Counting Our Way to Maine*, which follows a family on a trip to Maine and demonstrates counting to twenty. Ann Herbert Scott's *One Good Horse: A Cowpuncher's Counting Book* presents a cowboy and a son as they count things on the ranch from one good horse to one hundred cattle.

Counting books that provide additional information about a subject are Bruce McMillan's *Counting Wildflowers* and Muriel Feelings' 1972 Caldecott Honor book *Moja Means One: A Swahili Counting Book*, illustrated by Tom Feelings. Counting books like Bruce McMillan's *Jelly Beans for Sale* and Tana Hoban's *26 Letters and 99 Cents* include additional math concepts (*e.g.*, counting money).

After sharing a broad selection of counting books, young people may use the criteria listed above to compare their favorites to each other. They may also work in small groups to select a theme for their own counting book which can be created from illustrating objects, food items, or animals. Their counting book could be bound as a group or class book or displayed around the room as individual poster pages. A digital camera could also be used to photograph objects to create a "counting book" on a classroom Web page. Cathie Hilterbran Cooper's *Counting Your Way through 1–2–3: Books and Activities* is a professional resource for selecting and using counting books.

Couplet: Two lines of poetry that present a more or less complete thought. In the formal sense, the pair of words that end the two lines rhyme, which is known as an end-rhyme. In English language poetry a popular rhythm for a couplet has often been *iambic pentameter*, a rhythm that is composed of an unaccented syllable followed by an accented syllable:

* / * / * / * / * /* / * / * / * / * /

A formal couplet typically consists of eight (octosyllabic) or ten (decasyllabic) syllables. A couplet has often been used as a dramatic device to end a speech in a play. For a poem that demonstrates rhyming couplets descending from twelve syllables to one syllable, young people may read "Couplet Countdown" in Eve Merriam's *It Doesn't Always Have to Rhyme*. Rap music sometimes makes use of stanzas composed of couplets, which is an example of the adaptive nature of the verse form. Often a contemporary author will write a couplet that has no obvious rhyme scheme producing a two-line stanza or couplet that is composed in blank verse.

Young people can sense the playfulness that is inherent in the form as they listen to a reading of e. e. cummings' "maggie and milly and molly and may" from Jack Prelutsky's *The Random House Book of Poetry for Children*. The poem is also available on the Web at *www.poets.org/poems/poems.cfm?prmID=1188*. This particular poem demonstrates and offers students examples of couplet stanzas where an end-rhyme is present and couplet stanzas where blank verse is used. Students could compose their own ending for the poem by cummings if the reader withholds the last three words. Young people will also enjoy couplets, such as *"Upright, my tail! Forward, my feet! . . . I see a child across the street!"* composed by the courtly canine in Lois Lowry's novel *Stay!: Keepers Story* (Lowry, 1997: 50).

Crayon: Generally, a drawing or writing material in a stick form. These materials may be comprised of chalk, pastel, conté crayons, charcoal, lithographic and other grease crayons, as well as wax crayons. The popular meaning of "crayon" refers to colored paraffin sticks that have paper wrappings and are available in a variety of colors, sizes and shapes. David Small's *The Gardener*, a 1998 Caldecott Honor book incorporated mixed media including watercolor, ink pen line, and crayon. Leo Lionni used crayon on rice paper collage in his 1961 Caldecott Honor book *Inch by Inch*. Crayon was the single medium used in Margaret Wise Brown's 1944 Caldecott Honor book *A Child's Good Night Book*, illustrated by Jean Charlot. An interesting use of crayon is in Chris Van Allsburg's *Bad Day at Riverbend*, which follows Sheriff Hardy who is investigating a shiny slime invading a small western town that has been created through a series of black line drawings. As the picture broadens into full-color illustrations, the reader learns that this is actually a cowboy coloring book and that the "slime" has been created by a child using crayons. Young people may create their own crayon drawings, using a variety of papers for different effects.

Criticism or Literary Criticism: The evaluation, classification, analysis, and study of literary works; *decision* and *discernment* (from Greek *kritikos*). Among ways to categorize various approaches to criticism is that of M. H. Abrams in *A Glossary of Literary Terms*. He identifies four types of criticism: mimetic, which focuses on honest, realistic portrayals of plot (see *Sociological Criticism*), character (see *Psychological Criticism*), and setting (see *Sociological Criticism*); pragmatic, which considers the effect of the work on the audience (see *Reader Response Theory*); expressive, which is concerned with the author's life and state of mind (see *Biographical Criticism*); and objective criticism, which analyzes the text apart from other considerations (see *Formalism*). Young people engaged in book discussions may unconsciously use all four approaches by considering such questions as, "Was the protagonist believable?" "How did that event make you feel?" "What experiences prepared the author to write about the subject?" "Did you find examples of figurative language in the novel?"

Cumulative Tale: A narrative that has a simple chain-like plot developed through a pattern of repetition in which phrases, objects, or actions are added one to another until the complications are resolved. Cumulative tales may build to a climax and then reverse, becoming a circular tale that takes the reader back to the beginning as in Nancy Van Laan's *The Big Fat Worm*. Originating in the oral tradition, the cumulative tale is found among the folklore of all the people of the world. Examples of cumulative tales include Janet Stevens' *The House that Jack Built*, Audrey Wood's *The Napping House*, illustrated by Don Woods, Laura Joffe Numeroff's *If You Give a Mouse a Cookie*, illustrated by Felicia Bond, Jan Brett's *The Mitten*, and Simms Taback's *There Was an Old Lady Who Swallowed a Fly*.

Young people listening to a reading of these cumulative tales may be invited to participate by recalling what comes next. They may also sing along if the tale has accompanying music, as does Taback's *There Was an Old Lady Who Swallowed a Fly*. Young people who are introduced to cumulative tales as flannel board stories may encourage other young people to transfer the telling of a cumulative tale to flannel board, which is especially suited to the visual display of the repetition in a cumulative tale.

Dactyl: See *Meter*.

Decorative Frame: Elaborate designs created by an illustrator to frame picture book art or text. Decorative frames are pleasing to the eye, bring the reader into the story, and provide visual continuity. Decorative frames are often integral to the story as they are in the picture books of Trina Schart Hyman. Two of her award winning illustrated books, *Saint George and the Dragon*, retold by Margaret Hodges, and the Grimms' classic *Little Red Riding Hood* demonstrate her use of elaborately decorated frames surrounding the text as well as simple borders that function as window frames in *Saint George and the Dragon*. Having the action "framed," makes it seem that the reader is outside the story looking into the action. At times a character within the window motions the reader forward or catches the reader's eye. Other illustrators who have made use of frames or intricate borders include Jan Brett for *Berlioz the Bear* and *The Mitten: A Ukranian Folktale;* Felipe Davos for *The Secret Stars*, written by Joseph Slate; Juan Wijngaard for *Sir Gawain and the Loathly Lady*, retold by Selina Hastings; David Shannon for *The Amazing Christmas Extravaganza*; and Nancy Willard's *Pish Posh, Said Hieronymous Bosch*, which incorporates an elaborate frame created by Leo and Diane Dillon's son, Lee Dillon. Children will want to locate other books and illustrators who use this design. What information do they find in the frames? What do the frames contribute to the atmosphere of the story? For a follow-up activity, they may design a decorative frame for their favorite picture book illustration.

Dedication: An often-personal note prefixed on an opening page of a book that dedicates the work to one or more individuals as a token of affection, esteem, or tribute. Excellent examples of dedications are in Sarah Stewart's *The Library* and in Arnold Adoff's book of children's poetry called *Love Letters*, which he dedicated to his wife, Virginia Hamilton. The dedication reads as poetry:

> Dear Ginger Belle:
> These Love Letters,
> These Love Poems
> Are
> For
> You
> For All The Days
> Of All The Years
> Your Own Arn (1997).

Young people may wish to explore the dedications in other books, or they may write a dedication of their own in a book they self-publish.

Denotation: A word's literal dictionary meaning, without emotional associations. The opposite of *denotation* is *connotation*, which is the set of images and feelings that may be associated with the word. Developing an understanding that words can have emotional meanings beyond their dictionary meanings is important to the understanding of *poetry* and *style*. Without considering the terminology, young people can distinguish between literal and emotional meanings. For example, they can be led to consider what they associate with or think of when they hear or read the word, such as *puppy*, which will have strong connotations for many young people. They can compare their emotional associations and feelings with the dictionary definition: *a dog less than one year old*. They may carry out the same activity for other words encountered in stories and poems.

Denouement: The final clearing of the complications of a plot that occurs after the climax; French for *unknotting*. After the solution of the main conflict, an unraveling or explanation of untied conflicts or situations that made up the plot are revealed in order to satisfy the reader.

In a read-aloud story the teacher or librarian may wish to stop reading at the climax and ask children to suggest any questions that still remain concerning the plot complications. After the story is completed the children may discuss whether their questions were answered. If a book is read by several upper-grade children and discussed in a group setting, the leader may want to introduce the term denouement and ask the children to suggest any questions relevant to the plot that were explained after the climax. If all questions are answered, the denouement is complete and the plot is said to have a closed ending.

Detective Story: A type of mystery story in which a crime is solved by a detective who logically gathers and interprets evidence. Edgar Allan Poe developed the genre with the publication of *The Murders in the Rue Morgue*, establishing the genre's primary conventions: that there was a crime; clues but no red herrings; a detective; the detective's confidant who clarifies the situation; and a primary suspect who is proven innocent. In books for young people, the detective is typically not a real detective but rather another young person. For example, in Joan Lowrey Nixon's mystery, *The Name of the Game Was Murder*, fifteen-year-old Samantha must solve the murder of her great-uncle, famous novelist Augustus Trever. Series that feature child detectives include Crosby Bonsall's *Private Eyes Series*, Patricia Reilly Giff's *Polka Dot Private Eyes Series*, Marjorie Sharmat's *Nate the Great Series*, Terrance Dicks' *The Baker Street Irregulars Series*, and Donald Sobol's *Encyclopedia Brown Series*. Young people who are interested in these stories may predict how their favorite detective would solve a crime, perhaps one found in a current newspaper. They could support their predicted solution with details of plot and character from the detective stories they have read. And, young people who would enjoy exploring the concept of detective from a nonfiction perspective may read Donna Jackson's *The Bone Detectives: How Forensic Anthropologists Solve Crimes and Uncover Mysteries of the Dead*, with photographs by Charlie Fellebaum.

Dialect: A vocabulary or speech form that is limited to people from a particular region or area, social class, or occupation. It usually differs from what is normally the accepted pronunciation of the language and may contain different words and grammar usage.

One example of a United States dialect that is well represented in books for young people is Southern dialect. For example, among works that incorporate Southern Black dialect are the 1993 Caldecott Honor book, Sherley Ann Williams' *Working Cotton*, illustrated by Carole Byard, and Virginia Hamilton's *When Birds Could Talk and Bats Could Sing: The Adventures of Bruh Sparrow, Sis Wren and Her Friends*, illustrated by Barry Moser. Mildred Taylor's 1977 Newbery Award book, *Roll of Thunder, Hear My Cry* has dialogue from both educated and uneducated Southern voices during the Depression. Southern Cajun dialect is the basis of *Cajun Night Before Christmas* by Howard Trosclair (editor) and a variety of Southern dialects (from the Great Smoky Mountains to the bayous of Louisiana) abounds in Nancy Van Laan's *With a Whoop and a Holler*, a collection of Southern folklore.

Young people may be introduced to dialect by comparing the dialects in different versions of the same Brer Rabbit stories. Possible versions could include Van Dyke Parks' adaptation, *Jump!, Jump Again!, Jump on Over!* and Julius Lester's *The Tales of Uncle Remus*. To see changes in the interpretation of dialect over the years, young people can compare new versions and the original stories from Joel Chandler Harris' "Uncle Remus."

Young people may also listen to storytelling audiocassettes that feature a distinctive dialect. Two online resources for storytelling audiocassettes and professional materials are the National Storytelling Network (*www.storynet.org*) and August House (*www.augusthouse.com*).

Dialogue: The words spoken by characters in a story, play, poem, or any kind of narrative. Young people often favor literature that includes dialogue because the dialogue provides relief from descriptive passages. Dialogue also has other values: (1) it allows for the interplay of ideas; (2) it reveals a speaker's character; (3) it advances the action.

Young people can experience dialogue and explore its values by considering scenes from novels rich in dialogue, such as the one in Betsy Byars' *The Not-Just-Anybody Family* when Maggie and Vern are considering breaking into jail. This scene shows the interplay of ideas, moves the plot forward, reveals Maggie and Vern, and entertains the reader. Young people may further consider the role of dialogue in literature by adapting scenes from novels into readers' theatre scripts.

Several poems in Jack Prelutsky's collection *The Random House Book of Poetry for Children* are rich in dialogue that allow young people to assume a character's role. For example, included are E. V. Rieu's "The Flattered Flying Fish," the tale of a fish lured to dinner by a shark, demonstrates how action may be advanced through conversation; Roald Dahl's "Aunt Sponge and Aunt Spiker," an argument between two vain sisters, shows dialogue's capacity to reveal character, taken from *James and the Giant Peach*; and Lewis Carroll's "Father William," a discussion between a father and son, provides an example of the interplay through dialogue.

Diary or **Journal:** A journal is a recording of a writer's reflections and ideas on a fairly regular basis. These records, commonly with daily entries, were usually started because of a journey. The journey could be physical involving travel or emotional involving some important change in the author's life. *Diary* and *journal* are terms that are used interchangeably. Although a diary or journal is generally written for personal pleasure and private use, the result can be a publishable journal, such as Ted and Betsy Lewin's *Gorilla Walk*, which relates their journey into Africa's Bwindi Impenetrable National Park, or Sophie Webb's *My Season with Penguins: An Antarctic Journal.*

Frequently, in fiction for young people, authors may choose to create a work written in diary or journal form. This differs from a true account or actual diary of real events, which are classified as a form of biography. Fictional diaries have become popular since they immediately engage a reader in the character's life. Some notable examples of fictionalized diaries include: Joan W. Blos' *A Gathering of Days: A New England Girl's Journal, 1830–32;* Karen Cushman's *Catherine Called Birdy;* and Louise Fitzhugh's *Harriet the Spy.*

A journal or a diary can be a useful tool because young people can practice writing on a daily basis making use of this old and honored tradition. An activity could include the reading aloud of one of the above works and encouraging students to write a future diary entry for the main character or perhaps a peripheral character. For instance, what might Catherine's father have written in his journal? Another activity could involve the student in creating a diary or journal entry for a significant day in the life of a folktale character.

Dictionary: An alphabetical listing of words that includes information for each. A dictionary may be an inclusive one that lists many words, such as the *Oxford English Dictionary,* currently with 22,000 pages in 20 volumes; a general one, which may be targeted toward a specific user (*e.g.,* a second grade student); or a specialized one (*e.g.,* a biographical, legal, or geographical dictionary); a dictionary of idioms, rhyming words, slang, spellings, or pronunciations; a bilingual dictionary; or a thesaurus. Dictionaries may also be comprehensive and, thus, include a wide range of useful information (*e.g.,* meanings, grammar and usage, historical explanations of word origin and development of definitions, pronunciations, antonyms, and synonyms). Typically, the earliest dictionaries addressed the meanings of only the most challenging words; later dictionaries became more inclusive and comprehensive. The oldest existing dictionary is *Homeric Words,* a Greek lexicon developed two millennia ago. William Harmon and C. Hugh Holman, in their *A Handbook to Literature*, seventh edition, credit *The Dictionary of Syr T. Eliot, Knyght* with establishing the term *dictionary*.

Young people may explore the reference section in a school or public library and identify the various types of dictionaries and the ranges of information they include. They may also explore the Web sites such as *www.dictionary.msn.com/* or *www.m-w.com/* or *www.wordcentral.com/*. They may compare and contrast what is online with what is available in their library building.

Younger library users may be introduced to children's ABC books, which, as a type of dictionary, can lead to a better understanding of the concept of a dictionary. Young people may compare Tracey Campbell Pearson's *A-Apple Pie* with Kate Greenaway's classic illustrated edition and then with Arnold Lobel's Caldecott Honor book, *On Market Street*, illustrated by Anita Lobel. Older readers may consider ABC books through Cathi Hepworth's wild and wickedly funny *Antics!* in which illustrated ants demonstrate meanings (*e.g.*, flamboy**ant** is illustrated by a high-fashion lady ant). Older children may also examine Mike Wilks' *The Ultimate Alphabet* and create a dictionary using the page-packed illustration for each letter of the alphabet (*e.g.*, 360 items on one page begin with the letter *A*). A dictionary developed from any one page will require a number of reference tools to identify and define the objects, signs, sculptures, and paintings.

Didacticism: A term that describes literature created for the purpose of instruction. Didacticism shaped children's literature until the 18th century when publishers like John Newbery sought to introduce the concept of reading for pleasure, as well as for moral instruction. From ancient to contemporary times there has been a philosophical debate on these two functions of art. At its worst didacticism overwhelms the story. A term that has been used to describe literature that only preaches is *propagandist literature*. Such literature sacrifices literary quality to a moral message of some sort. Among contemporary sources of didacticism are new editions of the classics. For example, Robert Louis Stevenson's *A Child's Garden of Verses* includes the following stanza from "Good and Bad Children,"

> You must be bright and quiet,
> And content with simple diet;
> And remain, through all bewild'ring,
> Innocent and honest children (1885).

Such verses cannot offer children pleasure, and the condescending tone diminishes a young person's engagement with the text. In stark contrast to poems like "Good and Bad Children" is the lack of condescension toward the child audience in Stevenson's novel *Treasure Island.*

A successful use of didacticism is the fable, a story that artistically and imaginatively demonstrates the truth of a proverb. Aesop's fables have been successfully adapted into picture book format over the years. Young people can usually understand the message in a fable because it is explicit and because the message is conveyed in a playful and entertaining manner. For instance, Arnold Lobel's *Fables* presents lessons that do not dominate the story. As an activity, young people could listen to Lobel's fables read aloud and, using a master list, match the correct maxims to each story.

Die-cutting: A process of cutting material from a larger sheet into a desired shape and size by using a die, that is, by using a press and a steel shape. A steel rule is bent to form the design that may be used to create the outline form of a book such as Lois Ehlert's *Hands*, a book shaped like a gloved-hand. Die-cutting may also be used to create holes in the pages of a book as in Simms Taback's *I Know an Old Lady Who Swallowed a Fly,* which offers a view of the old lady's stomach through the die-cut shapes of the things she eats—a horse, a cow, a dog, etc. Additional books with die-cut holes include Tana Hoban's *Look! Look! Look!,* Simms Taback's 2000 Caldecott Award book *Joseph Had a Little Overcoat,* Lois Ehlert's 1990 Caldecott Honor book *Color Zoo* as well as her *Color Farm.*

An Ellison Letter Machine (or similar device) may be used by children to create die shapes, or they may trace around the outline of a cookie cutter to create a "die-cut" hole in a piece of construction paper. These "die-cuts" may be used to create note cards or small booklets.

Dime Novel: An inexpensive form of a melodramatic or sensational fiction story published from the last half of the 19th century until the 1920s when the reading shifted to pulp fiction. These paper novels usually sold for ten cents a copy, and first came into popularity with the Buffalo Bill Westerns of the late 1860s. Most of the novels used America as the setting and related stories of the romance, war, and particular periods of history. Stanford University offers young people a virtual tour of dime novel book covers, information about dime novel authors, and a time line of their history at "Dime Novels and Penny Dreadfuls" (*www.sul.stanford.edu/depts/dp/pennies/tour_guide.html*).

Documentary Novel: A realistic novel that incorporates such real life information as excerpts from legal reports, newspaper articles, and courtroom transcripts. Examples of documentary novels for older readers are Todd Strasser's *Give a Boy* *a Gun* and Barbara Snow Gilbert's *Paper Trail*. *Paper Trail* incorporates sections of factual data (titled "Snippets") among fictional chapters about a young protagonist's fight for survival against a militia group. Young people reading Gilbert's novel could track down the full articles and reports from which the "snippet" sections were taken and evaluate them as a whole; or, after reading another realistic novel which presents a social issue, they could research the topic to refute the author's implications or to identify data to support the plot as Gilbert did in her "Snippet" sections.

Double spread or Double-page Spread: The use of two opposing pages for one illustration. Picture books most often make use of this technique for presenting illustrations. For example, Marjorie Priceman uses double spreads so that there is space for the action of two stories in one in the 1996 Caldecott Honor book, Lloyd Moss' *Zin! Zin! Zin! A Violin*. The major story, told in verse, involves adding one instrument of the orchestra at a time until ten instruments become a chamber group of ten. Simultaneously, a dog, cat, and mouse chase to a happy resolution. In contrast another 1996 Caldecott Honor book, *Alphabet City* by Stephen T. Johnson, makes use of single-page spreads to present a wordless alphabet book. Some illustrators use a combination of double-spread and single-spread illustrations in a single book, such as the 1999 Caldecott Honor book, *Duke Ellington*, written by Andrea Pinkney and illustrated by Brian Pinkney, who uses a scratchboard technique on single and double-page spreads. Vertical double spreads were used by Janet Stevens in her 1996 Caldecott Honor winner, *Tops and Bottoms* and by Ann Jonas in *Aardvarks, Disembark*. Young people may review a group of Caldecott Award and Honor books, determine the type of spreads, and speculate on why they were so arranged.

Drawing: The creation of shapes and forms through lines applied to a surface using a variety of techniques and various media (*e.g.*, pencil, charcoal, ink, or crayon). Drawings are enhanced with the use of color and shading. Drawing is often used as a preliminary step in art creation although drawing itself is also considered to be a fine art technique.

Jerry Pinkney's pencil line drawings are evident in every book he illustrates, including Patricia McKissack's *Mirandy and Brother Wind*; Julius Lester's *John Henry*; and Julius Lester's *Black Cowboy, Wild Horses*. Excellent examples of pen and ink drawings can be found in the work of David Macaulay in books like *Cathedral: The Story of Its Construction*; *Castle*; *The New Way Things Work*; and *Building Big*.

Young people may enjoy experimenting with drawing books such as Ed Emberley's *Fingerprint Drawing Book* or his many other works, which may be found in the school library media center or public library. Another popular illustrator of children's drawing books is Lee J. Ames who created *Draw 50 Famous Caricatures* and others in the *Draw 50 Series*.

Dummy: A single physical layout plan for a printed publication such as a flyer, newspaper, magazine, or book. Simple dummies are composed of a collected group of pages in the same size and format of the intended publication. The most sophisticated is a blueprint of the publication, called a positive blue dummy.

Janet Stevens in *From Pictures to Words: A Book about Making a Book* defines a dummy as "a practice book." Stevens shares that she makes dummies from scratch paper in the same size as the final book. Her editor sends the story in typeface that Stevens cuts apart and tapes in the correct places on the pages of the dummy. Then, using earlier sketches and the storyboard map, Stevens draws in the sketches in their approximate size. This creation process provides a working plan for the book and is usually sent to the editor for further comment.

In Aliki's *How a Book Is Made*, cats narrate the steps in bookmaking. Aliki describes a dummy as a "handmade book" that is designed the way the artist wants the book to appear. The artist shows the dummy to the editor who may suggest changes in the text and then to the book designer who may suggest changes in the art.

After following the bookmaking process in the two books listed above, young people may try writing and illustrating their own stories. They may also create their own "handmade books" for a classroom library.

Easy Reader / Beginning Reader: A book with a controlled vocabulary designed for beginning readers. Many writers credit Dr. Seuss with creating this now popular genre with his *The Cat in the Hat* in 1957. This book, containing one hundred one-syllable words from the Dolch vocabulary list of 220 words, uses humorous illustrations to extend the story line. In 1957, Else Minarick's *Little Bear*, illustrated by Maurice Sendak, was published as the first title in Harper & Row's *I Can Read Series*.

At their best, easy readers provide a valuable transition from basic readers to library books, helping children develop confidence, interest, and independence in reading. However, consideration of audience is critical. Pre-schoolers need to listen to quality picture books with expanded vocabularies, and very young readers may find many books labeled *easy reader* or *beginning reader* too difficult because the vocabulary may be too advanced. Today a number of easy-to-read books on a slightly older level have curriculum value, especially in social studies and science.

A controlled vocabulary book that has demonstrated the genre's potential for literary excellence is the 1973 Newbery Honor book *Frog and Toad Together* by Arnold Lobel. Barbara Barstow and Judith Riggle address easy readers in depth in their professional resource *Beyond Picture Books: A Guide to First Readers*. And, the Multnomah County Library maintains a thorough beginning reader list on the Web (*www.multnomah.lib.or.us/lit/kids/beginreader.html*).

After children have read a number of easy readers, as a group they may identify favorite characters and graph the composite results.

Edition: All copies of a printing of a book from the same type image, such as 1ˢᵗ edition or 2ⁿᵈ edition, a paperback edition, or a special edition. The original printing, or 1st edition, is generally considered more valuable than later editions. A facsimile reproduction is a copy of the original work. The British Library published a facsimile of Lewis Carroll's original hand-written and illustrated *Alice's Adventures Under Ground*. A paperback edition of an original hardback is often cut down in size, has a different cover, is more up-to-date and appealing to young people, and is printed on a lower-grade paper.

Young people can compare several hardback and paperback editions of books they have read as well as different editions of the same hardback book. For example, Simon and Schuster publishers are reprinting newly illustrated books of selected classics. Eugene Field's *Poems of Childhood* was the sixteenth book to enter the series of reissued *Scribner Illustrated Classics*. Young people may compare one of these reprinted classics with a more recent edition. Young people may also be encouraged to check a bookshelf at home to see whether they have any first edition books. They can determine the printing history of a book, derived from numbers on the title page verso, commonly called the copyright page. For example, if the numbers printed are 10 9 8 7 6 5 4 3 2 — the book is the second printing (the number 1 has been dropped). Children find this trivia to be interesting; however, some books will not include the printing history. A professional resource that gives a clear and concise explanation of the parts of a book is the "*Introduction*" to Kathleen Horning's *From Cover to Cover: Evaluating and Reviewing Children's Books*.

Editor: A person who is in charge of printing a book or other medium. It is the editor to whom an author submits a manuscript, and the editor makes a decision on whether to publish the book. If the editor's decision is positive, he or she continues to work with the author to edit the book. A copy editor checks for grammatical and spelling accuracy. If illustrations are involved, created either by the author or someone else assigned by the editor, an art designer also participates. Editors who commonly work with children's books are referred to as children's book editors, and some publishers include the editor's name on the title page verso, commonly called the copyright page.

The editing role changes for the production of a picture book. The artist who will illustrate the picture book usually meets with the editor and the art director to consider the book's layout and design, and then the artist prepares pencil sketches (roughs). After the pencil sketches are approved, the artist begins work on the final illustrations which, when completed, are submitted to the designer who works with the printer to ensure proper placement of text and illustrations as well as proper color and alignment. The editor, art director, and artist typically review sets of the proofs, comparing them to the finished artwork and noting corrections and adjustments in the printing process before the picture book is printed and bound.

Younger children may consult Lucia Raatma's *How Books Are Made* for a simple explanation of the process. Older readers can locate books on the shelf, such as Marc Aronson's 2001 Sibert Award-winning book *Sir Walter Raleigh and the Quest for Eldorado* and a 2000 Batchelder Honor book, *Vendela in Venice*, by Christina Björk and Inga-Karin Eriksson, in which the book designer is listed. Understanding the concept of the relationship between an editor and an author may help young people appreciate the importance of editing their own written or illustrated work.

Embroidered Pictures: A design made with needlework consisting of colored threads and utilizing a variety of embroidery stitches. Embroidered pictures can be used to tell a story as the artistic medium in a children's picture book. For example, Dia Cha's *Dia's Story Cloth*, a story from the Hmong, is illustrated with embroidered pictures. Introducing readers to her life and that of her family, Cha based the story on an embroidered story cloth created by the author's aunt and uncle. Children may be interested in creating their own portion of a story cloth with embroidery that would depict a particular event from their own family history.

End Rhyme: Rhyme occurring at the end of a line of verse. Shel Silverstein's *A Light in the Attic* includes numerous examples, such as "Bored," in which each line ends with the word *afford* alternating with *skateboard, outboard, surfboard,* and simply *board*. Young people may write their own poetry with the end rhyme scheme, using Sue Young's *The Scholastic Rhyming Dictionary*. This compilation of over 5,000 rhyming words is a helpful tool in locating rhyming words.

Endpapers: A book's front and back two facing pages, usually of heavier paper than the pages of the text and illustrations. The left front endpaper and the right back endpaper are glued to the inside of the book's covering. Endpapers in trade picture books may be illustrated with a design that relates to the content of the book, as in Jerry Pinkney's illustrated picture book, *The Ugly Duckling*, written by Hans Christian Andersen, which shows the young swan on the front endpapers and the full-grown swan on the back endpapers. William Steig's *Pete's Pizza* has red paper for the front endpapers and green for the back endpapers; the jacket of the book reflects the red, white, and green of the Italian flag. At other times, endpapers may be of a solid color that is evidence of the mood of the work as in Arthur Yorinks' *Hey, Al,* illustrated by Richard Egielsky, which has beige front endpapers and bright yellow back endpapers. Rebound books and library editions may have plain white endpapers.

Illustrated endpapers add to the visual impact of picture books. Teachers and librarians should call attention to illustrated endpapers in books read aloud. Children may be encouraged to predict the meaning of a book's endpapers as the book is introduced and to interpret the meaning of a specific endpaper design after the book is read. For example, the endpapers in Ann Jonas' *The Quilt* duplicate the design of the underside of the little girl's quilt. The observant child will notice the duplication as the book is read. Daniel Pinkwater's *Jolly Roger* has endpapers that picture the Hoboken dog. They were created using the Mac Paint program and an Apple MacIntosh computer.

Children may develop a computer-produced design appropriate for a specific book, or they may paint an illustration they feel would be visually meaningful for the endpapers of a favorite picture book. After the productions are shared with the class, in order to explain the choice of design, they may be displayed in the classroom or library media center.

Epic: A long serious narrative poem presenting heroic actions of characters that are important to the history of a nation or a people. There are two types of epics: the folk (*e.g., Beowulf*) and the literary (*e.g.,* Spenser's *The Faerie Queene*). Although each type may have its origins in the oral traditions of a people, the literary epic has a distinct author who gives the work structure and form; and the folk epic has cumulative authorship that is evidenced by its episodic and repetitious nature. The epic probably developed from the myth, with the emphasis of the myth (*i.e.,* from actions of the gods) shifting to that of the epic (*i.e.,* the feats of extraordinary men).

The following characteristics are common to both folk and literary epics: (1) the style is formal and dignified; (2) the narrative is composed of events that relate to a main character; (3) there is much dialogue; (4) the epic hero has superhuman and/or divine traits; (5) the hero is important as a national or legendary figure; (6) supernatural forces are sometimes participants; (7) the setting is in the distant past which is portrayed to be of greater significance than the present; and (8) the values of the culture in which the epic was created are presented.

An award-winning example of epic literature for children is Margaret Hodges' *Saint George and the Dragon,* a retelling from Spenser's *The Faerie Queene.* Though not retold in poetic form, *Saint George and the Dragon,* with its revealing illustrations by Trina Schart Hyman, demonstrates various characteristics of the epic by presenting the Red Cross Knight who in ages past (1) engaged a fierce and destructive dragon in three separate encounters; (2) drew renewed strength from an ancient spring and a fair apple tree; (3) restored peace to the land; (4) exemplified the English ideals of justice, loyalty, and duty by continuing to serve the Faerie Queene and by giving his reward to the common people; and (5) earned national recognition as a future king and eventually as Saint George. After reading *Saint George and the Dragon* to intermediate-grade children, they may be led to discover the epic's characteristics seen in the work and then be introduced to the term.

Epigraph: A quotation or motto on the title page or at the beginning of a book; a chapter or a poem that indicates its theme. Noted children's author Sid Fleischman opens the first chapter of his autobiography, *Abracadabra Kid: A Writer's Life,* with a chapter title of "The Fateful Nickel" but he also includes an excerpt from a child's fan letter to him. The child had written, "Dear Sid Fleischman, I have read *Mr. Mysterious and Company.* It's the second best book I have ever read." Other quotes from letters are included at the beginning of each of the forty-three chapters of the book.

Young people may consider epigraphs in other favorite books of fiction. An "epigraph book report" would make an interesting exercise for young people. They may choose a fiction book and locate quotations or mottos that best fit several or all of the chapters in the book.

Epilogue: A brief concluding statement appended to a literary work. It often wraps up any unanswered questions, expands on relationships of characters and events to those in both the era of the setting and future times, introduces characters and events to be included in sequels, or points out a moral.

A work that includes an epilogue is Natalie Babbitt's *Tuck Everlasting.* In that epilogue Mae and Tuck have returned to Treegap, looking for recognizable buildings and people but not asking the questions they have about Winnie. Simultaneously Tuck and Mae thought about the cemetery and passed through the wrought iron arched gate. There they found the answer they sought:

> In Loving Memory
> Winifred Foster Jackson
> Dear Wife
> Dear Mother
> *1870–1948*

"'So,' said Tuck to himself. 'Two years. She's been gone two years'" (Babbitt, 1975: 138).

Young people may be encouraged to create epilogues for other stories they have read, considering what the characters might be doing ten or twenty or fifty years after a story ends.

Episodic Plot/Episodic Novel: A novel that is comprised of individual parts or episodes that are loosely connected with the same characters and setting but without an integrated plot. The structure is usually chronological although time may not be closely defined for any episode and the chapters may be read as complete stories. The 1999 Newbery Honor book, Richard Peck's *A Long Way from Chicago: A Novel in Stories,* represents a classic episodic novel for young people. In seven episodic chapters, over a period of seven years, Joey and Mary Alice make summer visits to see their colorful Grandma Dowdel in rural Illinois during the Great Depression. An example of a chapter book for younger readers with an episodic plot is Beverly Cleary's *Beezus and Ramona.* Books for beginning readers are often structured with an episodic plot, for example Arnold Lobel's *Frog and Toad Series* or Cynthia Rylant's *Henry and Mudge Series.* Young people may be encouraged to imagine new episodes for an episodic novel they have read or to compare the structure of an episodic plot to a progressive one, such as that of Natalie Babbitt's *Tuck Everlasting.*

Eponym: A person or place whose name is so obviously linked with something that it has become the designation for it. Examples of eponymous words include "Levi's," from Levi Strauss, a manufacturer of overalls; "leotards," from Jules Leotard, a French circus performer; and "geiger counter," from Hans Geiger, a German physicist.

Children may be introduced to the concept of eponymous words by listening to a reading of some of the stories in Marvin Terban's *Guppies in Tuxedos.* After they have heard some stories behind the eponyms in Terban's book, they may research those names and places in more detail, discover other eponyms, or create an imaginative product for which their individual names could become an eponym.

Etching: The process of creating a picture or design on a metal plate by using acid to eat away lines and indentions that when filled with ink can transfer the picture or design onto paper. Etching involves covering metal plates, typically copper, iron, or zinc, with wax or resin into which the illustration is scratched with a fine needle. Where the wax or resin remains, the metal is protected from the effects of the acid. Developed in Western Europe in the fifteenth century, etching became an art form in the 1600s. A children's illustrator who uses the process is Arthur Geisert. His picture books include *The Ark, Oink,* and *Pigs from A to Z.* Young people can better understand the etching process by reading Geisert's *The Etcher's Studio.*

Exposition: The part of a narrative that provides background information, creates the tone, defines the setting, and establishes the relationships of the characters. Exposition typically comes early in a linear plot, as indicated in *Freytag's Pyramid* (see *Progressive Plot*). However, it can also occur throughout a narrative. For example, Elaine Konigsburg in *The View from Saturday* uses a four-page exposition (p. 1–4) to introduce Mrs. Olinski, the Souls, and the Academic Bowl before Noah tells his story; she continues to use exposition to introduce other stories (Nadia's, Ethan's, and Julian's); and then Konigsburg concludes with one last exposition before the novel's closing scenes. This use of exposition knits the multiple perspectives and individual stories; it also allows the author to emphasize character, not plot. Young people who are reading *The View from Saturday* will find the exposition set apart with three bold dots from the individual stories.

Expressionism: Style of art that expresses moods and feeling through distorted or shocking colors with rapid brush strokes and slightly out of proportion shapes. The artist's emotions guide the painting rather than the intent to produce a realistic and life-like work. In modern art, this simplified style, which emphasizes emotional impact, is associated with twentieth century German movements and is sometimes referred to as German expressionism.

Ludwig Bemelmans' *Madeline* is an early example of the use of expressionistic art in children's books. Other examples of expressionism in children's books include Vera B. Williams' *A Chair for My Mother* and Gary Soto's *Chato's Kitchen,* illustrated by Susan Guevara. Guevara uses brilliant hues, dabs of color, and distorted perspectives to create a humorous mood and atmosphere for the story about Chato and his low-riding cat buddy from East L.A. and a family of mice who would have been the meal had not a friendly dog, Chorizo, joined the party.

Graphic art, such as that used by Donald Crews, is also considered to be a form of expressionism (*e.g., Sail Away* and *Freight Train*). Other picture books that demonstrate expressionism are the 2000 Caldecott Medal book, *Joseph Had a Little Overcoat,* by Simms Taback, and 1995 Caldecott Medal book, *Smoky*

Night, written by Eve Bunting and illustrated by David Diaz. Young people may visit the Expressionism exhibits at the National Gallery of Art (*www.nga/gov/*), and, focusing on the use of line, they may wish to reinterpret a realistic picture book illustration as expressionism.

Fable: A fictitious story leading to learning and insight. Because of the fable's sophisticated nature (satirizing human behavior and offering the discovery of insight), it is considered the product of a single author. Fables are found in a variety of literary genres—poetry, myth, novel, and so forth—and are identified as fables because of their focus on a single truth. Within the term diversities abound:

1) the narrative may be prose or verse
2) the pattern may be Aesopian, containing a brief narrative followed by an explicit or proverb-like moral (Michael Hague, *Aesop's Fables*), or the moral may be implied by the text as in Marcia Brown's *Once a Mouse*
3) the characters may be people (Brian Wildsmith, *The Miller, the Boy and the Donkey*, elements or objects ("The North Winds and the Sun" in Mitsumasa Anno's *Anno's Fables*), or animals (Leo Lionni, *Frederick*)
4) the narrative may appear to be the product of the oral tradition, or it may be the creation of a single author (Arnold Lobel, *Fables*)

Although diverse in subject and form, fables share a number of common characteristics. They often are satirical, but the satire is incidental, not the main purpose. Often they are described as didactic; however, experiential may be more accurate because any lesson should occur through discovery. Fables are both concrete (in terms of a simple narrative) and abstract (in terms of analogy and understanding). They are focused on a single matter, often a single incident. The goal of the fable is not to enlist reader identification and sympathy, but rather to stimulate thinking. Fables are typically in the past tense. Images of human behavior are more important than the particular actions presented. A detailed setting is missing; the language is economic; and the cast of characters is small (seldom more than three). Artistically, the fable's notable characteristic is incongruity (*e.g.*, stork serving dinner to a fox), which commands the attention of the reader and prepares him/her first for surprise and then discovery. Fables that include song are known as cante fables (*e.g.*, Virginia Hamilton's *When Birds Could Talk and Bats Could Sing.*

Because the fable's symbolism may be challenging to children, they should always be given the opportunity to discuss fables as well as any accompanying illustrations. *Anno's Aesop* offers young people many opportunities for pleasurable interaction. Anno's portrayal of the illiterate fox's reading of the pictures allows children first to tell the story from the pictures only, then hear the fox's interpretation, and finally to share the traditional tale. A follow-up activity could involve young people in drawing wordless Aesop fables which other children may try to interpret. Young people who are familiar with the content and structure of fables will enjoy Jon Scieszka's collection of contemporary fables with tongue-in-check morals addressing such topics as homework, curfews, and television commercials: *Squids Will Be Squids: Fresh Morals: Beastly Fables*, illustrated by Lane Smith. See *Beast Fable.*

Fabric: A generic term for all kinds of cloths. Fabric may be made by weaving, felting, bonding, or a variety of other techniques. They can be made of a wide variety of fibers including animal (obtained from animals such as wool or silk), vegetable (obtained from vegetables such as cotton, flax, or hemp), or synthetic fibers (man-made materials). Fabric may be used in bookbinding and is also sometimes used in children's book illustrations (*e.g.*, 1992 Caldecott Honor book Faith Ringgold's *Tar Beach*, which incorporates quilt blocks along the bottom of the pages). Angela Johnson's *Julius* (illustrated by Dav Pilkey) uses numerous print fabrics in the collage illustrations that also include acrylic, watercolor, instant coffee, crayon, and India ink. Tom Lynch's *Fables from Aesop* is composed of handsewn new and old fabrics of many different textures. Fabric designer Lindsay Gardnier used fabric to illustrate *Here Come Poppy and Max*, her first picture book.

After making their own book, young people may experiment with various fabrics to cover cardboard as a binding for their books. Young people may also experiment with collage illustrations that incorporate fabric scraps.

Fabric Relief: A form of artwork that consists of the application of fabric to a background surface. Portions of the fabric are raised from the surface to a greater or lesser degree with various types of padding. Examples of this technique, which provides depth, structure, and visual weight to the illustration, include Salley Mavor's illustrations in Josepha Hale's *Mary Had a Little Lamb* and Judith Benet

Richardson's *Come to My Party*. For *Come to My Party*, Mavor used different colors and textures of fabric to depict jungle animals on their way to a leopard's birthday party.

After an introduction to Salley Mavor's illustrations, young people may create their own fabric relief designs, using cloth in a variety of colors and textures.

Fairy Tale: A story that includes such supernatural characters as fairies, fairy godmothers, witches, ogres, trolls, giants, or wizards. These supernatural beings often exhibit one or more of the following characteristics: an unpredictable nature, the power to predict the future, control over humankind, and the ability to take on different forms. Based upon their origin, there are two types of fairy tales: the folk fairy tale, such as "Cinderella," which is a product of the oral tradition, and the literary fairy tale, which is the original creation of an author. The literary fairy tale has attracted many modern writers. Hans Christian Andersen (1805–1875) is the well-known Danish author of literary fairy tales. His tales exist in many collections, including *Michael Hague's Favorite Hans Christian Andersen Fairy Tales*. Other examples of the literary fairy tale include Jane Yolen's *Sleeping Ugly*, Kathleen Hague's *The Legend of the Veery Bird,* and Maurice Sendak's *Outside Over There*.

Young people should understand the difference between the folk fairy tale and the literary fairy tale because the two types are in different locations in the library. The folk fairy tale, developed in the oral tradition, is located in the Dewey Classification at 398.2; and the literary fairy tale, created by a specific author, is located in fiction sections. Children may explore the varied supernatural aspects of the fairy tale by individually reading one of the traditional tales found at 398.2 in the library and a modern tale, and identifying the characters' magical powers. The activity could be extended by their reading a literary fairy tale and identifying the characteristics that are also present in traditional fairy tales. See *Literary Tale.*

Falling Action: The element of a progressive plot that follows the climax. Its purpose is to resolve the conflict, answer any remaining questions, and explain what happens to the main characters. See *Plot* and *Denouement.*

Fantasy: A fictitious work in which the characters, actions, and/or setting are deliberately freed from reality. A fantasy, which may be a brief tale or a lengthy novel, is the creation of a specific author. There are two types of fantasy: high fantasy (which occurs in another world where physical and human laws do not exist) and low fantasy (which, though set in the real world, presents events which are magical).

High fantasy is categorized by archetypal quests, courageous and noble heroes, and an elevated style. The themes in high fantasy deal with global struggles between good and evil. Examples of high fantasy include C. S. Lewis' *Narnia Series* and Lloyd Alexander's *Prydain Series*. Other fantasy is often categorized by the nature of the imaginary elements, such as (1) talking animals, for example, E. B. White's *Charlotte's Web*; (2) toys and inanimate objects, for example, Margery Williams' *The Velveteen Rabbit*; (3) eccentric characters, for example, Peggy Parrish's *Amelia Bedelia*; (4) extraordinary worlds, for example, Norman Juster's *The Phantom Tollbooth*; (5) ghosts and other supernatural beings, for example Pam Conrad's *Stonewords*; and (6) time travel and/or space fantasies, for example Jane Yolen's *The Devil's Arithmetic*.

Modern fantasy evolved along with an interest in fairy tales in nineteenth century Britain. It developed more slowly in the United States, but it has become increasingly popular since World War II. The American acceptance of fantasy has been reflected in both the quality of the fantasies produced and in an increased appreciation of what fantasy offers a young reader. Among the values of fantasy in a children's literature program are: (1) fantasy may help a child develop imagination; (2) a well-crafted fantasy is not easily dated—it presents ageless themes and characters; (3) it can offer children an understanding of real life sometimes more effectively than realism. For example, the concept of mortality is considered in Natalie Babbitt's *Tuck Everlasting*, and the responsibility of friendship is portrayed in E. B. White's *Charlotte's Web*.

The criteria applicable to the evaluation of a modern fantasy are that the elements (characters and plot) are consistent, staying within the author's premise for the imaginary world, and that the story compels the suspension of disbelief (*i.e.*, the author has created a story that is believable).

Young people who do not typically read high fantasies may find them difficult; therefore, they will often benefit from responding in concrete ways to fantasies by building charts and maps of the settings, acting out scenes, and constructing dioramas.

Fiction: Imaginary narrative created by an author; not a record of fact (*i.e.*, not *nonfiction*). The narrative may be a novel, short story, drama, or a narrative poem. Fiction that is woven around historical persons or events is *historical fiction*; fiction that is imaginative but based on current events (such as Barbara Snow Gilbert's use of newspaper quotations in *Paper Trail*) is *documentary fiction*; fiction intertwined with the history of a person's life is *biographical fiction*; fiction that departs from reality is *fantasy;* fiction based upon extrapolations of scientific fact or theory is *science fiction;* and fiction set in a realistic and contemporary place is *contemporary realistic fiction.* All fiction is imaginative, but the work's genre determines how true to real life the work must be to be plausible.

One of the first literary distinctions that young people make is to separate "what is true" from "what is not true." To extend their understandings of fiction and nonfiction to the library setting, they may examine a library catalog entry and determine whether the work is fiction or nonfiction; also, they may use a photocopied diagram of the library floor plan to locate and color the areas where fiction can be found.

Fictional Biography: Biography based on memory or research of the factual record, but which includes conversations and incidents that are not found in recorded facts. The author bases the imaginary conversations and incidents upon what could have happened considering the evidence or recollections from his or her own background. The challenge for children and adults is to determine the differences among (1) biographical fiction, (2) historical fiction, and (3) fictionalized biography. Biographical fiction incorporates out-of-history events to enliven the story, such as the life of Ben Franklin told by a mouse in the fantasy *Ben and Me* by Robert Lawson. Historical fiction is a story based on the events and history of a particular era. It has non-historical main characters but actual historical events affect the events and resolution of the story, such as Eve Bunting's *Dandelions*, illustrated by Greg Shed. Jean Fritz's *Homesick: My Own Story* is an example of fictional biography. In *Homesick* Jean Fritz explained to readers that the stories about living in China until she was twelve years old are all true yet fictionalized because she could not recreate authentically her childhood in the 1920s.

Because the lines are blurred, it may be more useful to focus on biography and biographical fiction as opposite ends of a continuum upon which specific books can be compared. The major point is whether a biography is authentic or fictionalized. Young people should understand that, in the truest sense, biography is the history of a person's life and, therefore, that authenticity is important. As a member of a group, individual young people could examine a book that would fall within the boundaries of the continuum, look for clues of authenticity (*e.g.*, author notes, bibliographies, references, and classification), and share with the group their observations about where on the continuum their biography would fit. For example, after sharing Kathryn Lasky's *She's Wearing a Dead Bird on Her Head*, young people may discuss the author's note following the story and determine how closely the author followed historical facts.

Figurative Language: Language that applies literary devices known as figures of speech, most of which are comparisons of dissimilar entities. Figures of speech include alliteration, personification, simile, hyperbole, metaphor, understatement, and allusion. Figures of speech are often associated with poetry; however, they are also represented in the language of everyday speech. An entertaining source of figurative language is Julius Lester's *Ackamarackus*, which includes alliteration ("Crandall Crow from Colorado"), personification ("'No,' the tree responded. 'It's almost time for us to go to sleep for the winter'" [2001: 36]), simile ("'Well, I'm like a snake, I guess, but a lot bigger'" [2001: 38]), hyperbole ("snoring loud enough to be heard twenty miles away" [2001: 40]), metaphor ("she was history" [2001: 23]), understatement (". . , that turned out to be a mistake. A big mistake." [2001: 23]), and allusion ("Be all you can bee" [2001: 7]). Young people who listen to the six fables in *Ackamarackus* can be challenged to find the figurative language that makes the collection humorous.

Flashback: The technique of beginning a story in the middle of things (*in media res*) and then inserting a scene to explain what happened at an earlier time. Authors manage flashbacks by working them into dialogue and narration and by revealing them through dreams or recollections. The flashback provides an author with the opportunity to gain the reader's interest immediately and then to provide the background information. However, children who are not at least seven years old will be challenged by flashbacks because they cannot conserve and reverse their thinking.

Holes by Louis Sachar is an outstanding example of the use of this literary technique. Chapter 1 opens at Camp Green Lake. Stanley Yelnats has already caught the falling shoe, been tried and convicted of theft, and given his choice of incarceration sites—all details later to be revealed as flashbacks. Ruth White also began *Belle Prater's Boy* in the middle of things: Woodrow's mother had left and Gypsy's father had died; it is only through flashbacks that the reader can understand these life-altering experiences.

Young people may discuss the use of flashbacks in these books as well as others with a progressive plot, such as that in Jean Craighead George's *My Side of the Mountain*. Young people may find a plot diagram useful; see *Progressive Plot*.

Flat Character: A two-dimensional character; an undeveloped character that does not possess diverse personality traits. Flat characters take on different roles in different genres. For example, they are expected in folktales where a beautiful character is typically good and wise, and an ugly character is mean and greedy. In longer works, authors have the opportunity to create round characters; however, the author of a novel with a variety of characters does not have the space to develop all of them. The flat characters in novels have different roles from those in folktales. Flat characters in novels may be *foils* (*e.g.*, the rat Templeton is for Charlotte in E. B. White's *Charlotte's Web*); *villains* (*e.g.*, the villainous captain in Avi's *The True Confessions of Charlotte Doyle*); or *functional background characters* (*e.g.*, Toby's dad in Kimberly Holt's *When Zachary Beaver Came to Town*). In book discussions, young people may consider which characters are flat, why they determine them to be flat, and why the author chose to make them flat.

Foil: A character whose qualities contrast and, thus, underscore those of another character. The concept of foil developed from the use of thin sheets of metal placed under jewels to intensify their color and brilliance. Examples of foils include Jamie, Claudia's thrifty and less imaginative brother who with her runs away from the boring tyranny of home in Elaine Konigsburg's *The Mixed-Up Files of Mrs. Basil E. Frankweiler*; Templeton, whose selfish rodent ways accentuate the nurturing ones of Charlotte in E. B. White's *Charlotte's Web*; and Cinderella's lazy and mocking stepsisters who underscore her princess-like qualities. Young people could explore the concept of the foil by acting out what a foil like Jamie or Templeton thinks of the main character.

Folk Art: A style of painted artwork created by traditional artists who sometimes have no formal training in the arts. Marked characteristics of folk art may include a highly decorative design, repeated patterns, repeated bright bold colors that are used in an imaginative way, flattened perspective, strong forms in simple child-like arrangements, lack of perspective, and immediacy of meaning. The artwork of one of America's most well-known folk art painters is featured in W. Nikola-Lisa's *The Year with Grandma Moses* (Henry Holt, 2000).

Primitive or folk art styles enable a book's illustrations to define a particular era or culture. For example, Barbara Cooney won the 1980 Caldecott Award Book for folk art illustrations that create the mood of nineteenth century rural New England in Donald Hall's the *Ox-Cart Man*. Mattie Lou O'Kelly's *From the Hills of Georgia: An Autobiography in Paintings* offers an autobiography that is enhanced with distinctive folk art paintings. Artist Kathy Jakobsen has illustrated several children's picture books in a recognizable folk art style including: *Johnny Appleseed: A Poem*, written by Reeve Lindbergh; *My New York*; and *This Land Is Your Land*, written by Woody Guthrie. Aminah Brenda Lynn Robinson has created children's books depicting African American culture through folk art including *To Be a Drum*, written by Evelyn Coleman; *A Street Called Home; Elijah's Angel: A Story of Chanukah and Christmas*, written by Michael J. Rosen.

Folktales from tribal societies also present occasions for artists to choose a folk art style reminiscent of the art from earlier cultures. One example is Baba Wague Diakite's *The Hatseller and the Monkeys: A West African Folktale*, which features a definitive West African art style of paintings on tiles.

After being introduced to children's books featuring folk art paintings and studying the characteristics of folk art, young people may create some of their own paintings in this style. They may also research the lives of well-known folk artists, or learn about the connection between folk art and folk music.

Folk Song: Song, of often unknown origin, inspired by the traditions, experiences, and emotions of the people of a particular region, country, or era. Folk songs are a universally common form of expression within the oral tradition. Passed down through generations and, thus, preserved, folk songs are often adapted in more than one version and many are eventually written down. The term *folk songs* includes not only ballads but also lyric love songs, carols, sea shanties, lullabies, marching songs, work songs, hobo songs, and African American spirituals. The various types of folk songs usually have the shared feature of an easily remembered melody.

Folk songs may be featured as the text in individual picture storybooks or in folk song collections with accompanying music. Collections of American folk songs include Kathleen Krull's *Gonna Sing My Head Off! American Folk Songs for Children*, illustrated by Allen Garns and Amy L. Cohn's *From Sea to Shining Sea: A Treasury of American Folklore and Folk Songs*.

More recent folk songs are included in Woody Guthrie's *Grow Big Songs*, volumes 1 and 2, available in both book and audio forms. Guthrie's well-known folksong *This Land Is Your Land* serves as the text in a children's picture book and is combined with Kathy Jakobsen's folk art paintings depicting scenes from Americana.

Sometimes children's folk songs or ballads are featured as the text in a children's picture book like the 1956 Caldecott Medal Book by John Langstaff, *Frog Went A-Courtin*. This song is featured in Gary Chalk's *Mr. Frog Went a Courting*, and most recently it was illustrated with a New York City backdrop in Marjorie Priceman's *Froggie Went A-Courtin*. Another full song illustrated as a children's picture book is Floyd Cooper's *Cumbayah*.

Young people may enjoy singing along with the music audiotape or CD *A Child's Celebration of Folk Music*, which includes thirteen folk favorites, including "She'll Be Coming 'Round the Mountain," "Crawfish Song," and "Skip to My Lou."

Folklore: The traditional customs, songs, rhymes, riddles, ballads, superstitions, charms, omens, legends, beliefs, fairy tales, fables, myths, dances, rituals, proverbs, riddles, tall tales, etc. of a people. Because elements of folklore have been incorporated into literature throughout the ages, it is important for children to develop an understanding of the forms and patterns of folklore. Children systematically may learn about folklore through teachers or librarians introducing various forms and encouraging children to compare and contrast them. Upperelementary level students may use a list of dictionary definitions of various folklore forms and participate in a library treasure hunt to locate examples of each.

Folktale: Any timeless story that developed within the oral tradition and, therefore, represents the cumulative authorship of many storytellers. The term applies to such diverse forms of traditional literature as fairy tales, fables, myths, legends, tall tales, and elaborate framework stories, as for example, *One Thousand and One Arabian Nights*, retold by Geraldine McCaughrean. However, it does not include literary tales—that is, original tales created in the form of a folktale, such as *Hans Christian Andersen: The Complete Fairy Tales & Stories*, translated by Erik Haugaard.

Frequently in children's literature folktales are classified by subject, style, or technique. Such classifications may include the following types: cumulative ("The House That Jack Built"); pourquoi or why ("Tikki Tikki Tembo"); humorous/ nonsense ("The Three Sillies"); talking beast ("The Three Billy Goats Gruff"); realistic ("Dick Whittington and His Cat"); and magical ("Cinderella").

The universal qualities of the folktale are evidenced by basic similarities in plot, characterization, style, and motif that are present in the tales of all cultures. Plots have a direct, concrete nature; an early disclosure of the conflict; brisk, often repetitious action that mounts steadily until the climax; and a swift and just conclusion. Folktale characters, often serving as symbols of good or evil, are typically uncomplicated, changeless, and quickly introduced. Stylistically, the folktale relies on both prose and rhyme, employs figurative language and imagery, avoids descriptive passages, and contains simple, unexplained dialogue. Motifs (*i.e.,* recurrent images, words, objects, and actions) such as three wishes, a magical object, or a wicked stepmother have also underscored the similarities of all folktales. The shared characteristics of folktales make them a rich source for comparative studies by students of all ages.

Introducing children to many versions of the same tale offers avenues to explore content similarities between tales, visual interpretations, and language differences that indicate the tale's national origin. Among the many versions of Cinderella which are useful for such comparisons are: the Chinese *Yeh Shen*, retold by Ai-Ling Louie and illustrated by Ed Young; the English *Tattercoats*, retold and illustrated by Bernadette Watts; the French *Cinderella*, written by Charles Perrault and illustrated by Marsha Brown; *The Egyptian Cinderella*, written and illustrated by Shirley Climo; and *Cendrillon: A Caribbean Cinderella*, retold by Daniel San Souci and illustrated by Brian Pinkney.

Foot: See *Meter*.

Foreshadowing: The literary technique of preparing the reader for later plot events and outcomes by presenting clues within earlier action. If the foreshadowing is skillfully managed, readers will not be aware of the hints until after completing the story, but when the clues are later recalled, their believability is ensured. In picture books, endpapers may foreshadow events to come; for example, the end papers of Maurice Sendak's *Where the Wild Things Are* suggest an exotic jungle setting. A title, such as Robin Friedman's *How I Survived My Summer Vacation and Lived to Write about It*, can foretell a story's resolution. However, foreshadowing is usually woven into the text. For example, the narrator in Betsy Byars' *The Midnight Fox* (Byars, 1968: 2) remembers that on a stormy August night a small fox leaves footprints away from a cage and is greeted by the high, clear bark of the Midnight Fox; thus, he suggests significant events to come.

Young people may experience an effective use of foreshadowing in Lynd Ward's *The Biggest Bear*. The reader sees Johnny feeding the little bear maple sugar that he brought from the store. Then, on the next four pages, the text and illustrations show all the food that the bear has eaten. On the fifth page the reader is startled by the picture of an enormous bear that is unbelievable until the food clues are remembered. Then, the size seems entirely appropriate. After being introduced to foreshadowing in *The Biggest Bear*, young people may find examples of foreshadowing in books they read individually.

Formalism (or Formalistic Criticism): A critical approach that emphasizes analysis of a work's form or structure rather than the effect on the reader, social implications, issues of truth and morality, relationship to life, or intentions of the author. The formalistic approach encourages a close reading of the text with attention to basic literary elements (*i.e.*, plot, character, tone, theme, point of view, setting, and style). However, the goal is not to consider how the literary elements function individually but rather how they work together to build a unified structure. During the 1940s the approach came to be known as the *New Criticism*, a term introduced in John Crowe Ransom's *The New Criticism*. By the 1960s formalism had lost much of its popularity with critics who faulted its focus on poetry, lack of success with the novel, attention to tedious details, and philosophical rejection of any understandings beyond the text. However, the formalistic principles of carefully reading the text and considering the unity of the literary elements are still considered to be the foundation of literary criticism.

Young people may be introduced to the concept of formalism by discussing the relationship of a work's literary elements, especially the relationship of plot and character. The critics Cleanth Brook and Robert Penn Warren defined plot as "character in action" in *Understanding Fiction*, second edition (Brook and Warren, 1959: 80). As they gain understanding, young people may consider more complex interrelationships of literary elements. For example, Katherine Paterson's novel *Jacob Have I Loved* offers a rich consideration of the interrelationships of a protagonist, Sara Louise, and her beautiful and talented sister, Caroline. They are entrapped in sibling rivalry, a conflict, which according to Paterson's Newbery-acceptance speech, began "east of Eden." The symbolic setting, Rass Island, is isolated and bound by the social parameters of the 1940s. The first person point of view reveals the protagonist's thoughts and motivations. Paterson's style is rich in biblical allusions; and the theme emphasizes the capacity for family relationships to shape the lives of children for as long as they live. A careful reading of a rich literary work can reveal a unity of plot, character, setting, style, point of view, and theme in which every element counts.

Format: The general size, shape, and general make-up of a book or magazine. Additional elements of a book's format include the design of the pages, typography, illustrations, type of paper, binding, and dust jacket. In the creation of nonfiction books additional format decisions include bibliographies, indexes, glossaries, and other aids. Charlotte Huck, et al. in *Children's Literature in the Elementary School*, seventh edition, states, "There are no absolute rules for format; the look of a book should be responsive to its purpose and its content" (Huck, et al., 2001: 516). Huck also notes that the Dorling Kindersley *Eyewitness Series* marked a change in direction for the nonfiction or information book format.

Format decisions in children's book publishing are usually made by some combination of the illustrator, author, and art director of a publishing house. All of the elements must work together to create the whole; for example, the size and shape of the book may relate to the content of the story or to the illustrations as in Janice May Udry's *A Tree Is Nice*, which is a book about the value of a tree and is in a "tall" format. In this book, the type is clear and easy to read, and the placement of the words on the pages works well with the illustrations. The book is available in a durable sewn binding.

Young people may examine a selection of children's books pulled from the library shelves and look closely at the general size, shape, and make-up of the books. They may also look at the design of the pages, typography, illustrations, type of paper, binding, and dust jacket to determine if they would have made changes in the book's format if they had been the "art director" of the project.

Formula: A predictable sequence of action that typifies some popular novels as well as television series and movies. The most well-known source of formula fiction in children's literature has been the Stratemeyer syndicate, origin of *Hardy Boys, Bobbsey Twins, Nancy Drew*, and numerous other series. Leading the way in formula fiction, Stratemeyer developed book and chapter outlines that were sent to ghost authors who followed a strict formula that included such details as when to mention the previous book in the series and when to mention the next title. Children from nine to twelve years old find pleasure in reading formula fiction series, some in the numbered order. Mysteries are a common type of formula fiction, which use cliff-hangers to move the reader through the book, and usually result in a satisfactory conclusion. Among popular formula fiction series for older readers is the *Sweet Valley High Series*.

Children who are reading formula fiction probably will be happy to share their favorite series and the number of books they have read. If small groups of young people in a school or library are reading the same series, they could participate in a discussion of a set of books in that series. They may pretend to be literary detectives and compare the chapters across the set of novels in search of similarities and patterns. They could look for patterns in where the previous books in the series are mentioned in a novel (often chapter two), how chapters end, where there is a hint of the next book to come, and in which chapter the climax occurs. These points could be graphed on a progressive plot line. Young people may be led to more creative literature through a literature program rich in motivation and opportunities for readers to respond. See *Series*.

Fractured Tale: A traditional tale retold with twists in such story elements as characters, plot, point of view, and setting. Most often the fractured tale is a decidedly humorous retelling that features nontraditional art. Fractured tales should contain enough similarities to the original story so that young people can respond to the connection. It is important that young people should have a thorough understanding in the original tale in order to appreciate the humor.

An earlier fractured fairy tale is Brinton Turkle's *Deep in the Forest*, a wordless parody of "Goldilocks and the Three Bears" in which a little bear visits a human family's home and tries out the porridge, chairs, and beds. Another early example of a fractured tale is Jane Yolen's classic small chapter book retelling of "Sleeping Beauty" in *Sleeping Ugly*.

Many fractured fairy tales retell the original story but use a different setting. Susan Lowell made such a change in *The Bootmaker and the Elves*, which is the "The Shoemaker and the Elves" set in the Wild West. Authors also make dramatic changes in the main characters as in Michael Emberley's *Ruby*, which sets "Little Red Riding Hood" in New York City with "Red" as a mouse who has been warned by her mother to stay away from cats, or in Eric Kimmel's *The Runaway Tortilla* which retells "The Gingerbread Boy" as a southwest tale. Mary Pope Osborne's *Kate and the Beanstalk*, illustrated by Giselle Potter, portrays a girl who climbs to the top of the beanstalk where she outsmarts the giant and makes her fortune.

The children's book creation team of Jon Scieszka (author/reteller) and Lane Smith (illustrator) has collaborated on several tales that gave rise to the popularity of this sub-genre in the early 1990s. Lane Smith received a Caldecott Honor for his illustrations in the team's *The Stinky Cheeseman and Other Fairly Stupid Tales*, which in addition to a retelling of a collection of such favorites as "The Gingerbread Boy" and "Little Red Riding Hood," is a creative venture of bookmaking and picture book artwork. Other popular collaborations by Scieszka and Lane include *The True Story of the Three Little Pigs* and *The Frog Prince, Continued*.

One of the most popular fairy tales that has been retold in "fractured" versions is Cinderella. Some of the retellings in picture storybook form include: Caralyn Buehner's *Fanny's Dream*; Babette Cole's *Prince Cinders*; Ellen Jackson's *Cinder Edna*; Susan Lowell's *Cindy Ellen: A Wild Western Cinderella*; Susan Meddaugh's *Cinderella's Rat*; and Frances Minters' *Cinder-Elly*. William J. Brooke includes a portrayal of a Cinderella who does not want to try on the glass slipper in *A Telling of the Tales: Five Stories*. Fractured fairy tale retellings of Cinderella in chapter book format include Gail Carson Levine's *Ella Enchanted* and Phillip Pullman's *I Was a Rat!*

Young people may compare the versions of Cinderella listed above for literary devices, allusions, and patterns that make up each of the retellings. They may list or graph common elements in the stories and work together to locate folklore elements. An additional natural extension of this topic is for young people to create their own fractured fairy tales using traditional retellings of "Sleeping Beauty,"

"Goldilocks and the Three Bears," "Little Red Riding Hood," "The Princess and the Pea," and" "Jack and the Beanstalk." See *Parody*.

Framework Story: A single story or collection of stories enclosed within a frame story that serves as a narrative setting. The plots of the framework and the internal story may or may not be integrated. A classic use of a framework structure is the set of tales narrated by the character Shahrazad as in, for example, Geraldine McCaughrean's *One Thousand and One Arabian Nights*. An example of a work that uses the technique for a single story is Patricia Polacco's adaptation of Ernest Thayer's "Casey at the Bat" integrating the single poem into her picture storybook version, *Casey at the Bat: A Ballad of the Republic Sung in the Year 1888*.

After hearing Polacco's *Casey at the Bat* read aloud, young people may be encouraged to notice the differences in the formats of the internal and the framework stories. The framework story is in narrative prose printed directly on the white background of the illustrations. The enclosed story is Thayer's classic narrative poem printed in a series of boxes with gray backgrounds outlined in red. Using the brainstorming technique, young people may create a framework story for a folktale or poem they have shared, or, working in small groups, they may invent a frame for a set of three or four poems or folktales they have read.

Free Verse: Unrhymed poetry that does not follow a fixed metrical pattern, though sometimes the words within a single line will rhyme. Verses are dependent upon natural speech rhythms and the counterpoint of stressed and unstressed syllables. Distinctions of free verse can include the arrangement of words on the page and the use of line or word breaks as a kind of punctuation. Free verse differs from blank verse in that blank verse does observe a regular meter in its unrhymed lines. Early origins of free verse include the "Song of Solomon" and "Psalms" in the King James translation of the *Bible*. Free verse represents the most widely used verse pattern in the English language.

A recent award-winning example of free verse is Karen Hesse's 1998 John Newbery Award book, *Out of the Dust*. Kristen O'Connell George has written several collections of poetry with examples of free verse, including *The Great Frog Race and Other Poems*, *Old Elm Speaks: Tree Poems*, and *Little Dog Poems*.

Young people may listen to free verse read aloud on audiotapes of Karen Hesse's *Out of the Dust*. They may also write their own free verse poetry on a favorite hobby or pastime.

Genre: A term of French origin used to differentiate types or categories of literary works. Problems in using the term arise from the fact that it is often applied loosely and that the boundaries of the term have shifted and changed across literary eras. For example Plato and Aristotle wrote about three genres: lyric, narrative, and drama; however, William Harmon and C. Hugh Holman in *Handbook to Literature* (Harmon and Holman, 2000: 23) designate genre types "according to form, technique, or, sometimes subject matter." Under that definition, they describe the television series *Dallas* as a combination western and soap opera. Applying the definition of Harmon and Holman, a picture storybook like Chris Van Allsburg's *The Polar Express* may also be typed as a fantasy; and a novel, such as Nancy Farmer's *The Ear, the Eye, & the Arm* is also recognized as science fiction. Although somewhat arbitrary, genre labeling is a useful device that functions as a contract between the reader and the author, preparing the reader for what can be expected and laying the groundwork for understanding. Thus, the *Polar Express* may be analyzed and discussed as a title that meets criteria of the picture storybook as well as those of fantasy.

Professional sources for linking young people with books in specific genres are *What Do I Read Next?* by Neil Barron, et al.; Diana Tixier Herald's *Genreflecting*; and Bridget Dealy Volz's *Junior Genreflecting: A Guide to Good Reads and Series Fiction for Children.* Young people may be introduced to the term through Sandy Asher's collection of short stories *But That's Another Story: Favorite Authors Introduce Popular Genres.* An adult could read aloud one of the twelve short stories, discuss the accompanying author interview, and booktalk other books within the genre. Robin Friedman's *How I Survived My Summer Vacation and Lived to Write About It* presents a protagonist who can only develop first lines for the novel he is attempting to write. Each new first line shows a dramatic shift from one genre to another (*e.g.*, from science fiction to survival to detective story). Like the aspiring novelist in *How I Survived My Summer Vacation and Lived to Write About It*, young people could apply the concept of genre by writing first lines for novels in different genres.

Glossary: A partial dictionary of specialized terms appended to the end of a book. Young people could be encouraged to browse the 500s of the Dewey classification system, find examples of glossaries, and identify some of their characteristics (*i.e.*, alphabetical, specialized terms, brief definitions, placement at the end of a work, a valuable feature of many information books). An important feature in many books, both fiction and nonfiction, is the use of the glossary for non-English words; for example, Gary Soto includes a Spanish-English glossary in *Chato and the Party Animals*, and Joseph Bruchac includes one for Native American-English words in *Squanto's Journey: The Story of the First Thanksgiving*, illustrated by Greg Shed.

Young people could work in groups to compile a glossary for a unit of study or for a book that does not have a glossary. They could also develop a crossword puzzle for the terms in a glossary, and they could apply puzzle-making software, such as that found on the Web (*www.puzzlemaker.com/*).

Gothic Novel: A type of romance that was popularized in the seventeenth and eighteenth centuries, beginning with the publication of Horace Walpole's *The Castle of Otranto: A Gothic Story*. Early Gothic novels were characterized by a medieval setting, a castle, underground passages, sliding doors and panels, an innocent heroine, a villain, unexplained disappearances, terrifying visions, and supernatural or apparently supernatural happenings. Today the concept of Gothic novel has been expanded to other settings and other horrors, thus including the adult novels of Stephen King as well as the novels for young people by Phyllis Reynolds Naylor, such as *Jade Green: A Ghost Story*. Avi's *Midnight Magic* includes many details that characterize the classic Gothic novels, and after reading the book, young people could discuss the ways Avi incorporated those elements and what their effects on the story were. Young people who understand the elements characteristic of Gothic novels are prepared to enjoy Sheila Greenwald's parody *It All Began with Jane Eyre: Or, The Secret Life of Franny Dillman*.

Gouache: (Pronounced *gwash*.) Poster paint; a painting medium made from mixing opaque pigments, water, and chalk or a gum; or a painting in the medium. Gouache is intense and bold, and it has the characteristic of drying to become lighter in tone than when it is wet. Because its effects are somewhat like oil paint, artists use it to create studies for larger paintings to be done in oil. Publishers often identify the art media/medium on the title verso page.

Caldecott (Award and Honor) illustrators who have been recognized for their use of this medium are Molly Bang in *When Sophie Gets Angry—Really, Really Angry*; Marjorie Priceman in *Zin! Zin! Zin! A Violin*, written by Lloyd Moss; and Arnold Lobel in *Fables*. Other Caldecott-honored illustrators used gouache in addition to other media: Simms Taback in *Joseph Had a Little Overcoat*; Christopher Myers in *Harlem: A Poem*, written by Walter Dean Myers; and David Macaulay in *Black and White*. Young people may be given opportunities to paint with both gouache and watercolor and to compare the two media. They may use the experience to hypothesize why an illustrator may prefer one medium over another or may prefer to use mixed media to illustrate a book.

Graphic Art: A term that includes pictorial art outside painting (*e.g.*, engraving, lithography, silk-screen, and other techniques that involve a printing process. Graphic art is linear in nature, relying more on drawing than color. See *Etching*.

Graphic Design: The laying out of illustrations and texts in printed and digital formats. Picture book illustrators skilled in design include Ann Jonas who created the imaginative *Round Trip* and Gail Gibbons who was a graphic designer in NBC's children's programming before creating such information books as *Gulls . . . Gulls . . . Gulls . . .* , *Apples*, and *Rabbits, Rabbits & More Rabbits!* After young people have examined the layout of texts and illustrations in a book like *Apples* (with visual and textual information about apple parts, products, and types), they may as individuals in a group create and contribute pages to a graphically designed book on a science topic they are studying.

Graphic Novel: A broad term, originated by Will Eisner in 1978, to describe a work created in the format of a comic book. Eisner applied the term to his graphic novel *A Contract with God: And Other Tenement Stories* although the format had previously been in existence. Typically published in trade paperback format and released monthly, these stories are told with a sequential combination of printed graphical pictures. Words are optional. Artwork media range from pen and ink to colorful painted frames, and the printed illustrations are usually either full size (seven inches × ten inches) or digest size (five inches × eight inches). Widely applied, the term refers to short stories or full-length novels and to fiction or nonfiction, including autobiography. Subsets of graphic novels feature specialized super hero comic stories.

Art Spiegelman won a Pulitzer Prize in 1992 for his underground *Maus Series*, the first of which was *Maus: A Survivor's Tale*. Professional resources that address graphic novels include D. Aviva Rothschild's *Graphic Novels: A Bibliographic Guide to Book-Length Comics* and Stephen Weiner's *100 Graphic Novels for Public Libraries*. Two awards that have honored (among other comic formats) the graphic novel are The Eisners (selected by creators, publishers, and booksellers) and The Harveys (selected by creators and publishers). An example of a graphic novel honored by The Eisners is Howard Cruse's *Stuck Rubber Baby*, and one honored by The Harveys is Harvey Pekar and Joyce Brabner's *Our Cancer Year*. Judd Winick's *Pedro and Me: Friendship, Loss and What I Learned* won the 2001 Sibert Honor award, presented by the Association for Library Service to Children for outstanding nonfiction. The Berkeley Public Library's teen Web site provides a booklist of graphic novels (*www.infopeople.org/bpl/teen/graphic.html*).

Young people may be introduced to a selected graphic novel through overhead transparencies; afterward, they may write the language they imagine could accompany the illustrations. Also, young people could collaborate in groups to create their own graphic novel developed by one group writing the storyline and another group creating the accompanying illustrations.

Graphite: A form of carbon that consists of a soft black mineral substance. Artists use graphite pencils and graphite in stick form for drawing. Most graphite has a metallic luster when applied to paper or other surfaces.

Graphite is often used with other media to illustrate a children's book. In a 1972 Caldecott Honor book, Tom Feelings used collage with graphite to illustrate *Moja Means One*, written by Muriel Feelings, and also to illustrate his 1975 Caldecott Honor book *Jambo Means Hello*, also written by Muriel Feelings. John Steptoe's 1985 Caldecott Honor book *The Story of Jumping Mouse* is illustrated with graphite pencil and India ink on paper. More colorful books incorporating graphite include Tomie de Paola's 1976 Caldecott Honor book *Strega Nona* in which he used watercolor and felt-tip pen over graphite. Stephen Gammell's 1986 Caldecott Honor book *The Relatives Came*, written by Cynthia Rylant, incorporates graphite and colored pencil.

Young people may experiment with artist's graphite sticks obtained from an artist supply store. They may create black and white illustrations alone, or mix the graphite with the other artistic media mentioned above (*e.g.*, collage, India ink, watercolor, felt-tip pens, or colored pencils).

Gutter: The deep indention at the margin of the sewn or glued centerfold of a book; the place where the inner margins of two facing printed pages adjoin. The gutter plays an important role in children's picture books where the double-page illustration spreads must be aligned correctly to ensure that the original illustration is not distorted or clipped. A classic example of such a distortion is the cropped duck in Robert McCloskey's *Make Way for Ducklings.*

Young people can select the Caldecott Award and Honor books for a particular year, identify the double-page spreads, and evaluate whether the illustrations were properly aligned.

Haiku: A Japanese poem whose three lines of five, seven, and five syllables present an often seasonal, nature theme and elicit a mood or feeling for the reader to contemplate. Because many Japanese syllables are shorter than English syllables, the English haiku will probably be longer than Japanese haiku. The preciseness of the syllable count should not be of a concern as much as the nature content and the capacity to evoke emotion.

Young people will find information about two classic Japanese poets in Matthew Gollub's *Cool Melons—Turn to Frogs! The Life and Poems of Issa*, illustrated by Kazulo G. Stone, and Dawnine Spivak's *Grass Sandals: The Travels of Basho*, illustrated by Demi. An illustrated anthology of haiku poetry is *Stone Bench in an Empty Park*, edited by Paul B. Janezko with photographs by Henri Silberman. Young people may enjoy illustrating a favorite haiku, perhaps photographing objects in a special place as Henri Silberman did for *Stone Bench in an Empty Park*. They may also illustrate a haiku by selecting a painting photo on a museum's Web site and simultaneously share the art and read the haiku poem as part of a group presentation. A group nature walk may be helpful for inspiration.

Hand-lettering: Letters, words, and sentences created by hand by the illustrator and typically used in illustrated pages. One way to determine whether a book is hand-lettered is to compare the same letters across the text to see whether the multiple uses are identical. Beautiful and classic examples of hand-lettering are found in old illuminated manuscripts which use elaborately illustrated letters to begin a section of a prayer book or biblical text. Barry Moser used this technique on the title page of Margaret Hodges' *St. Jerome and the Lion*.

With new technologies and a wide variety of typefaces available to illustrators, hand-lettered texts are becoming less common. Young people have access to a number of hand-lettered books, including a classic example of hand-lettering in picture storybooks, Wanda Gag's *Millions of Cats*. Vera B. Williams is a master at this technique. In *"More More More" Said the Baby: 3 Love Stories* she not only painted in gouache the letters in a variety of colors and shades, but also painted all around them. Lettering that becomes part of the book, not the typeface for the text, may be observed in Peter Der Manuelian's *Hieroglyphs from A to Z: A Rhyming Book with Ancient Egyptian Stencils for Kids*. Stephen Johnson in *Alphabet City* uses his illustrations to create the alphabet with everyday sights found in Brooklyn, *e.g.,* the end of a saw horse becomes an "A." Also of interest to children might be the books for which illustrators have created an entirely new typeface, such as the 1995 Caldecott Award book, *Smoky Night,* for which David Diaz hand-lettered the title type.

Children may enjoy hand-lettering the first letter of their last name, making it as elaborate as possible and applying color and gold ink as in an illuminated manuscript. See *Typography*.

Hans Christian Andersen Awards: Children's literature awards presented every other year by the International Board on Books for Young People to an author and an illustrator, living at the time of the nomination, whose complete works have made a lasting contribution to children's literature. The award was first presented to an author in 1956 and to both an author and an illustrator in 1966. Young people may find information about the award and the sponsoring organization at *www.ibby.org/Seiten/04_andersen.htm.*

Hatching: The technique of using closely formed parallel lines to give the effects of tone, form, and shading in an illustration. It is most commonly used in drawing and engraving. Lines may vary in size and closeness, and placing additional lines across the first set at an angle is known as crosshatching.

The 1966 Caldecott Medal book, Sorche Nic Leodhas' *Always Room for One More,* was illustrated by Nonny Hogrogian who used black pen for prominent hatching and crosshatching, and pastels and wash for color. Other examples of crosshatching include John Steptoe's 1988 Caldecott Honor book, *Mufaro's Beautiful Daughters: An African Tale*; Paul Fleischman's *Shadow Play,* illustrated by Eric Beddows; and Hannah Roche's *My Mom Is Magic!,* illustrated by Chris Fisher. Young people may also find hatching and crosshatching in the pen and ink work of David Macaulay in books such as *Cathedral, Castle,* and *Pyramid*. Young people may create their own illustrations that incorporate this method.

Historical Fiction: Realistic fiction with an integral setting that portrays significant historical events (*e.g.*, World War II) or past social phenomena (*e.g.*, the Westward Expansion). Sir Walter Scott's novels, such as *Waverley* and *Ivanhoe*, established traditional expectations for the historical novel: the portrayal of invented characters and historical figures whose lives are inevitably influenced by the cultural and social conflicts and challenges of their times. Historical fiction for young people is typically more loosely defined than that for adults. Charlotte Huck in *Children's Literature in the Elementary School* explains, "The term *historical fiction* can be used to designate all realistic stories set in the past" (2001: 464). With that definition historical fiction can include not only realistic fiction about historical events but also realistic stories developed from author experiences and memories and older contemporary realistic fiction that can authentically illuminate history with settings and events of significance.

The Scott O'Dell Award for Historical Fiction honors an author of outstanding historical fiction published in the United States and set in North, Central, or South America. Historical novelist Scott O'Dell established the award ($5,000 prize) in 1981. Young people may find listings of past O'Dell Award winners at their libraries (*e.g.*, *www.mcpl.lib.mo.us/readers/awards/teen/odell.htm*). Among the O'Dell Award winners are Karen Hesse's *Out of the Dust*, set in the Dust Bowl days of the 1930s in the Oklahoma Panhandle. Developed in free verse, *Out of the Dust* is a compelling tale of loss, misery, and the indomitable spirit of a young girl, Billie Jo, whose world seems to hold little hope for folks who refuse to move west.

Historical fiction is a popular genre that draws many outstanding authors, including Newbery Award winners, such as Richard Peck for *A Year Down Yonder*; Christopher Paul Curtis for *Bud, Not Buddy*; Karen Hesse for *Out of the Dust*; Karen Cushman for *The Midwife's Apprentice*; and Lois Lowry for *Number the Stars*. Primary criteria for evaluating historical fiction are accuracy and authenticity. Young people may be involved with the assessment of a work's accuracy and authenticity by individually reading different novels set in the same era, constructing timelines of relevant historical events, and comparing the events in their novels with the historical time line. They may be encouraged to speculate why authors often choose certain times/places (*e.g.*, the Great Depression) for historical settings. Also, young people may choose historical fiction from a variety of eras and, as a group, develop a timeline of the settings represented. Because the genre is now represented in many picture books, such as Eve Bunting's *Dandelions*, illustrated by Greg Shed, even the young reader or listener may be drawn into a discussion of a distant setting.

Homonym: One or more words spelled and pronounced alike but having a different meaning (*e.g.*, *bear, bear*). Closely related is a homophone, a word that is pronounced the same as another word but which has a different meaning and spelling.

Young people may be challenged by some of the eighty homonym/homophone riddles and puzzles in Marvin Terban's *Hey, Hay! A Wagonful of Funny Homonym Riddles*. Young people may also make a list of homonyms and homophones.

Hornbook: A small wooden paddle on which was pasted a lesson sheet of parchment or vellum that usually contained the alphabet, numerals, and the Lord's Prayer. For preservation, the text was covered by a thin sheet of hammered transparent cow's horn, tacked down with thin brass strips. Usually a hornbook was 3 1/2 inches by 2 1/2 inches, and it might have had a hole in the handle in order to be carried on a cord around the child's neck or waist. The hornbook was used for reading instruction from the sixteenth to the eighteenth centuries. It was brought to the New World and used in the teaching of Puritan children.

Although the wooden hornbook was the most common, a number of different materials such as silver, copper, bone, and even gingerbread were used. The gingerbread hornbook was prepared in an iron mold, producing a cake with a raised letter alphabet. It is said that it was eaten as the child learned. As a letter was named, it was consumed.

A replica of a hornbook can be obtained from The Horn Book, Inc., 56 Roland St., Suite 2000, Boston, MA 02129. Phone 1–800–325–1170 (contact to inquire about cost). After the facsimile is acquired and shown to an upper grade group, the history of the hornbook may be researched in the media center by a committee and shared with the class. Young people may create their own hornbooks with graham crackers for the base and alphabet cereal and icing for the text.

Hyperbole: A figure of speech that relies on exaggeration or overstatement. The origin of the term is from the French for "to throw more at the devil." Young people are familiar with the obvious exaggeration in such everyday statements as "I could eat a horse" and "He is as old as the hills." They will also recognize hyperbole in tall tales which rely on the device not only for descriptions but also to set plot sequences in motion. For example, Suzanne Williams' *Library Lil*, illustrated by Steven Kellogg, is a tall tale in which Lil, who was born with a book in her hand, changes the townspeople and a motorcycle gang from television junkies into readers. Another tall tale rich in hyperbole is Debbie Dadey's *Will Rogers:*

Larger Than Life, which relates the exaggerated exploits of Will Rogers, including his trick of roping the world and his current activities with Wiley Post, "flying around and roping the stars." Dadey concludes this exaggerated story with "The Truth." Other examples are in Patricia C. McKissack's *A Million Fish . . . More or Less,* illustrated by Dena Schutzer, a tall-tale yarn set in lower Louisiana where young Hugh Thomas relates the problem of catching three small fish and then a million more.

Although humorous, hyperbole may also be used to make a serious point as Beauty often did as narrator in Ruth White's *Belle Prater's Boy.* For example, Beauty described the town's surprise at Woodrow's mother's disappearance by observing ". . . folks were fairly jolted out of their ruts" (1996: 4); she also noted that Residence Street was "the only place around for miles where you could build a house without . . . hanging it off the side of a hill" (1996: 4). Less seriously, Beauty declared that Grandma's newfangled vacuum "was so mighty it could pick up a steel ball" (1996: 4).

To experiment with hyperbole, young people may look for examples in everyday speech and in the books they read; and they may develop their own about a current happening or by describing a tall tale character, seeing who can make up the biggest whopper.

Iamb or **Iambus:** See *Meter.*

Idiom: Well-known phrases or expressions that have a meaning different from what are grammatical or logical. They usually are not translated from one language to another because the meaning would change and could not be understood. The English language has numerous idioms. Historic collections of idioms are Charles Earle Funk's *A Hog on Ice and Other Curious Expressions* and Funk's *Heavens to Betsy and Other Curious Sayings.*

Marvin Terban's *In a Pickle and Other Funny Idioms* describes an idiom as "groups of words that don't mean what they say." Terban says that what idioms actually say may even sound silly and that they can be confusing because each one has a special meaning. He shares the special meaning of thirty idioms in this book including such phrases as: "To get in everyone's hair," "Bury your head in the sand," and "Straight from the horse's mouth." Terban also published *Punching the Clock: Funny Action Idioms* that explains more than 100 expressions such as "raise the roof," "hold your horses" and "beat around the bush." Terban's most complete collection is the *Scholastic Dictionary of Idioms* that explains the meanings and origins of over 600 idioms and proverbs.

Illustrated Book: John Warren Stewig in *Looking at Picture Books* defines an illustrated book as one with fewer illustrations than picture storybooks and with pictures that are included usually printed in either limited color or only in black and white. Stewig notes that the pictures in an illustrated book are extensions of the text and possibly add to the interpretation of the story but are not usually included to help with understanding the story. Illustrated books are usually intended for students with competent reading skills. Examples of illustrated novels include Ann M. Martin and Laura Godwin's *The Doll People*, illustrated by Brian Selznick, and Hans Magnus Enzensberger's *The Number Devil: A Mathematical Adventure*, translated by Michael Henry Heim. Young people may select a favorite chapter book and create a few illustrations to extend the text of the book.

Illustrator: An individual who draws pictures, especially for books, magazines, or advertisements. The illustrator strives to interpret, enhance, and enlarge upon a written text. A children's book illustrator's work is defined in Eileen Christelow's *What Do Illustrator's Do?*, which depicts two illustrators creating the same picture book, "Jack and the Beanstalk." Christelow introduces the topic with a question: "What do illustrators do? They tell stories with pictures." She explains the process of illustrating, using terms such as *point of view*, *layout*, and *design*. To understand the work of an author and illustrator, young people may also read Janet Stevens' *From Pictures to Words*, which explains the use of a storyboard, shows the different artistic media, and discusses the artist's creative process.

The *Caldecott Medal* was named in honor of nineteenth-century English illustrator Randolph Caldecott. It is awarded annually by the Association for Library Service to Children, a division of the American Library Association, to the artist of the most distinguished American picture book for children" (American Library Association, 2001). Leonard Marcus' *A Caldecott Celebration: Six Artists Share Their Paths to the Caldecott Medal* presents six illustrators' own stories about the creation of their medal-winning books: Robert McCloskey's *Make Way for Ducklings*; Marcia Brown's *Cinderella or The Little Glass Slipper*; Maurice Sendak's *Where the Wild Things Are*; William Steig's *Sylvester and the Magic Pebble*; Chris Van Allsburg's *Jumanji*; and David Wiesner's *Tuesday*.

Young people may look at the illustrations featured in these Caldecott Medal books and others to compare the media used through the years. The most definitive information on artistic media used in the Caldecott Award and Honor books was originally compiled by Christine Behrmann. A compilation is included in each annual edition of *The Newbery and Caldecott Guide Awards: A Guide to the Medal and Honor Books*. Online information about the Caldecott Medal and a complete list of award books can be found at the Caldecott Medal homepage (*www.ala.org/alsc/caldecott.html*).

Information about a number of children's book illustrators and their work can be found in Pat Cummings' series: *Talking with the Artists, Talking with the Artists*, Volume Two, and *Talking with the Artists*, Volume Three. Young people may assemble a collection of children's books illustrated by the one the illustrators listed in Cummings' books and create a display or bulletin board. Additional connections to information about individual children's book illustrators and their work may be found on various sites linked from David Brown's at *www.ucalgary.ca/ ~dkbrown/*.

Imagery: A general literary term that refers to the formation of mental images that are summoned by words and expressions that appeal to the senses. A device often used in poetry, imagery can convey instantaneous mental pictures. Imagery can also clarify an action, a thing, a place, or an idea. It may be literal or figurative. Literal meaning is directly conveyed through the words as they are written. When using figurative imagery, the writer speaks indirectly through the language in order to entice the reader's imagination.

Gary Paulsen's use of imagery in *The Winter Room* vividly brings to life this story of a young boy's growing up on a northern Minnesota farm. Excerpts from "Tuning," the book's introduction, include imagery such as,

> "If books could be more, could show more, could own more, this book would have smells . . . It would have the smells of old farms, the sweet smell of new-mown hay as it falls off the oiled sickle blade when the horses pull the mower through the field, and the sour smell of manure steaming in a winter barn. . . .
>
> "If this book could be more and own more and give more, this book would have sound . . . It would have the high, keening sound of the six-foot bucksaws as the men pull them back and forth through the trees to cut pine for paper pulp. . . .
>
> "And finally if books could be more, give more, show more, this book would have light . . . Oh, it would have the soft gold light—gold with bits of hay dust floating in it—that slips through the crack in the barn wall . . . " (1989: 2–6).

Picture books that feature strong imagery include Beatrix Potter's *The Tale of Peter Rabbit*; Paul Goble's *The Girl Who Loved Wild Horses*; Michael Bedard's *Emily*, illustrated by Barbara Cooney; and Jane Yolen's *Welcome to the Icehouse*, illustrated by Laura Regan.

Young people may listen to a children's book read aloud such as one previously listed or Jane Yolen's 1988 Caldecott Award book *Owl Moon*, illustrated by John Schoenherr, or Ezra Jack Keats' 1963 Caldecott Award book *The Snowy Day*. They may respond to the imagery in the story by painting a picture with watercolors to depict what they "saw" and "felt" as the book was read aloud.

Impressionism: A style of art that emphasizes light and reflected light, as it is first perceived by the eye. The term was derogatively developed from Claude Monet's painting "Impression, Sunrise" (circa 1872). Impressionism was early associated with Monet, Edouard Manet, Edgar Degas, Alfred Sysley, and Pierre-August Renoir. The First Impressionistic Exhibition was held in Paris in 1874. Influenced by nineteenth-century physicists who studied light and color as well as photography, impressionist painters typically developed landscapes rapidly outdoors. Often painting the same scene in different daylights and applying small areas of pure color, they created spacious landscapes, quiet in tone and shimmering with light.

Still very popular today, the style can be found in contemporary picture books. Among examples of impressionism in children's book illustrations are Emily Arnold McCully's Caldecott Award book, *Mirette on the High Wire*; Sherley Anne Williams' Caldecott Honor book, *Working Cotton*; Ed Young's Caldecott Award book, *Lon Po Po*; Raúl Colón's illustrations for Sharon Dennis Wyeth's *Always My Dad*; Libba Moore Gray's *My Mama Had a Dancing Heart*; James Stevenson's illustrations for Charlotte Zolotow's *Say It!* (1980); and Charlotte Zolotow's *Mr. Rabbit and the Lovely Present*, illustrated by Maurice Sendak. In creating the illustrations for Zolotow's story about Mr. Rabbit who helps a young girl gather fruit for her mother's birthday basket, Sendak was a master at the use of splashes of color to represent objects and to portray the background and foreground.

Christina Björk's *Linnea in Monet's Garden* offers young people an introduction to impressionism, to Monet, to Paris and its museums and sun-lit Seine, and to Monet's home in Giverny. Young people may read or browse picture books illustrated in the style of impressionism, examine impressionistic art prints, and visit the National Gallery of Art online at *www.nga/gov/* to view "French Painting of the 19ᵗʰ Century" and "American Paintings, Impressionism of the late 1800s and Early 1900s." They may be encouraged to identify the primary characteristics of the works of art they have considered.

India Ink or **Indian Ink** or **Ink:** A permanent black ink made from the pigment of lampblack (derived from non-electric lamps) or soot (obtained by burning vegetable oils, such as sesame or wood) and glue binder. It is the common name for black ink used in the United States. It can also be purchased in solid forms that are often called Chinese ink, Japanese ink, or sumi ink.

India ink has often been used as the sole medium or as a defining medium in Caldecott Medal and Honor books including the following selections (illustrators are listed first in each entry because they are the recipient of the award for the distinguished artwork):

1944 (Award): Louis Slobodkin for *Many Moons*, written by James Thurber. Pen and ink; watercolor.

1958 (Honor): Paul Galdone for *Anatole and the Cat*, written by Eve Titus. Pen and ink with gray wash over graphite with paper collage.

1962 (Honor): Maurice Sendak for *Little Bear's Visit*, written by Else Holmelund Minarik. Pen and ink with wash separations.

1974 (Honor): David Macaulay for *Cathedral*. Pen and ink.

1978 (Honor): David Macaulay for *Castle*. Pen and ink.

1980 (Honor): Rachel Isadora for *Ben's Trumpet*. Pen and ink.

1985 (Award): Trina Schart Hyman for *Saint George and the Dragon*, retold by Margaret Hodges. India ink and acrylic.

1988 (Award): John Schoenherr for *Owl Moon*, written by Jane Yolen. Pen and ink and watercolor.

1989 (Honor): James Marshall for *Goldilocks and the Three Bears*. Pen and ink and watercolor.

1990 (Honor): Trina Schart Hyman for *Hershel and the Hanukkah Goblins*. India ink and acrylic paint.

1994 (Honor): Kevin Henkes for *Owen*. Watercolor paints and black ink.

1997 (Honor): Dav Pilkey for *Paperboy*. Acrylics and India ink.

1998 (Honor): David Small for *The Gardener*, written by Sarah Stewart. Watercolor, ink pen line, and crayon.

1999 (Honor): Uri Shulevitz for *Snow*. Ink and watercolor washes.

After examining a set of the books listed above, young people may compare the illustrations by counting and comparing the use of black ink by decades. They may also compare some of the books that are totally pen and ink, such as Macaulay's *Castle*, with those that have used the ink to define the illustrations in, for example, Shulevitz's *Snow*. Young people may also be interested in creating their own pen and ink drawings.

Information Book: A book that provides factual information about anything (*e.g.*, real objects, phenomena, events, people, animals, and plants). Information books may include realistic illustrations or photographs and address any subject broadly or narrowly. They may be published in a variety of formats, including chapter books, picture books, concept books, photo essays, and fact books. Broad criteria for selection of information books may include: excellence in writing style, organization, accuracy, authenticity, currency, child appeal, developmental appropriateness, appealing format and design, and reference aids where appropriate. It is also important that information books clearly distinguish fact from opinion.

Two books that provide helpful professional selection information and background information about nonfiction books are Patricia J. Cianciolo's *Information Picture Books for Children* and Beverly Kobrin's *Eyeopeners II: Children's Books to Answer Children's Questions About the World Around Them*. An annual social studies selection may be found at Notable Social Studies Books for Young People on the Web at *http://socialstudies.org/resources/notable/home.html*, and a science book selection may be found at the Web site for Outstanding Science Trade Books for Children at *www.nsta.org/pubs/sc/ostblist.asp*.

The Orbis Pictus Award for Outstanding Nonfiction for Children is awarded each year by the National Council of the Teachers of English (NCTE). The Orbis Pictus Award "promotes and recognizes excellence in writing for children. . . . The name Orbis Pictus, commemorates the work of Johannes Amos Comenius, *Orbis Pictus—The World in Pictures*, considered to be the first book actually planned for children" (NCTE, 2000). More information about this award may be found at *www.ncte.org/elem/pictus/index.html*, which also provides the award criteria and the past winners.

The Robert F. Sibert Information Book Award was made for the first time in 2001 by the Association for Library Service to Children (ALSC of the American Library Association [ALA]). It is awarded each year to the author of the most distinguished information book published the preceding year. The first award was presented to Marc Aronson for *Sir Walter Raleigh and the Quest for El Dorado*.

Young people may be interested in comparing their own favorite information books to the Sibert criteria listed at *www.ala.org/alsc/sibert_terms.html* and to the Orbis Pictus award criteria at *www.ncte.org/elem/pictus/criteria.html*.

Integral Setting: See *Setting*.

Internal Rhyme: An occasion when two or more words rhyme within a single sentence or single line of verse; also called middle or medial rhyme. David Vozar's *Yo, Hungry Wolf! A Nursery Rap*, illustrated by Betsy Lewin, has many examples, including "at the door with a roar" and "eyes are the size of those mean wolf guys." Jane Yolen also used internal rhyme in *Welcome to the Green House*, illustrated by Laura Regan, which includes "a slide of coral snake, a glide of butterflies" and "from the water's edge, from the rocky ledge." Young people may create their own sentences that feature internal rhymes or they may look for the device in other children's books.

International Reading Association Children's Book Awards: Children's literature awards given by the International Reading Association for an author's first or second published book. There are four awards presented for fiction and non-fiction in two age categories: younger readers (ages 4–10) and older readers (ages 10–17). Books from any country and in any language copyrighted during a calendar year will be considered. Each award carries a monetary stipend. Young people may find more information about the awards, including past winners, on the Web at *www.reading.org/awards/awardaut.html.*

International Standard Book Number (ISBN): A unique number assigned to each published book, found on the back of most books and also in the cataloging information on the verso of the title page. Created originally in the early 1970s by the International Federation of Library Associations and Institutions (IFLA), the International Standard Book Number (ISBN) is a part of the International Standard Bibliographic Description (ISBD), which is a set of international standards created to describe all forms of library materials. Standardization in the cataloging of library materials and identification of materials eases a user's search for specific materials and enables libraries to share information about their collections with each other. ISBN numbers are composed of nine digits plus one check digit and divided into three parts usually separated by hyphens. The first part of the number indicates the language or country of origin, the second part denotes the publisher and the third part is the book's specific number.

When a class writes, illustrates, and binds their own books, a classroom set of simulated "ISBN" numbers could be created. The first part of the number could be a number assigned for the school or for the English language; the middle part of the number could denote a classroom number; and the last part of the number would be the book's specific number.

Irony: A literary device that expresses the contrast or difference between reality (what is) and appearance (what seems to be). Two types of irony are verbal and situational. Verbal irony, a figure of speech, enables an author to contrast what is said with what is really meant. When read or spoken, verbal irony is communicated by tone of voice; however, verbal irony is more difficult to recognize in print. An activity to encourage young people to consider verbal irony is for them to interpret how the old sheep in E. B. White's *Charlotte's Web* would have told Wilbur that he would be bacon by fall. They may also consider the factors that help them interpret the old sheep's attitude. Authors use situational irony to contrast what is expected with what actually occurs. An example of situational irony is David Wiesner's *Tuesday* in which illustrations convey characters' inability to reconcile what they have seen with what they know is possible. After reading *Tuesday* aloud, young people may explain why characters' facial expressions are humorous. However, irony does not have to be humorous.

There are many examples of situational irony in children's literature. In E. B. White's *Charlotte's Web*, Charlotte's impending death in juxtaposition to her efforts to save Wilbur's life is ironic. Younger readers can find humorous uses of irony in Ellen Raskin's *Nothing Ever Happens on My Block*, which portrays a small boy sitting on the curb wondering why nothing exciting ever happens, while the reader observes all sorts of excitement. Older readers may refer to Raskin's Newbery Award book, *The Westing Game,* for outstanding use of irony as Turtle Wexler and an odd assortment of characters receive clues to solve the mystery from the song "America the Beautiful." For children of all ages, an excellent use of irony is readily observed in Jon Agee's *The Incredible Painting of Felix Clousseau.* This unknown painter's works "come to life" and just when we think we can live with that, Agee presents us with a surprise ending that demonstrates irony at its best. Chris Van Allsburg's use of irony in *The Sweetest Fig* gives readers a chance to cheer when Marcel the dog eats the last magic fig and he becomes the master and the horrible Monsieur Bibot becomes the dog. Gifted children seem to find irony easier to understand than the average reader does. Therefore, a teacher or librarian may read aloud one of the picture books mentioned above and have children point out the use of irony. Verbalizing irony will help all readers understand and appreciate its use in the stories that they read. See *Mode* and *Irony/Satire*.

Irony/Satire: One of four modes described by Northrop Frye in *Anatomy of Criticism: Four Essays.* Together the four modes reflect the full range of human experiences. In irony/satire, the protagonist is not the capable and enduring hero of tragedy and romance but rather an average individual who has ordinary human problems that never transcend the everyday world. In children's literature, the use of animals and toys allows the depiction of ironic victims without losing optimism and hope. Often irony is a parody of romance. For example, Glenna Sloan in *The Child as Critic* identifies "The Gingerbread Boy" as "a good primer introduction to the ironic myth." The Gingerbread Boy escapes being eaten until he agrees to let the pig or fox carry him, thus ending his quest. Young people may compare and contrast romance and irony/satire by comparing romantic and ironic protagonists, for example, using Peter Rabbit as a romantic hero and the Gingerbread Boy as an ironic hero. See *Mode* and *Romance*.

John Newbery Medal: An annual children's book award named in honor of John Newbery (1713–1767), the first publisher of children's books. The John Newbery Medal was first awarded in 1922 by the Association for Library Service to Children, a division within the American Library Association. The medal is presented to the author of the most distinguished children's book written by a United States citizen and published in the United States in the preceding year. The John Newbery Medal is the oldest of all children's book awards. Young people may find information about the award, its history, selection criteria, and past award winners on the Web at *www.ala.org/alsc/nmedal.html.*

Kamishibai: Paper drama; a traditional form of Japanese storytelling that uses a set of illustrated story boards. From its origins in medieval Japan, *kamishibai* took its contemporary form in the 1920s and was especially popular in the 1950s when *kamishibai* men rode bicycles through neighborhoods, selling candy to young people and then telling them illustrated stories. Often the stories would be serials that would continue another day. Today young people can be introduced to Japanese folktales through *kamishibai* story cards (*Kamishibai* for Kids [*kamishibai. com*]). They may illustrate a set of story cards for a Japanese folktale and use them to tell their folktale. Story cards (approximately 11" × 15") may be mounted on a small stage or held on a table or in a lap. For selecting a story to tell, young people may use Yoshiko Uchida's *The Dancing Kettle*, a collection of 14 authentic Japanese folktales, or they may choose a single illustrated folktale, such as Marguerite Davol's *The Paper Dragon*.

Kate Greenaway Medal: A medal, named after British children's book author and illustrator Kate Greenaway (1846–1901), presented annually since 1956 by the British Library Association to the outstanding illustrator of a children's book first published in the United Kingdom in the preceding year. Young people may find information about the award and a list of the award-winning books on the Web at *http://la-hq.org.uk/directory/medals.html*.

Laura Ingalls Wilder Award: A children's book award presented by the Association of Library Service to Children of the American Library Association since 1954 to an author or illustrator whose books, published in the United States, have over a period of years made a substantial contribution to literature for children. Since 1980 the award has been presented every three years. Young people may find more information and a list of the award-winning authors on the Web at *www.ala.org/alsc/wilder.html.*

Legend: A traditional story. Often containing supernatural elements, it may resemble a myth; but unlike a myth it typically has historical basis and less emphasis on the supernatural. Legends sometimes appear to develop when a place (*e.g.,* the town of Hamelin) or a person (*e.g.,* William Tell) has become intertwined with the local folklore. The elements of many legends, including "The Pied Piper of Hamelin" and "The Story of William Tell" are found in the tales of many countries.

Young people may read a familiar legend, such as Marcia Brown's *Dick Whittington and His Cat*, and research its historical elements (*i.e.,* that in the 1400s London was served by Lord Mayor Richard Whittington and that rats were common) and speculate on that tale's boundaries of folklore and truth. They may also explore the tale's social dilemma, relating it to both the lore in, for example, Robert Holden's *The Pied Piper of Hamelin* (retold), illustrated by Drahos Zak, and the facts in, for example, Gail Haley's *The Post Office Cat*, which describes a more recent struggle against mice.

Leitmotif: See *Motif.*

Letters: A written or printed communication from one person to another person or organization, usually placed in an envelope and sent by the postal service. Books comprised of a collection of letters are formally known as epistolary picture books or epistolary novels.

Authors include letters as story elements in a variety of ways. For example, Janet and Allan Ahlberg's *The Jolly Postman: Or, Other People's Letters* was the first of their three books which featured correspondence in fairy tale land through pocket envelopes and removable letters, cards, postcards, party invitations, etc. The other two in the series included *The Jolly Christmas Postman* and *The Jolly Pocket Postman*. Alma Flor Ada uses letters instead of text to loosely weave together stories in the fairy tale world in two picture books, *Dear Peter Rabbit* and *Yours Truly, Goldilocks*. Lydia Grace sends letters home in the 1998 Caldecott Honor book, Sarah Stewart's *The Gardener*, illustrated by David Small. The secret to the story of William Joyce's *Santa Calls* can be found at the end of the story with two facsimile letters that can be removed from the envelopes. Letters were used as a plot device in the 1984 Newbery Award book *Dear Mr. Henshaw*, written by Beverly Cleary, and in Karen Hesse's *Letters from Rifka*.

Young people may keep their own "epistolary novel" by composing a collection of sequential letters to their favorite book character, a family member, or a special friend. Topics for each of the letters could be assigned to the class as a progressive assignment over a course of several months.

Lettrism: A mode of visual communication through the placement of letters and symbols. Lettrism developed in the 1950s when it was also known as *typewriter art*. The purpose of lettrism is visual effect, although, as in concrete poetry, the technique can also convey verbal content. Young people will be familiar with a contemporary use of lettrism in e-mail messages: : -)." A contemporary work that contains lettrism is Roberto De Vicq De Cumptich's *Bembo's Zoo: An Animal ABC* that includes illustrations of twenty-six animals created with the Bembo font. Young people may experiment with lettrism by producing an illustration like those in *Bembo's Zoo*. Or, they may apply the concept to an original concrete poem.

Lexicon: An older term used for a dictionary; a list of words; linguistically, a language's total morphemes; and, less commonly, a dictionary of Hebrew or Greek. See *Dictionary*.

Limerick: A humorous form of verse composed of five lines in which the first and second lines rhyme, the shorter third and fourth lines rhyme, and the fifth line rhymes with or repeats the first line. Although the origin of the limerick is not clear, the form is usually associated with Edward Lear whose *Book of Nonsense* was first published in 1846.

Young people may listen to limericks read aloud from collections like John Ciardi's *The Hopeful Trout and Other Limericks*, Edward Lear's *Of Pelicans and Pussycats*, Arnold Lobel's *Pigericks*, James Marshall's *Pocketful of Nonsense*, and Myra Livingston's *Lots of Limericks*. They may begin to play with the form if they are challenged to create a fifth line after hearing a limerick's first four lines. Young people who wish to write limericks may create group limericks until they are comfortable with the form and the often-surprising ending. Or, they may wish to create individual limericks.

Linoleum Block (Printing): Describes the block or plate made of linoleum that is used for making relief prints. Sometimes utilized as a covering for floors, the material is durable and washable, and it is easily cut with knives or small gouging tools in a similar way that woodcuts are produced. Details are not as fine as those in a woodcut because the softness of the material causes the linoleum to break off, and linoleum blocks lack the grain that characterizes woodcuts. In the printing process, a different block is usually cut for the application of each color if there are two or more colors in the illustration. Linoleum blocks are often backed with burlap or canvas and can be attached to a wood block for easier handling. Linoleum cuts were made by Henri Matisse (French, 1869–1954) and Pablo Picasso (Spanish, 1881–1973).

Ashley Wolff has illustrated several books with linoleum block printing, including *The Bells of London*, *A Year of Birds*, and *A Year of Beasts*. Robert Sabuda has also used the medium to illustrate children's books, such as *I Hear America Singing*, written by Walt Whitman, and *Earth Verses and Water Rhymes*, written by J. Patrick Lewis. Among recent Association for Library Service to Children Notable Books is Angela Shelf Medearis' *Seven Spools of Thread: A Kwanzaa Story*, illustrated with linoleum block prints by Daniel Minter.

Literary Tale: An original tale developed according to the themes and structures of a folktale, but created by a specific author. Jane Yolen's *Touch Magic: Fantasy, Faerie and Folklore in the Literature of Childhood* offers librarians and teachers information about the literary tale as well as the traditional tale.

Hans Christian Andersen (Denmark, 1805–1875) is considered the master of the literary tale. Children have long been familiar with the tales of Andersen because many of his stories were translated into English in 1846. Among Andersen's classic tales that continue to be retranslated, retold, and re-illustrated for children are *The Emperor's New Clothes*, illustrated by Angela Barrett; *The Steadfast Tin Soldier*, illustrated with woodcuts by Jonathan Heale; *The Steadfast Tin Soldier*, illustrated by Fred Marcellino; and *The Ugly Duckling*, illustrated by Jerry Pinkney, which is reported to be a symbolic retelling of Andersen's life.

Young people, who may already be familiar with the stories of Andersen but are unaware of the concept of the literary tale, may each read a different Andersen tale and list its similarities to folktales they know. They may compile their findings on a bulletin board using a grid with one axis representing folktale characteristics and the other axis listing the Andersen tales read by the group.

Lithograph: An illustration created from a printing method invented by a German named Alois Senefelder in 1798. This process of lithography requires drawing with a greasy crayon (usually called a lithograph pencil or crayon) on a flat surface of stone, metal, or plastic, then covering the surface with water and finally greasy ink. The ink only sticks to the surface where there are crayon marks. A dampened paper is then applied to the surface with a press, and a print or lithograph of the drawing is the result. Lithographs in more than one color require separate drawings for each color. Due to changes in the printing process, this technique is no longer a usual feature in children's book illustration.

The first Randolph Caldecott Medal was awarded in 1938 to Helen Dean Fish's *Animals of the Bible*, illustrated by Dorothy P. Lathrop, which consisted of black and white lithographs. Other Caldecott Award books created from lithographs include: Ingri and Edgar Parin d'Aulaire's *Abraham Lincoln*; Robert McClosky's *Make Way for Ducklings*; and Maud and Miska Petersham's *The Rooster Crows*.

This process can be imitated using materials from an art supply store. Young people may create their own drawings on a flat metal surface such as a cookie sheet and then "print" off their own "lithograph."

Lullaby: A soothing song that is sung to babies and young children to quiet them and to lull them gently to sleep.

"Hush Little Baby" is a classic lullaby depicted individually in several children's picture books. Three versions of the illustrated song include: Marla Frazee's *Hush Little Baby: A Folk Song with Pictures* ; Shari Halpern's *Hush Little Baby*; and Sylvia Long's *Hush Little Baby*. Winning a 1997 Caldecott Honor, Minfong Ho's *Hush!:*

A Thai Lullaby, illustrated by Holly Meade, portrays a young mother who quiets all the creatures so her baby can sleep.

Songbooks of lullabies include *Lullabies: An Illustrated Songbook*, illustrated by Holly Meade, and Shona McKellar's *A Child's Book of Lullabies*. Cheryl Mattox's *Shake It to the One That You Love the Best: Play Songs and Lullabies from Black Musical Traditions* is a songbook and audiotape combination which includes a selection of African American lullabies.

Numerous collections of lullabies are also available on audiotape and compact disc. Selected versions include *Lullaby: A Collection* and *A Child's Collection of Lullaby*. *The World Sings Goodnight*, volumes 1 and 2, is a collection of authentic lullabies from around the world, all sung in their native tongues. Other specialized audio collections include *'Til Their Eyes Shine: The Lullaby Album* (all female vocalists) and *Daddies Say Goodnight* (all male vocalists).

Young people may compare the illustrations in the various picture books featuring the song "Hush Little Baby" and may listen to the lullaby on audio. Young children may listen to lullaby tapes during quiet times. Young people may also express themselves through free hand drawing with crayons as they listen to the soothing music of the lullabies. Others may want to share the lullabies they have heard elsewhere.

Lyric: A poem that describes a single speaker's personal contemplations, feelings, and perceptions and that emphasizes sound and imagery. Lyrical poetry originated in ancient Greece where it was sung, usually to the accompaniment of a lyre, and today *lyric* also means the words of a song. In English, lyrical poetry does not have a set form, and generally lyrical poetry is considered one of two broad classifications (narrative being the other). Young people may be introduced to the qualities of sound, the expression of personal feelings, and a visual interpretation of imagery in picture book editions of such lyrical poems as Robert Frost's *Stopping by Woods on a Snowy Evening*, illustrated by Susan Jeffers, and William Blake's *The Tyger*, illustrated by Neil Waldman. Young people will have an opportunity to compare their interpretations of the poem's visual imagery with those of the illustrators if they first hear it without seeing the illustrations.

Magical Realism: A twentieth-century approach in pictorial and literary arts of centering a work in reality but also incorporating elements of fantasy or the supernatural. The trend began after World War II with such well-known writers of adult fiction as Jorge Luis Borges and Umberto Eco. Bruce Brooks has demonstrated the technique in *Throwing Smoke*, a sports novel about Whiz who is frustrated with the losing record of his baseball team. The team's win-loss ratio changes after Whiz begins printing baseball cards of talented imaginary players who magically appear on his team. A picture storybook in which magical realism is communicated through the illustrations is David Wiesner's Caldecott-winning *Tuesday*, a surreal and humorous account of a very ordinary evening when frogs did fly and next morning when characters try to make sense of the memories and evidence. The finale causes readers to ponder, "What if pigs could fly?"

Young people could share a work of magical realism and discuss where the magical and real elements begin and end and how they interrelate. Young people could also speculate how certain magical elements would affect a realistic work that they have read together.

Metaphor: A figure of speech in which one object or idea is used in place of another. The result is an implied comparison that suggests a likeness through the creation of an image. Children's experiences with figurative language should include their exposure to and discussion of images that are suggested by rich metaphors. Although it is not necessary for children to dwell on the term itself, they can be led to appreciate the beauty of a metaphor's image and its enhancement of a text's meaning. A good way to present metaphoric language to children is to read aloud Myra Livingston's *Up in the Air*. This work includes a number of examples of figurative language. Re-read and ask children to find examples of the author's use of one object in place of another that has one or more similar characteristics. Examples of metaphors to be discovered and discussed are: "ropes of road . . ." and "[u]mbrella forests."

Meter: The rhythmic pattern in a line of poetry. Typically the rhythm is described in units of stressed and unstressed syllables called a *foot*. Standard feet in English poetry are iambic (' ^), trochaic (^'), anapestic (^^'), and dactylic ('^^). Meter is further described by the number of feet in a line: *monometer*, one foot; *dimeter*, two; *trimeter*, three; *tetrameter*, four; *pentameter*, five; *hexameter*, six; and *heptameter*, seven. Although the technical conventions of rhythm are useful to adults who are reviewing, criticizing, or describing poetry, young people should be encouraged to respond critically simply by hearing poetry read aloud and considering why a poet created a particular rhythm for a poem. For example, hearing Diane Siebert's *Train Song* for a second time, young people could be encouraged to hear the sound of the train on the tracks as they clap or sway to the rhythm. David McCord's "Song of the Train" in *One at a Time: His Collected Poems for the Young* also creates the recognizable sound of a train as it gains speed on the tracks.

Mildred L. Batchelder Award: A citation awarded to an American publisher for a children's book considered to be the most outstanding of those books originally published in a language other than English and in a country other than the United States and subsequently translated into English and published in the United States. The award, named in honor of Mildred Batchelder, a former executive director of the American Association of Library Service to Children, was first presented in 1968. Young people may find information about the award and lists of award-winning books on the Web at *www.ala.org/alsc/batch.html.*

Mixed Media: The use of more than one medium in the creation of an illustration. Many award-winning artists have combined media to create picture book illustrations. Among Caldecott Honor illustrators who have used mixed media are Simms Taback who mixed watercolor, gouache, pencil, ink, and collage in *Joseph Had a Little Overcoat*; Brian Pinkney who mixed scratchboard renderings with gouache, luma dyes, and oil paints in Andrea Pinkney's *Duke Ellington*; and Peter Sis who mixed watercolor, pen and ink, and oil pastel to illustrate *Tibet: Through the Red Box*. Also, Janet Stevens used paper made from carrots, corn, potatoes, beans, radishes, tomatoes, a pair of gardening pants, and a shirt with the mixed media of watercolor, colored pencil, and gesso for her original art in the 1996 Caldecott Honor book *Tops and Bottoms*.

After young people have considered the mixed media used in a set of award-winning picture books, they may use a different set of media to produce an adaptation of one illustration they select from the set. A "guess the media" activity with a variety of Caldecott books may extend children's knowledge of media used in picture books. Use *The Newbery and Caldecott Awards: A Guide to the Medal and Honor Books* as a guide to the correct media/medium.

Mode: A framework by which to consider categories of treatment of all literature. Northrop Frye in *The Anatomy of Criticism: Four Essays* explained that *mode* is a broader concept than genre because it facilitates comparing and contrasting literary works of all types across all eras. Frye identified (in order of complexity) four basic modes or stories: romance, which tells of wishes fulfilled and the triumph of good over evil; comedy, which presents a positive view of the world in which people and circumstances can change toward the ideal; tragedy, which presents the limits of human power to fulfill wishes and to ensure the protection of the innocent or the good; and irony/satire, which reveals the discrepancies between the ideal and reality. He considered each mode to be a reflection of the author's attitude about the powers of the protagonist in relation to other characters or the environment. See *Comedy*, *Romance*, *Tragedy*, and *Irony/Satire*.

Modeling Clay: Any non-hardening clay that contains various additives and can be shaped. One well-known type is Plasticine. This clay can be used repeatedly and comes in a variety of colors. It may be used for making models for casting larger works, for creating three-dimensional objects, or for the artistic medium in children's picture books.

Canadian illustrator Barbara Reid is best known for work in this medium. In sculpting picture book illustrations in clay, she has been able to achieve incredible artistic detail. Reid received the Ezra Jack Keats Award in 1988 for *The New Baby Calf*, written by Edith Newlin Chase, and *Have You Seen Birds?*, written by Joanne Oppenheim. The award recognizes and celebrates promising new children's book illustrators.

Children may create flat pictures using modeling clay. Barbara Reid's *Playing with Plasticine* and her *Fun with Modeling Clay* show young artists how to shape modeling clay into flat pictures and three-dimensional objects. Young people may also compare the clay illustrations in Reid's books with books on the same topic though created in other media (*e.g.*, Reid's clay illustrations in *Two by Two* with

Peter Spier's pen and ink illustrations in *Noah's Ark*; Arthur Geisert's etchings in *The Ark*; and Mordicai Gerstein's oil on vellum illustrations in *Noah and the Great Flood*).

Mood: The author's attitude toward his or her subject. The distinction between *mood* and *tone* can be subtle, and many critics (*e.g.*, Rebecca Lukens in *A Critical Handbook of Children's Literature*, sixth edition, describe tone as the author's attitude toward the subject and the reader. Tony Johnston's *The Iguana Brothers: A Tale of Two Lizards*, illustrated by Mark Teague, demonstrates how mood and tone can differ in a single work. The lizard brothers, Tom and Dom, blink, think, eat bugs, and imagine that they are dinosaurs; they are silly. Yet, the book is hilarious because the author expects readers to know how ridiculous the iguanas are. In contrast is Arnold Lobel's *Toad and Frog Are Friends* in which, despite the foibles of Toad and Frog, the qualities of mood and tone are similar. Toad's and Frog's weaknesses are amusing but never insipid because the author respects them and their friendship and expects the readers to do the same. Young people could explore the moods of these two books by acting out episodes and discussing differences between the voice interpretations of Tom and Dom and those of Toad and Frog.

Mother Goose: See *Nursery Rhymes*.

Motif: In literature, a recurring character, word, action, verbal pattern, phrase, object, or idea. A source, accessible to young people and rich in examples, is folklore. A scholarly work on motif in folklore is Stith Thompson's six-volume work, *Motif-Index for Folk-Literature*. In the manner of Stith Thompson, young people could examine a set of folktales and document the common, recurring elements, such as

- deep sleeps—*e.g.*, Trina Schart Hyman's retelling *The Sleeping Beauty* and Jacob and Wilhelm Grimm's *Snow White*, translated by Randall Jarrell and illustrated by Nancy Berkert;
- witches—*e.g.*, Paul Zelinsky's *Rapunzel* and Jacob and Wilhelm Grimm's *Hansel and Gretel*, translated by Elizabeth Crawford and illustrated by Lisbeth Swerger;
- wishes—*e.g.*, Gerald McDermott's *The Stonecutter* and John Warren Stewig's *The Fisherman and His Wife*, illustrated by Margo Tomes;

- trickery—*e.g.*, Gerald McDermott's *The Raven* and Tony Johnston's *The Tale of Rabbit and Coyote,* illustrated by Tomie de Paola.

When the concept of motif is applied to a single work, it is known as *leitmotif,* examples of which abound in single works of folklore. There are several sets of recurring action in "Jack and the Bean Tree" from Richard Chase's *The Jack Tales* (Chase, 1971, 1943: 31–39): Jack runs to see the bean on three mornings; he is punished by his mother for lying each morning; he climbs the bean tree three times; each time he climbs the tree he encounters the giant's wife; on each visit the giant hunts for him while chanting the well-known refrain; and three times Jack steals the giant's personal property. Young people, working in small groups, could examine a set of folktales and identify the recurring characters, actions, and objects. They could compile their results with those from other small groups and communicate the results in a chart

---

Mystery: A story or novel in which a mystery is the central focus. Mysteries include detective stories, suspense novels, tales of terror and the supernatural, and Gothic novels. Characteristics of mysteries include realistic dialogue, puzzling events, a fast moving plot, and suspense. The author controls the suspense by planting clues and creating a plot with twists and turns. Sometimes part of the mystery is deciding in which genre the book should be considered. For example, the reader of Virginia Hamilton's *The House of Dies Drear* is not certain until the conclusion whether the book is realistic fiction or fantasy. The ability of the author to manage clues is a primary criterion for evaluating a mystery. Clues too transparent or too obscure can spoil the mystery for readers who consider mysteries to be suspenseful, problem-solving games.

The mystery genre is one of the most popular with young people, and they may share their enjoyment of mysteries in book discussion groups, in book review writing, by consulting the Web for the listing of the Edgar Awards (*www.story-house.com/welcome.html*). Also, as an activity young people could listen to or read a mystery, such as Ellen Raskins' *The Westing Game*; Joan Lowery Nixon's *The Other Side of Dark*; Eve Bunting's *Coffin in the Case*; Natalie Babbitt's *Goody Hall*; John Bellairs' *The Mummy, the Will and the Crypt*; or Willo Roberts' *Babysitting Is a Dangerous Job,* and make individual lists of perceived clues as the book is read. At the book's conclusion, they could discuss when they accurately determined the solution, which clues were most significant, and how the story's structure maintained suspense.

Myth: An anonymous story that is set in the distant past. Myths have three characteristics that set them apart from other forms of traditional literature: (1) they are presented as truth; (2) the main characters have extraordinary powers; and (3) each story is related to a body of stories. Typically myths attempt to explain phenomena in nature, the history of rituals, creation, death, or the adventures of great heroes. Myths give humans an opportunity to name and explain what they do not understand, thus, according to Pierre Grimal in *Larousse World Mythology*, making humans more secure in their world.

Comparing two related myths is an activity that would involve intermediate children in the analysis of the nature and characteristics of myths. For example, Warrick Hutton's *Persephone* is a Greek nature myth that may be compared to Gerald McDermott's *Daughter of the Earth: A Roman Myth*. Demeter and Persephone from the Greek myth and Ceres and Proserpina from the Roman myth are parallel characters, a goddess of agriculture and her daughter. The myths tell of the crisis (*i.e.*, unending winter) that befalls the earth after the daughter is kidnapped and taken to the underworld. The gods intervene, and the daughter is freed except for one season each year. Thus, winter is limited to a quarter of the year. Many young people would enjoy exploring the words that originated in mythology and have become part of the English language, and Isaac Asimov's *Words from the Myths* would support efforts to search for allusions to mythology as well as the origins of words from mythology.

Narrative Poetry: Ballads, epics, and other poems of disparate types that tell a story. In all of literature narrative poetry is among the oldest of literary genres and includes *The Odyssey, The Iliad, Beowulf,* and *Canterbury Tales.* Narrative poetry was popular until the end of the nineteenth century when the novel became the primary genre for telling a story and when poets began to focus on subjects that could not be presented sufficiently well in prose. However, the nineteenth century was the beginning of narrative poetry for children when there appeared in 1822 "'Twas the Night Before Christmas," attributed to Clement C. Moore. Among the poem's many picture book editions is Jan Brett's *The Night Before Christmas.* The poem was immensely popular in the nineteenth century and remained so, as did Edward Lear's narrative poetry in *A Book of Nonsense,* first published in 1846; Henry Wadsworth Longfellow's *Paul Revere's Ride,* illustrated by Nancy Parker; and Ernest Lawrence Thayer's "Casey at the Bat," which is in Patricia Polacco's *Casey at the Bat: A Ballad of the Republic, Sung in 1888.* Among twentieth century children's narrative poets are Shel Silverstein, Colin McNaughton, and Jack Prelutsky.

Studies of young people's preferences in poetry have consistently shown narrative poetry to be a favorite, and young people should have opportunities to enjoy hearing narrative poems read loud.

National Council of Teachers of English Award for Excellence in Poetry for Children: An award established and presented since 1977 by the National Council of Teachers of English to a living American poet for his or her aggregate work. The award was given annually until 1982, at which time it was decided that the award would be given every three years. The collection of poetry books of all winners of the NCTE Award for Excellence in Poetry for Children, past and future, will be sustained and preserved in the Boston Public Library's Rare Books and Research Division. Young people may find information about the award, including selection criteria and past award-winning poets on the Web (*www.ncte.org/ elem/poetry*).

Newbery Medal: See *John Newbery Medal.*

Nonlinear Text: Verbal and/or visual communication that does not have a predetermined sequence to the elements of text or illustrations. Thus, the sequence can shift from reading to reading, requiring the reader to assume responsibility for the text and presenting multiple stories. The reader takes an active role in the construction of the text by responding to conventions such as branching, collage, split or folded pages, movable components, and unstructured page layouts. Nonlinear texts may take many forms (including hypertext). The term has also been applied to stories, often about diverse and conflicting perspectives, woven from multiple formats and points of view, such as Virginia Wolff's *Bat 6* in which the voices of 21 narrators merge to tell of tragedy in their post Word War II small town; Paul Fleischman's *Bull Run* and *Seedfolks*, both using multiple points of view to weave complex stories of individual differences; Walter Dean Myers' *Monster*, which uses journal entries and a script to reveal complex emotions not always understood by the indicted narrator; and Virginia Walter's *Making Up Megaboy* in which multiple perspectives (teacher, attorney, witness, police officer) contribute puzzling clues to a murder committed by a thirteen-year-old.

Nonlinearity is the dominant characteristic of David Macaulay's *Black and White*. After exploring this, young people may identify the qualities (*e.g.*, the unusual shape, arbitrary sequence, the open-ended nature, and the special role of the reader) that set it apart from a traditional one.

Nonsense Verse: Light, playful verse, usually lyric or narrative, that defies logic. Its characteristics include strong rhythm, invented words, figurative language (*e.g.*, alliteration, personification, and hyperbole), and ridiculous characters and events. A classic source of nonsense poetry is Edward Lear's *The Complete Book of Nonsense*, first published in 1846, or a collection of four Lear poems in *Nonsense Songs*. One of the most famous nonsense poems, Lewis Carroll's "Jabberwocky," in *Through the Looking Glass*, has led to the acceptance of the term *jabberwocky* to mean nonsensical speech or writing. Creators of nonsense verse also include Shel Silverstein and Jack Prelutsky. Young people who read or listen to nonsense verse may be challenged to find the sense in nonsense or to identify examples of the poet's use of rhythm, coined words, figurative language, or absurd characters and situations.

Noodlehead Story: Type of folktale in which the bumbling, sometimes witless, underdog usually comes out on top through no efforts of his own; numbskull tale; simpleton tale. A noodlehead story often has a simpleton male for a main character, who, given a set of instructions will make a mess of them, happily stumbling along and leaving chaos behind. Almost all cultures have noodlehead stories within their oral traditions, and examples include the Grimms' "Hans in Luck," the English "Jack" stories, some *Hodja* tales from Mediterranean countries, and stories about Juan Bobo, a character popular in Puerto Rico.

Martha Hamilton and Mitch Weiss' *Noodlehead Stories: World Tales Kids Can Read and Tell* demonstrates the universality of the noodlehead tale; and the short, funny tales can inspire adults and young people to join in a noodlehead storytelling session. The book also addresses the appeal of the numbskull story, specific information about each tale, and tips for storytelling. Young people can explore the simpleton tale in such single folktale picture books as Ehud Ben-Ezer's *Hosni the Dreamer: An Arabian Tale*, illustrated by Uri Shulevitz; Eric Kimmel's *Onions and Garlic: An Old Tale*, illustrated by Katya Arnold; and Jane Kurtz's *Trouble*, illustrated by Durga Bernhard. Each offers an opportunity to discuss the tale's appeal and the characteristics it shares with other noodlehead stories.

Nostalgia: A sentimental longing to return to a former time and place in one's life, usually to a home, home place, or homeland with memories of family and friends. Nostalgia usually focuses on happier times and incidents of deep personal significance, such as those related to a particular age or to economic or social backgrounds. In children's literature, a sentimental or negative tone in which the author maintains an adult perspective, not relating to that of the child; does not respect young readers, approaching them with condescension; or allows sentimentality to erase the daily realities of past times.

However, author's memories of family and friends in other times and places have been rich sources for children's literature. Among the titles representing child-centered, emotionally honest stories are Cynthia Rylant's *When I Was Young in the Mountains*, illustrated by Diane Goode, which is a personal reminiscence of her childhood in the Appalachia Mountains; Patricia Polacco's *The Keeping Quilt*, which provides a glimpse of the author's family history by sharing the origin of the pieces of fabric in a quilt; Crescent Dragonwagon's *Home Place*, illustrated by Jerry Pinkney, which features a present-day family searching through an old home place and wondering about a family of long ago; and Anne Shelby's *Homeplace*, which follows a grandmother and a grandchild as they trace their family history.

As a follow-up activity, young people may write or tell their own story of personal memories about a particular place they have lived or visited, a happy occasion spent with family or friends, or an event that happened when they were younger.

Novella: A short fictional prose narrative that has more depth than a short story but does not possess the complexity of a full-length novel. Novellas usually concentrate on a single subject or a chain of events and sometimes include a surprising event or conclusion. Although the term had been applied to early tales (*e.g.*, Boccaccio's *Decameron*), Goethe and other German writers established the short novel as a literary genre at the end of the nineteenth century.

War, historical events, and social issues are often popular novella topics. Gary Paulsen's *The Rifle* is a 105-page story of an American Revolutionary War rifle that is passed down through the years and fires again on a fateful Christmas Eve in 1994. Gary Paulsen's *Soldier's Heart* is a 106-page novella that presents fifteen-year-old Charley Goddard's story of the horrors of serving as a Union soldier in the Civil War. In a 97-page story, Cynthia Rylant's *I Had Seen Castles* tells of an older man named John as he relives his life-changing experiences from World War II.

Young people may read the three novellas listed above and prepare booktalks on them. Joni Bodart features books with fewer than 200 pages (not limited to novellas) in *The World's Best Thin Books: What to Read if Your Book Report Is Due Tomorrow*, which identifies 100 "world class" thin books. (This reference was originally published as *100 World Class Thin Books*.)

Numbskull: See *Noodlehead*.

Nursery Rhymes: Traditional verses of often exaggerated rhyme and rhythm that may be shared aloud with babies and very young children as an introduction to the sounds of the language. They are an important part of children's literary heritage and include songs, riddles, and ballads. Bernice Cullinan and Lynn Galda (in *Literature and the Child*) define four characteristics of nursery rhymes that have contributed to their enduring popularity: powerful rhythm; imaginative use of words and ideas; compact structure; and wit and whimsy of the characters.

John Newbery was the first to associate the term "Mother Goose" with nursery rhymes and publish them (*Mother Goose's Melody, or Sonnets for the Cradle,* commonly thought to have been published in 1780). This collection was attributed to Mother Goose, though there is no conclusive evidence of the origin of the rhymes or even of a person with that name. Iona and Peter Opie authored two definitive works, *The Oxford Nursery Rhyme Book* and *The Oxford Dictionary of Nursery Rhymes.* Although most nursery rhymes originate in the oral tradition, some do have a known author. For example, Sarah Josepha Hale wrote "Mary Had a Little Lamb" in 1830.

Selected nursery rhyme collections include: *The Helen Oxenbury Nursery Rhyme Book,* selected by Brian Alderson; *The Arnold Lobel Book of Mother Goose: A Treasury of More Than 300 Classic Nursery Rhymes*; Michael Hague's *Mother Goose: A Collection of Classic Nursery Rhymes*; *The Lucy Cousins Book of Nursery Rhymes*; Zena Sutherland's *The Orchard Book of Nursery Rhymes,* illustrated by Faith Jaques; Rosemary Wells' *My Very First Mother Goose,* edited by Iona Opie; and Rosemary Wells' *Here Comes Mother Goose,* edited by Iona Opie.

In addition to collections, there are some single-verse nursery rhyme children's books, such as Janet Stevens' *The House that Jack Built*; Paul Galdone's *The Three Little Kittens*; and Sarah Josepha Hale's *Mary Had a Little Lamb,* with photographs by Bruce McMillan.

Young people may listen to nursery rhymes read by older students or adult volunteers who use a variety of collections from the library. Young readers will enjoy Anne Miranda's *To Market, To Market,* a take-off on Mother Goose, illustrated by Janet Stevens. Older students who have access to William Baring-Gould's *Annotated Mother Goose* may be inspired to research further the history of a rhyme. Others may write a parody of a rhyme or a new ending to a favorite nursery rhyme, such as "Jack and Jill went up a hill. . . . "

Oil Paint: Artistic medium made from mixing dry colored powder evenly into linseed oil. The technique of oil painting entails priming a canvas (or other absorbent surface such as a board) and applying one or more layers of paint. Artists may paint on the surface with little planning; or, like many Old Masters, they may sketch the painting in detail, cover the surface with monochromatic layer(s), and then paint in the color. Depth can be built into the painting with the use of layers. The medium most used by the Old Masters, it is still often chosen by artists for large or important works and by illustrators of children's picture books.

There are several illustrators of note that have used this art form to produce award-winning books. Paul O. Zelinsky used oil painting to produce one Caldecott Medal book, *Rapunzel,* and three Caldecott Honor books: Anne Isaacs' *Swamp Angel; Rumpelstiltskin,* retold by Paul Zelinsky; and *Hansel and Gretel,* retold by Rika Lesser. Others who have made effective use of this technique include Thomas Locker for such books as his own *Where the River Begins* and Jean Craighead George's *The First Thanksgiving;* Floyd Cooper for Joyce Carol Thomas' *Brown Honey and Broomwheat Tea;* and Mike Wimmer for Robert Burleigh's *Home Run: The Story of Babe Ruth.* Among the 2001 Association for Library Service to Children's Notable Books are two illustrated with oil painting: James Cross Giblin's *The Amazing Life of Benjamin Franklin,* illustrated by Michael Dooling, and Andrea Davis Pinkney's *Let It Shine: Stories of Black Women Freedom Fighters,* illustrated by Stephen Alcorn.

Young people may enjoy these picture books along with a field trip to a nearby museum or a virtual trip to the National Gallery of Art *(www.nga.gov)* to view old and new master works using oil painting to develop a rich appreciation of this medium. They may also have guest demonstrations of oil painting by local artists or picture book illustrators.

Omniscient Point of View: The third-person perspective of a narrator who knows all events (past, present, and future) and the thoughts and motivations of all characters. Limited omniscient point of view describes the use of a third-person narrator who reveals the thoughts and motivation of one or only a few characters. An all-knowing narrator offers the author the possibility of revealing the views and feelings of all the characters in a story. Because everything can be explained without losing consistency and, therefore, credibility, omniscient point of view is especially useful in fantasies such as E. B. White's *Charlotte's Web*, in which the reader knows the desires and feelings of Templeton as well as those of Charlotte and Wilbur. C. S. Lewis' *The Lion, the Witch, and the Wardrobe* also makes use of the omniscient point of view, and the reader knows what forces drive each character, good or evil. And, in Jane Langton's Newbery Honor book *The Fledgling*, an omniscient point of view creates a mythic atmosphere, permits Georgie and the goose to be both wise and innocent, and allows the reader into the satiric insights revealed by Mr. Preek's and Miss Prawn's conversations and thoughts.

Young people can most easily understand the concept of third-person narrator. One avenue for extending that understanding to omniscient point of view is to read aloud a novel with that point of view so that young people may ponder and discuss the characters' motivations, feelings, and thoughts, and the author's consistent use of the same point of view to communicate to the reader. Young people often find the clearest contrast to the omniscient point of view is the first-person point of view in a realistic story in which the reader can know only what the narrator knows.

Onomatopoeia: A word whose sound suggests and emphasizes its meaning; also known as *echoism*. An example of the suggestion of meaning is "Hickory, Dickory, Dock," which uses a combination of rhythm and onomatopoeia (echoing the *tick, tock* sound of a clock) to emphasize the poem's intent. Some onomatopoeic words (*e.g., crack, sizzle, buzz*) sound like what they represent. The words may be real words as, for example, when Woodrow showed his new clothes and comic books to Gypsie, he "jabbered" and "gushed" in Ruth White's *Belle Prater's Boy*. Or, they may be imaginary words as in Lewis Carroll's "Jabberwocky" ("O frabjous day! Callooh! Callay!," from *Through the Looking-Glass and What Alice Found There*) (*www.emule.com/poetry/dispoem.cgi?poem*). Some philologists have hypothesized that all language originated as onomatopoeic words.

Young people enjoy hearing and participating in this playful element of prose and poetry. A potential read aloud that introduces multiple examples of this term is Verna Aardema's *Jackal's Flying Lesson: A Koikhoi Tale*. Like many African folktales, this picture book invites the vocal participation of young people who can join in such activities as the fox's smacking his lips (*mik, mik, mik*) and gulping (*dilak*) and the dove's crying (*woo, woo, woo*). For other activities, young people may choose a favorite animal tale and describe how they could use onomatopoeia to enhance their own adaptations.

Open Ending or **Open-Endedness:** The lack of complete closure to a structural element of a literary work. The lack of closure may range from an incomplete poetic foot to a story that stops in mid-sentence. In children's literature *open ended* almost always refers to the lack of complete resolution to the conflict in a novel. For example, Lois Lowry's *The Giver* ends with the reader's not knowing what happens to Jonas and the baby after they leave for "Elsewhere." The open ending frustrates many readers. An open ending is, however, perhaps the most realistic ending to any story, and an open ending can accommodate the diverse perspectives and beliefs of all readers. Encouraged to see an open ending as one with many possibilities, young people can brainstorm potential closed endings for a story and discuss their likelihood and their potential to please readers. An open ending also invites a sequel, and young people may speculate how a sequel might begin.

Orbis Pictus Award for Outstanding Nonfiction for Children: A children's book award presented annually since 1990 by the National Council of Teachers of English to promote and recognize excellence in the writing of nonfiction for children. The award's name commemorates the work of Johannes Amos Comenius, *Orbis Pictus—The World in Pictures*, considered to be the first book actually planned for children. Young people may find more information about the award as well as a list of the award-winning books on the Web (*www.ncte.org/elem/pictus*).

Origami: The process or art of folding paper into three-dimensional shapes, such as birds, dragons, or flowers. The term may also refer to the paper objects produced. Molly Bang used photographed origami for the illustrations in *The Paper Crane*, as did Jim LaMarche to illustrate *Little Oh*, written by Laura Krauss Melmed.

After sharing *The Paper Crane*, young people may develop their own skills in origami through such books as Florence Temko's *Origami Magic* and Steve Biddle and Megumi Biddle's *Origami Safari*.

Page Layout: The actual creation of a camera-ready page that consists of the placement of text, pictures, and other design elements of the pages in a book. Illustrations and accompanying text can be variously placed on one page, on facing pages, alternating pages, or on a part of a page. The extension of illustrations across two pages is known as a double-page spread or double spread.

James M. Deem's *Bodies from the Bog* incorporates an interesting page layout of captioned photographs and illustrations accompanied by well-placed sections of text. Featuring double-page spreads that are turned vertically is Janet Stevens' *Tops and Bottoms*, a story about Hare's outwitting a rich and lazy bear throughout the gardening season.

Young people may select a number of children's books for examination and compare the differences in the page layouts in both fiction and nonfiction books.

Page Shape: The outline shape of the internal pages of a book. Occasionally, the pages in books for children are shaped to an outside outline of a book that is different from the traditional square or rectangle. And, sometimes a book features pages of varied sizes, including half pages or graduated pages. Shorter pages may or may not create a different scene on the left-hand side of the book as the page is turned. As John Stewig noted in *Looking at Picture Books* (Stewig, 1999: 145), "the use of the half page moves the action along, by showing two half pages of difference between the double page spread." Stewig notes that John Goodall was an artist who used the half page device as early as 1970 in *Shrewbettina's Birthday*.

Sometimes the internal pages of a book are shaped or cut differently. Lois Ehlert's *Waiting for Wings* incorporates pages cut in various sizes while sharing the story of caterpillars waiting to become butterflies. Pages in the back of Lois

Ehlert's *Planting a Rainbow* are die-cut in a graduated fashion beginning with the color red, then orange, yellow, green, blue, and purple to show all the colors of the rainbow of flowers planted by a mother and child. The same technique of graduated page sizes is also used in Eric Carle's *The Grouchy Ladybug*, the story of an anti-hero. Lark Carrier's *There Was a Hill* features die-cut pages that reveal surprising parts of a story as the pages are turned.

Unique page shapes in children's books include Kees Moerbeek's *Six Brave Explorers*, which is cut on a diagonal producing a book in a triangular shape. Lois Ehlert's *Hands* is shaped like the gloved hands of her father who used his skills and talents in crafts.

Some board books have a die-cut page shape such as *Pooh* (Pooh Giant Shaped Board Books) that is die-cut to the outline of Pooh's body. Stephen T. Johnson's large board book called *My Little Red Toolbox* is in the rectangular shape of a toolbox and has removable cardboard cut-outs of a hammer, wrench, screwdriver, and other tools.

After young people have examined a number of books with varying page shapes, they may illustrate a book cover for a favorite folktale on a piece of paper shaped like an object in the tale.

Pageant: Originally, the movable platform upon which medieval religious plays were performed. Set upon wheels so that it could be used in processions, this medieval stage had two rooms, a lower one for costume changes and an upper one for the presentations. A pageant was usually designed and constructed for a specific play. Later, the term *pageant* designated the plays that were performed upon a movable platform. In the twentieth century, the term has been applied to an exhibition that can include costumes, tableaux, drama, songs, and dances. The modern pageant is often performed outdoors and presents local history.

An example of a Christmas pageant for children is Richard Kennedy's adaptation of Hans Christian Andersen's *The Snow Queen*. Kennedy's adaptation includes songs and notes on how to produce this holiday pageant.

Palindrome: A word, phrase, or sentence that reads the same if it is read forwards or backwards and disregards punctuation and spaces between words. Examples of words that are palindromes include kayak, civic and radar. Phrases that are palindromes include "Rise to vote, Sir," "No lemons, no melon," and "We'll let Dad tell Lew."

Marvin Terban's *Too Hot to Hoot: Funny Palindrome Riddles* is a collection of palindrome letter and number puzzles. Two additional collections of palindromes for children include John Agee's *Go Hang a Salami! I'm a Lasagna Hog!* and Agee's *So Many Dynamos! And Other Palindromes.*

Louis Sachar's 1999 Newbery Award book *Holes* features a famous palindrome of note. The book's central character is Stanley Yelnats whose name is indeed a palindrome and speaks to the circular theme of the story.

Young people may select a favorite palindrome, transcribe it to a colored piece of paper cut to represent an object in the palindrome, and post it on a palindrome bulletin board.

Paper Cuts or Paper Cutting: An artistic form of cutting paper to create designs by hand. It is also known as *scherenschnitte*, which is German for paper cutting and describes traditional craft only requiring paper and scissors. The art of paper cutting has probably been practiced in China since the invention of papermaking in A.D. 105, and it became popular in Europe in the sixteenth century. For children's books, the cut paper designs are attached to a base sheet of paper and may be raised from the surface to create depth in the illustration. Tools required include sharp scissors, razor-edged knives, and quality paper often in a variety of colors. Sometimes the cut paper designs are pricked with various sized needles to create further definition.

The 1997 Caldecott Award book, David Wisniewski's *Golem*, is made of cut papers of Color-Aid, coral, and bark. Other books illustrated by Wisniewski are also illustrated with the same technique: *Elfwyn's Saga*; *Rain Player*; *The Wave of the Sea-Wolf*; and *Sundiata, Lion King of Mali*. Other paper cutting achievements in children's books include Ed Young's Caldecott Honor book, *The Emperor and the Kite*, written by Jane Yolen, and Marguerite W. Davol's *The Paper Dragon*, illustrated by Robert Sabuda. In *The Paper Dragon* the text is printed on the right side, and the left-hand pages open up to triple page spreads of elaborately cut and painted tissue paper collage. The 2000 Pura Belpré Illustrator Award-winner was Carmen Lomas Garza for her papel picado (cut-paper art) in *Magic Windows/Ventanas Mágicas*. She also wrote *Making Magic Windows*, which provides instructions for using this art form.

Young people may be introduced to David Wisniewski paper cutting techniques through the explanation he provides on the Children's Book Council Web site (*www.cbcbooks.org/columns/archives/dwisniew.htm*). For further information, one may consult Kay Vandergrift's shadow puppet and paper cutting bibliography related to Wisniewski's art at: *www.edu/special/key/shadowpuppets.html*. Young people may wish to create their own paper cutting designs.

Parallel Story: A parallel event or situation is one that is happening at the same time as and/or is similar to another event or situation. The full-page illustrations in Jan Brett's *Trouble with Trolls* shares the aboveground story of Treva's trouble with the trolls as they try to steal her dog. At the same time the illustrations in the borders depict the story of a hedgehog visiting the troll's home underground while they are away. David Macaulay's *Black and White*, the 1991 Caldecott Award book, is comprised of four illustrated "stories" that seem to be happening at the same time. Edith Baer's *This Is the Way We Go to School* and *This Is the Way We Eat Our Lunch* share common transportation modes and the various lunch menus for children from different places around the world.

Young people may enjoy reading a parallel story by showing what is happening above ground and below ground at the same time, or they may share how a common event is different and similar among various groups of people, such as the celebration of birthdays.

Parody: An amusing imitation of a familiar piece of writing. The form of the earlier work is retained but the words are changed and the tone is designed to be humorous. In order for children to enjoy parodies, they must be aware of the content of the original work.

The hilarious illustrations of James Rice and the humorous lines in Trosclair's *Cajun Night Before Christmas* provide an enjoyable introduction to the term because most children are familiar with the rhythm and lines of Clement Clark Moore's *The Night Before Christmas or a Visit of St. Nicholas*. Sharing James Rice's *Prairie Night Before Christmas* or Dav Pilkey's *Twas the Night Before Thanksgiving* adds to the fun. After reading these parodies, young people might brainstorm other "nights" that could be a setting for similar ones. See *Fractured Folktale*.

Participation Book: Books with special features that either physically or visually engage the reader. Young children are asked to actively engage in an interaction with the book such as touching a furry surface like that of an animal's body, smelling a flower, or putting their finger in a hole to simulate a worm in an apple. They may also lift a flap, open a "door," or manipulate pieces in the book.

Dorothy Kunhardt's *Pat the Bunny* invites both physical and visual participation by looking in a mirror, playing peek-a-book by raising a cloth, and feeling a scratchy beard. Eric Hall's *Where's Spot?* has a format that motivates young readers to lift flaps and look for Spot. Lorinda Bryan Cauley's *Clap Your Hands* encourages physical participation through clapping, jumping, spinning, patting, rubbing, and stretching in a variety of ways. In Carol Jones' *Old MacDonald Has a Farm* children are asked to look through a peephole and guess which animal comes next. Janet and Allan Ahlberg's *Each Peach Pear Plum* involves exploring the pages to find familiar folktale characters that are hidden in the illustrations. Also by the Ahlbergs, *The Jolly Postman* allows readers to remove letters, cards, and other mail that is tucked inside envelope pages.

Young children will simply enjoy an adult's participation in the book; other young people could work as a group to create and present their own participation book to a younger audience.

Pastels: An artistic drawing medium in dry stick form that is used similar to a crayon. Pastels are created when colored pigments are pressed together with gum. Well known for rich and sometimes brilliant color, pastels come in a wide range of shades and densities (from soft to hard). The color stays the same as it is applied because no drying time is required like other types of painting media. Due to the powdery nature of the medium, the finished product should be sealed with a fixative or protected under glass. Another kind of pastel is water-soluble and can be used as a wash, rather than as a direct application.

Examples of illustrations created with pastels include Eleanor Coerr's *Sadako*, illustrated by Ed Young, and Joe Hayes' *A Spoon for Every Bite*, illustrated by Rebecca Leer. Pastels are often used as a part of the mixed media in a children's picture book. For example, Brian Pinkney used oil pastels on scratchboard to illustrate *Sukey and the Mermaid*; Cathi Hepworth selected pastels and colored pencil for *Antics!*; Nancy Tafuri used watercolor ink, pastel, and pen to illustrate Mira Ginsburg's *Asleep, Asleep*; and Patricia Polacco created *Thunder Cake* with Pentel markers, acrylic paint, ink, pencil, and oil pastel.

Young people will enjoy experimenting with pastels to create their own renderings of a favorite character or setting from children's literature.

Pattern Book: A book with strong repetitive language patterns created for younger children. These books usually have short sentences and few words per page. Classic examples of pattern books include: Gene Baer's *Thump, Thump, Rat-a-Tat-Tat*; Margaret Wise Brown's *Goodnight Moon*; Eric Carle's *The Very Hungry Caterpillar*; Barbara Emberley's *Drummer Hoff*; Robert Kraus' *Whose Mouse Are You?*; and Bill Martin's *Brown Bear, Brown Bear*. Mother Goose books include rhymes that feature simple patterns in language with much repetition. Among the numerous choices are Iona Opie's *Here Comes Mother Goose*; Tomie de Paola's *Mother Goose*; and Brian Wildsmith's *Mother Goose*.

Young people may identify other pattern books in their school library or public library collection, or they may use some of the books mentioned above to write their own simple pattern books.

Personification: A figure of speech created by giving human qualities (*e.g.*, emotions, motivations, actions, and personalities) to ideas, abstractions, animals, or other things. Letters of the alphabet are personified in a rhyme from *The Jessie Willcox Smith Mother Goose* (Derrydale, 1986: 40):

A was an Apple;	I inspected it.	Q quartered it;
B bit it;	J jumped for it;	R ran for it;
C cut it;	K kept it;	S stole it;
D dealt it;	L longed for it.	T took it;
E eat;	M mourned for it;	U used it.
F fought for it;	N nodded at it;	V viewed it;
G got it;	O opened it;	W wanted it;
H had it;	P peeped in it;	X, Y, Z and &,
	All wished for a piece in the hand.	

As an activity to explore this figure of speech, younger children could mime the human actions of the various letters. After reading Shel Silverstein's *Where the Sidewalk Ends* (1974), older children may find examples of personification. They may also wear big cardboard boxes and act out the poem "Two Boxes" (p. 41) in which two boxes meet, converse, decide they are brothers, and walk home hand in hand to dinner. In discussing "Two Boxes," older children will find multiple examples of personification.

Perspective: The technique of depicting spatial relationships on a flat surface, especially one that signifies distance or a different point of view; the geometric technique of linear perspective.

In Chris Van Allsburg's *The Polar Express* a reader views the train from the ground as it comes toward the North Pole. Later, at the stroke of midnight when Santa leaves on his journey, a reader views the departure from above the sleigh. Likewise, David Wisniewski's *Golem* presents an aerial view looking down on Golem as he tries to protect the ghetto from the enemies of the Jews. A reader of Alice and Martin Provensen's *The Glorious Flight: Across the Channel with Louis Bleriot, July 25, 1909*, looks upward from the ground on pages 12 and 13 to see an airship fly over the city of Cambrai. Stephen Huneck's *Sally Goes to the Beach* presents a dog's-eye view of summer. Robert Burleigh's *Home Run: The Story of*

Babe Ruth, illustrated by Mike Wimmer, presents shifting perspectives from the field to the stands and from the spectators to Babe Ruth. In each of these cases, perspective is used to create an illusion of height and size and, thus, to affect the reader's relationship to the elements of the story.

A humorous perspective is presented in Livingston and Maggie Taylor's *Pajamas*, illustrated by Tim Bowers, which features an illustration of a child looking through his legs and seeing his room upside down. April Wilson's wordless book *April Wilson's Magpie Magic* depicts a child's drawn magpie coming to life and interacting with other drawings.

To gain an understanding of perspective, young people may use disposable cameras to take photographs from different perspectives (aiming upward, downward, and at different angles) on a playground, in their classroom, or another location.

Photo Essay: Exploration of a theme or interpretation of a story through a group of often sequential photographs. Photo essays are used in both books and magazines. Examples of children's books that are photo essays include: Joan Anderson's *Cowboys: Roundup on an American Ranch*, with photographs by George Ancona; Diane Hoyt-Goldsmith's *Buffalo Days*, with photographs by Lawrence Migdale; Donna M. Jackson's *The Bone Detectives: How Forensic Anthropologists Solve Crimes and Uncover Mysteries of the Dead*, with photographs by Charlie Fellenbaum; Bruce McMillan's *Night of the Pufflings*; Dorothy Hinshaw Patent's *Feathers*, with photographs by William Muñoz; and Walter Wick's *A Drop of Water: A Book of Science and Wonder*.

Young people may decide on a topic for a photo essay for their class, possibly on their own school. After writing a story about their school and creating a storyboard to outline the photographs, young people may use digital or disposable cameras. After the photographs have been produced, they may lay them out according to the storyboard and begin the process of creating their own photo essay book. Their photo essay may be added to the school's Web site.

Photography: The reproduction of permanent images of objects or individuals on a light-sensitive surface by the action of radiant energy, especially light. It was first developed by Louis Daguerre in 1839, and the picture was known as a daguerreotype. Barbara Morrow's *Edward's Portrait* presents the story of a family that has individual portraits made in the early days of the daguerreotype.

A selection of children's books with color photograph illustrations includes: Bruce McMillan's *Growing Colors*; Tana Hoban's *Look! Look! Look!*; Nikki Grimes'

It's Raining Laughter, with photographs by Myles Pinkney; Walter Wick's *A Drop of Water*; Joy Cowley's *Red-Eyed Tree Frog*, with photographs by Nic Bishop; George Ancona's *Carnaval*; *LIFE: Our Century in Pictures for Young People*, edited by Richard B. Stolley, which presents the last century through 380 photographs; and Sandra L. Pinkney's *Shades of Black: A Celebration of Our Children*, with photographs by Myles Pinkney.

Some children's books include photographs that have been artistically altered. Patricia Lillie's *When This Box Is Full*, with photographs by Donald Crews, includes black and white photographs that were reproduced from line conversions screened with a "Lasergrain" pattern with color added by hand-placing film overlays. Peggy Christian's *If You Find a Rock*, with photographs by Barbara Hirsch Lember, is composed of hand-tinted black and white photographs. Donald Crews' *Carousel* includes three paintings of the carousel, each prepared as full-color collages. The carousel with children was then photographed, and the camera was moved to simulate motion. For the sound pages, three pieces of full-color art were prepared and similarly photographed. Nina Crews' *You Are Here* incorporates full-color photo collages that were created digitally using Adobe Photoshop.

Some picture book photographers include detailed information about how the photographs were taken. For example, in *Jelly Beans for Sale*, Bruce McMillan makes the following statement, "I used a Nikon F / MF23 with a 105 mm micro lens, sometimes with a polarizing or light blue filter. I shot with full sunlight in the late afternoon and early evening, and used Kodachrome 64 film, which was processed by Kodak. The coins were photographed on the part of the stand I made of red cedar" (1996).

Young people may learn more about photography in Dave King's *My First Photography Book*.

Photorealistic Art: Artwork, in the form of paintings or sculpture, which is characterized by meticulous attention and precise reproduction of detail; superrealism. Photographs or slides are often used as an aid for technical proficiency, and the finished product is often likened to them. Photorealism was essentially an American movement that began in the United States, but the style was also popular in Europe during the mid-1960s and 1970s. A pioneer American photorealistic painter is Chuck Close. His life, career, and art are presented in *Chuck Close, Up Close* by Jan Greenberg and Sandra Jordan. Stephen Johnson used pastels, watercolors, gouache, and charcoal on hot pressed watercolor paper in his 1996 Caldecott Honor book, *Alphabet City*, to create a collection of realistic paintings. Young people may try their own hand at photorealistic art by using photographs of street scenes or individuals as aids in their creation of artwork.

Picture Book: Often used as the broader term to encompass children's literature in which pictures and words are integrated into a book form that typically has 32 pages. Charlotte Huck, et al. in *Children's Literature in the Elementary School*, seventh edition, states that a picture book "is not made up of single illustrated pictures but conveys its message through a series of images. The impact of the total format of the book is what creates the art object known as the picture book" (Huck, et al., 2001: 188). Barbara Z. Kiefer in *The Potential of Picture Books: From Visual Literacy to Aesthetic Understanding* defines the picture book as a "unique form of art" and further defines the picture storybook as one in which "pictures and words tell a story" (Kiefer, 1995: 6). Together the author's words and the illustrator's pictures share importance in the book's effectiveness.

John W. Stewig in *Looking at Picture Books* explains the term defines a book in which "different objects or ideas appear on each page, linked by the artist's style, but not necessarily by a sequential story line" (Stewig, 1995: 3). This definition of a picture book could include many alphabet books, counting books, concept books, and wordless books—those where the message of the book is carried primarily through the illustrations. Excellent picture book examples using this criteria would include Stephen Johnson's *Alphabet City*; Lois Ehlert's *Color Zoo*; Bruce McMillan's *Growing Colors*.

The Randolph Caldecott Medal is administered by the Association for Library Service to Children of the American Library Association. It is awarded to the "artist of the most distinguished American picture book for children published in the United States during the preceding year" (American Library Association, 2001). Additional information about terms, criteria, history, and award-winning titles can be found at the Caldecott Medal Home Page (*www.ala.org/alsc/caldecott.html*) and in the annual edition of *The Newbery and Caldecott Awards: A Guide to the Medal and Honor Books*.

Examples of finely crafted picture storybooks where pictures and words tell a story are numerous on the Caldecott Medal list and include Peggy Rathmann's *Officer Buckle and Gloria*; Allen Say's *Grandfather's Journey*; and Emily Arnold McCully's *Mirette and the High Wire*.

Young people may look at other children's picture books and picture storybooks on the Caldecott Award and Honor lists. They may also be interested in holding their own mock Caldecott election in the fall of the year by following the Kathleen Staerkel's *Newbery and Caldecott Mock Election Kit: Choosing Champions in Children's Books*. The reading level of picture books often exceeds that of easy readers; and, therefore, most picture books are designed to be read aloud by adults to young people who are learning to read.

Plot: The arrangement of a story's events to achieve an artistic effect. Plot is the literary element that forces an artistic order on incidents that in real life are often chaotic. Because plots vary in their structure and their effects, few generalizations hold true for all narratives. However, most readers and play-goers since the time of Aristotle expect a plot to have a beginning, a middle, and an end; and a beginning and an ending that illuminate each other are considered to be plot strengths that add meaning to the entire narrative. Another expectation for plot is that it involves character(s) in conflict; and, therefore, plot and character are inextricably linked in cause and effect, requiring compatibility (unity) of character and action. However, young people will typically be more interested in plot than characters.

Readers also expect plots to have order, and younger readers are most comfortable with a chronological plot. Two basic plot patterns are episodic or progressive. Episodic plots move from one incident to another, never building to a major turning point (crisis or climax). Examples of episodic plots may be found in early chapter books like Beverly Cleary's *Ramona the Pest*, in which chapter by chapter, Ramona wants the proper boots, questions how Mike Mulligan found a bathroom, and refuses to go to kindergarten. A more sophisticated episodic novel for an older audience is Richard Peck's *A Long Way from Chicago: A Novel in Stories*. Progressive plots move from a beginning through complications and conflict to a climax or crisis and then to resolution. The progressive plot is not always linear, it may rely on flashbacks to explain past events, as, for example in Ruth White's *Belle Prater's Boy*. In addition to the basic episodic and progressive plots there is also a freer plot structure: the nonlinear or radial plot, which allows the story to unfold with multiple and shifting points of view and formats, including reader participation.

Regardless of the structure, the plot ending or resolution will be more satisfying if the author has used foreshadowing to make it seem inevitable rather than coincidental. Also, most young people more easily accept a closed ending (where the outcome is known) rather than an open ending (where some questions remain). Narrative hooks, conflict, complications, inciting incidents, and the crisis create suspense that motivates readers to continue the story; and after the crisis, the suspense of the final resolution motivates readers to finish the story. See *Cliff-Hanger, Climax, Closed Ending, Coincidence, Complication, Conflict, Denouement, Episodic Plot, Exposition, Falling Action, Flashback, Foreshadowing, Nonlinear Text, Open Ending, Progressive Plot, Resolution,* and *Rising Action.*

Young people's first experiences with plot may be to summarize the sequence of events, to discuss the nature of the conflict, and to consider whether the work's ending is satisfying. If the ending is not satisfying, young people can suggest alternative endings.

Poetic Justice: The literary concept that the good are rewarded and the bad are punished. Thomas Rhymer first used the term in *Tragedies of the Last Age* to set forth the idea that individuals should be encouraged toward good behavior. The idea was so accepted in the seventeenth and eighteenth centuries that theater directors used rewritten versions of Shakespearean tragedies so that the endings would seem happier and more just. Young people typically hold expectations for fairness and justice, and their expectations are fulfilled in stories and novels like Beatrix Potter's *Peter Rabbit*, which presents Peter's disobedience, endangerment, and ultimate reconciliation; Richard Peck's *A Long Way from Chicago*, which emphasizes Grandma's brand of law and order; and Jacob and Wilhelm Grimm's *Hansel and Gretel*, retold and illustrated by Paul Galdone, which ends with the witch's destruction. However, just and happy endings do not always reflect life, and today's realistic literature allows for the honest portrayal of tragedy in stories like William Armstrong's *Sounder* and Katherine Paterson's *Bridge to Terabithia*. Older children could compare the ending of *Bridge to Terabithia* to what might happen in real life. As a discussion activity, young people could be encouraged to predict the endings in genres where poetic justice is still expected (*e.g.*, in folktales, fables, and mysteries).

Poetry: Literature in its most compact and imaginative form, using imagery, sound, and rhythm to create an emotional and intellectual experience. Poetry has significance, and, therefore, it is more than verse. And, poetry has a form and a concentrated capacity for expression that sets it apart from prose. In *Rainbows Are Made*, Carl Sandburg offers imaginative and nontraditional definitions of poetry that emphasize its capacity to achieve an emotional impact beyond literal words. Among those definitions are "Poetry is a series of explanations of life, fading off into horizons too swift for explanations" (1984: 2); "Poetry is a phantom script telling how rainbows are made and why they go away" (1984: 46); and "Poetry is the sequence of dots and dashes, spelling depths, crypts, cross-lights, and moon wisps" (1984: 68).

A philosophy that should guide sharing poetry with young people is that the purpose of poetry is pleasure. Children from the youngest to the oldest should experience poetry read aloud, and they should be provided opportunities to participate by responding to rhythm, joining in refrains, presenting choral readings, and dramatizing poems. Young people can develop an understanding of the dimensions of poetry by browsing poetry collections in libraries and by examining poetry anthologies. An anthology that can engage upper elementary students in deeper understandings is *Inner Chimes*, edited by Bobbye Goldstein. Young people should also be encouraged to compile a myriad of poets' definitions of poetry. And, most importantly they should be freed from expectations that a poem has a single meaning. Eve Merriam's poem "'I,' Says the Poem" in *It Doesn't Always Have to Rhyme* (1966: 46) concludes by emphasizing the creative partnership between poem and reader. The poem declares that it is a cloud, a tree, a city, the sea, and a mystery that waits for the reader to come to it.

Point of View: A term used to identify the author's choice about who will tell the story and how much the narrator will know about the thoughts of others. When the story is told from a first person point of view, the narrator uses "I" and records his/her own thoughts and actions but cannot retell the thoughts of others unless those characters reveal themselves in conversation. An excellent example of how first person point of view can control the conflict in a novel is Wheeze's first personal account of sibling jealousy in Katherine Paterson's *Jacob Have I Loved*.

In the omniscient point of view, the author tells the story in third person and is not limited in reporting details of the thoughts, actions, and conversations of all characters. An example of omniscient point of view is Jane Langton's *The Fledgling*, a fantasy made more accessible because the author can explain the motivations of all the characters. In the limited omniscient point of view, the author tells the story in third person and is limited to reporting the thoughts and feelings of only one or a few characters. The thoughts of the remaining characters become part of the story only if they are presented through conversation. Laura Ingalls Wilder used limited omniscient point of view in *Little House on the Prairie*, enabling young Laura to interpret the world with childlike simplicity.

In the objective point of view, the author does not reveal the thoughts of the characters. Instead, the reader's interpretation results from the straightforward presentation of action and conversation. Demands on the reader's imagination and comprehension skills make this point of view less used in children's books. An example of objective point of view is Avi's *Nothing But the Truth* in which memos, news clippings, dialogues, and diary excerpts can be misinterpreted by well-meaning individuals who do not have access to any character's thoughts or motivations.

As an activity emphasizing point of view, upper grade children can be encouraged to read the first person diary account of Leigh Botts in Beverly Cleary's *Dear*

Mr. Henshaw. After reading Leigh's last diary entry, the young people may write a paragraph in first person as either Mom or Dad might recount the scene or in third person with the author interpreting the scene through a limited omniscient point of view in which the thoughts of Leigh and his mom and dad are revealed. Young people may also consider Roberto Innocenti's *Rose Blanche* in which the point of view shifts from first person to third person in the middle of the book.

Pointillism: A neo-impressionist art technique in which light effects are produced by crowding small spots of various colors on a white ground. The eye of the viewer blends colors and shapes to discern meaning. Georges Seurat (French, 1859–1891) is best known for using the technique, and young people may view his most famous painting, *La Grande Jatte* on the Web (*www.artic.edu/aic/kids/dots.html*). Young people may also find examples of pointillism in children's book illustrations in Sally Grindley's *A Flag for Grandma*; Karen E. Lotz's *Can't Sit Still*; and Gyo Fujikawa's *A to Z Picture Book*.

Potato Printing: A simple printing technique in which raw potatoes are cut in half and carved to function as a printing block. A pencil can be used to mark a pattern in the potato, and the pattern can be cut on the potato raised or recessed. The potato is then dipped into a saucer of thick paint and the design is printed onto a paper or other surface.

Two children's books that feature potato printing are Diana Pomeroy's *One Potato: A Counting Book of Potato Prints*, which illustrates fruits and vegetables created by potato prints and features the numbers one to one hundred, and Pomeroy's *Wildflower ABC: An Alphabet of Potato Prints*, which has illustrations of wildflowers from Aster to Zigadenus fremontii as botanical portraits created with potato prints.

Directions for creating potato prints are included in *One Potato* along with suggestions for printing greeting cards and gift-wrapping paper. Younger children may enjoy this activity but will need to have the potatoes cut for them. Small cookie cutters can also be used to imprint a design in the potato that can be cut away to provide a raised surface for printing.

Pourquoi: French word meaning *why*. In children's literature *pourquoi* or *why* stories are often from the oral tradition and explain natural phenomena. Many traditional pourquoi tales are retold in individual picture books, such as Tomie de Paola's *The Legend of the Bluebonnet*, which explains why there are bluebonnet flowers, and Verna Aardema's Caldecott Award book, *Why Do Mosquitoes Buzz in People's Ears*, illustrated by Leo and Diane Dillon. There are also collections, such as Virginia Hamilton's *In the Beginning: Creation Stories From Around the World*, which explains creation from a multicultural perspective.

Pourquoi stories are a significant element of traditional Native American stories, including Joseph Bruchac and Gayle Ross' *The Story of the Milky Way*, which explains the nature of the universe; Paul Goble's *The Gift of the Sacred Dog*, which explains how Plains Indians received sacred dogs (horses), and *Her Seven Brothers*, which explains the origin of the Big Dipper; and John Steptoe's Caldecott Honor book, *The Story of Jumping Mouse*. A professional resource for pourquoi tales is Anne Marie Kraus' *Folktale Themes and Activities for Children: Pourquoi Tales*.

After being introduced to pourquoi tales, young people may work in pairs to find an imaginative explanation for a phenomenon in nature (*e.g.* why oceans have waves, or why puppies cry at night). They may enjoy telling or illustrating their stories. Or, they may read a pourquoi tale and brainstorm other imaginative explanations for the natural occurrence.

Predictable Book: Books helpful to beginning and emergent readers that possess particular language devices such as repetitive phrases, rhyming words, refrains, language patterns, or an organized theme (such as the days of the week). Predictability helps young readers to guess what is coming next as they develop their reading strategies and their understanding of basic story structure. Some examples of predictable books include:

- language patterns and repetition, Eric Hill's *Where's Spot?* and Bill Martin's *Brown Bear, Brown Bear*
- familiar themes, Eric Carle's *Today Is Monday* and Cindy Ward's *Cookie's Week*
- repetitive story patterns, Paul Galdone's *The Three Bears* and Ruth Krauss' *The Carrot Seed*
- predictable plots, John Burningham's *Mr. Gumpy's Outing* and Pat Hutchins' *Rosie's Walk*

Other types of predictable books include: question and answer; chair or circular stories; cumulative stories; and songbooks. Books often have more than one predictability device.

Young people may enjoy creating their own "predictable" book that has a particular rhyme pattern or organized theme. They may also examine picture books in the school library media center or public library and identify books that fit into the different categories of types of predictable books.

Prequel: A literary work that takes place or is concerned with a time period prior to an existing published work. Prequels sometimes are created because readers have questions about what might have happened to characters in a previous time or place.

Theodore Taylor wrote *The Cay* twenty-four years before he wrote *Timothy of the Cay*. *The Cay* takes place when twelve-year-old Phillip is rescued by a Black man during World War II, and they are stranded on a Caribbean island. It is a classic novel of survival and racial prejudice. In the prequel, *Timothy of the Cay*, the reader learns more about Phillip's previous life as a cabin boy and also learns about his life since the event. Walter and Steven Farley's *The Young Black Stallion* is a prequel to the first book in the *Black Stallion Series*. The book traces the early life of the black stallion in the mountains of Arabia before he was captured and brought to the West. Young people may select a favorite fiction title and write a "prequel" chapter to the book.

Problem Novel: A contemporary realistic novel that focuses on problem(s) that affect the main character. Problem novels for preteen readers often address such issues as physical disabilities, developmental disabilities, mental illness, aging, and death. A young adult problem novel often presents a young person coping with such challenges as drug abuse, psychological disorders, abandonment, or physical or sexual abuse. The realistic problem novel is typically first associated with modern young adult literature because in the late 1960s young adult literature was defined by the novels *The Outsiders*, by S. E. Hinton, and *The Pigman*, by Paul Zindel. Because young people currently have wide access to talk shows and tabloids that exploit personal problems daily, the problem novel does not meet the 1960s need to assure readers they are not alone and to suggest consequences and solutions. Thus, a genre in which social problems were a primary focus does not hold the center stage it once did.

Many problem novels during the 1970s emphasized social issues to the neglect of character development. In explaining the writing of *Dear Mr. Henshaw*, Beverly Cleary made the point that she wrote about a boy with a problem, not a problem with a boy. Other realistic novels with well developed characters who confront contemporary problems include two by Kimberly Willis Holt: *When Zachary Beaver Came to Town* is a National Book Award-winning account about three boys, one coping with obesity, another with abandonment, and the third with the loss of a brother; *My Louisiana Sky* is a story about smart Tiger Ann Parker who is ostracized because of her childlike mother and learning-disabled father.

Contemporary realistic fiction is the most popular genre with many young people, and booktalks that address diverse contemporary problems can increase their awareness of books they might choose to read. However, linking a specific problem in a book to a specific reader who might have the problem assumes that the reader probably does have the problem, wants to read about it, and will respond to the book in a predictable and positive way—all assumptions that do not respect the reader and can produce negative results. Young people reading contemporary realistic fiction today may encounter social problems and discuss whether the author handled them realistically. Furthermore, they can also explore the development of the main character and consider the question posed by Beverly Cleary: Was the central focus a problem that possessed a character or a character who dealt believably with conflict and challenge?

Progressive Plot: A plot in which complications and conflict create increasing tension to the point of a crisis that is followed by a resolution. Gustav Freytag (Germany, 1816–1895) in *Technique in Drama* drew upon Aristotle's description of dramatic action to create what is known as *Freytag's Pyramid*:

CRISIS /
CLIMAX

RISING ACTION   FALLING ACTION

complications   denouement/
inciting incident   unraveling/
exposition   resolution
BEGINNING   **END**

Youngest readers can plot simple stories, such as the folktale "The Gingerbread Man," and older readers can plot novels, such as Christopher Paul Curtis' *Bud, Not Buddy.*

Prose: Speech or writing that may have rhythm but does not have a rhythmic pattern. Prose naturally develops more slowly in languages than does poetry. And, in the English culture, prose was especially slow to develop because Latin, not

English, was the official written language, and the influence of Latin structures on English remains evident today.

Generally, speech or writing that is not poetry is prose. Illustrating that point is one of the humorous lines in Moliere's *The Bourgeois Gentleman*: Monsieur Jourdain remarks that he has been speaking prose all his life and did not even know it. The truth in his discovery is one way to introduce the concept of prose to young people. Another way to introduce the concept is to sketch a continuum illustrating the range between prose and poetry, as indicated in the following table:

PROSE	⇔	⇔	⇔	POETRY
ordinary spoken language	written language	poetic prose (King James Bible)	free verse w/ rhythm and line breaks	poetry

For examples of prose in the library, young people may find excerpts of fictional dialogue that is like ordinary spoken language, and they may find short stories, novels, and articles that illustrate prose as written language. Typically, prose is characterized by a logical order and the presentation of ideas and concepts.

Protagonist: The principal character in a literary work. The term originated in ancient Greek drama when the *pro (first)* actor led the chorus in the *agon (contest)* and, thus, opposed the antagonist. Young people can understand that every story has a main character, that the reader usually knows more about the main character (*i.e.*, that the main character is more developed than other characters), and that the main character is at the center of a work's conflict. They may engage in a discussion of main characters by playing a game (in groups) to see how many protagonists they can identify in stories and novels. See *Antagonist.*

Proverb: A succinct, popular saying that expresses a general truth. Proverbs originated in the oral tradition, but their written forms are also very old, having been found in writings from ancient Egypt and Sumer. Closely related to fables and riddles, proverbs exist in every spoken language, and a proverb may have many variants.

Benjamin Franklin's annual almanac, *Poor Richard's*, is the best-known collection of American proverbs. An examination of his proverbs will allow children to recognize many of them and to explore the various styles that typically make proverbs memorable and enjoyable. For example, "Fools make feasts and wise men eat them," uses opposites (antithesis); "Forewarned is forearmed," is a play on words; "He that goes a-borrowing goes a-sorrowing," is an example of the use of rhyme; "Early to bed and early to rise, makes a man healthy, wealthy and wise," demonstrates the use of alliteration; and the use of parallel structure may be considered in, "Waste not, want not." All of the above examples can be found in Robert Lawson's *Ben and Me*, a fantasy told by Amos, a mouse who lives in Benjamin Franklin's fur hat. Children reading this work will develop an understanding of the proverb's relationship to everyday life as Amos explains his version of the origins of Ben's maxims.

A Word to the Wise and Other Proverbs, selected by Johanna Hurwitz, presents a list of common proverbs as well as an explanation of their meanings and origins. In an afterward Hurwitz notes that proverbs often contradict one another (*e.g.*, "Look before you leap." "He who hesitates is lost."). Young people may be challenged to look for other pairs of proverbs that contradict each other.

Pseudonym: A fictitious name that, when used by a writer, is also known as a pen name or nom de plume. Perhaps the most famous pseudonym in children's literature is Dr. Seuss. For an activity, young people may look up Dr. Seuss in a resource such as the series *Something About the Author* where they will be directed to Theodore Geisel. Volume 67 of *Something About the Author* also reveals two other pen names for Theodore Geisel: Theo LeSieg (Geisel spelled backwards) and the joint pseudonym Rosetta Stone. Young people will enjoy the play on the word *pseudonym* in Sue Denim's *Dumb Bunnies*, illustrated by Dav Pilkey. And, young people who understand the concept of anonymous will appreciate the play on words in Jack Prelutsky's *The Poems of A. Nonny Mouse*, illustrated by Henrik Drescher, and *A. Nonny Mouse Writes Again!*, illustrated by Marjorie Priceman.

Psychological Criticism: An approach to interpreting literature that applies the principles of psychology to analyses of the author's intentions (See *Biographical Criticism*), the responses of readers (See *Reader-Response Criticism*), the meaning of symbols (See *Symbol*), and the authentic portrayal of characters and their motivations. The technique primarily originated from the writings of Sigmund Freud, who in 1896 was the first to use the term *psychoanalysis*. A strength of psychological criticism is its capacity to illuminate the emotions of characters. For example, readers could determine if there are similarities between their lives and those of a character such as Palmer in Jerry Spinelli's *Wringer*, which portrays the effects of peer pressure. Or, they could explore other psychological perspectives, including that of finding the strength to face the truth in Ruth White's

Belle Prater's Boy, of friendships as in Elaine Konigsburg's *The View from Saturday*, or of the challenges faced in school as in Beverly Cleary's *Dear Mr. Henshaw*.

Pulp Painting: Creating paintings with colored paper pulp. Well known for her work in this medium is Denise Fleming who builds boldly colored illustrations one layer at a time by pouring colored pulp through hand-cut stencils onto wire mesh supports. After drying in a press for three days, the paper is the painting. Among her books illustrated with pulp paintings are *The Everything Book*, *Lunch*, and the Caldecott Honor book *In the Small, Small Pond*. To make their own pulp paintings, young people may use Denise Fleming's kit, *Painting with Paper: Easy Papermaking Fun for the Entire Family* or consult Denise Fleming's Web instructions (*www.bcplonline.org/kidspage/kids_flem_papermaking.html*).

Pun: A usually humorous play on two or more words that share similar sounds but which have different meanings. In the past, the pun in literature has been criticized, and many people find the pun irritating. However, it is a form found in plays by Shakespeare as well as in the works of contemporary children's authors.

A Rocket in My Pocket (compiled by Carl Withers) includes examples of puns from folklore. First lines of some of those verses are:

> I bought a wooden whistle,
> And it "wouldn'" whistle (1988: 192).
> and,
> Do you carrot all for me?
> My heart beets for you... (1988: 193).

Children may be introduced to the term and encouraged to brainstorm pairs of words that have similar sounds. Children may then use the words to create their own poetic puns.

Pura Belpré Award: A children's book award presented in honor of Pura Belpré, the first Latina librarian from the New York Pubic Library who enriched the lives of children through her sharing of Puerto Rican folklore. It was established in 1996 and co-sponsored by the Association for Library Service to Children (ALSC), a division of the American Library Association (ALA) and the National Association to Promote Library Services to the Spanish Speaking (REFORMA), an American Library Association affiliate. The award is presented to a Latino/Latina author and artist whose work best celebrates and affirms the Latino cultural experience in an outstanding work of literature for children and youth. Young people may learn more about the award at *www.ala.org/alsc/belpre.html*.

Radical Change: Defined by Eliza Dresang in *Radical Change: Books for Youth in a Digital Age* (Dresang, 1999: 4–5) as "fundamental change, departing from the usual or traditional in literature for youth, although still related to it," as it is applied to the creation of contemporary literature for children and young adults in today's digital society. Three broad types of change are defined in Dresang's work:

- changing forms and formats as in the nonlinear organization of Anthony Brown's *Voices in the Park* and new forms like the graphic presentations in Virginia Walter's *Making Up Megaboy*
- changing perspectives, including the multiple perspectives in Paul Fleischman's *Bull Run* and Virginia Euwer Wolff's *Bat 6*
- changing boundaries about subjects and issues, such as Russell Freedman's book about child labor, *Kids at Work*, or Walter Wick's management of science information in *A Drop of Water*

Young people may enjoy perusing many of the books that are included in Dresang's bibliographies.

Randolph Caldecott Medal: A children's book award named in honor of the English illustrator Randolph Caldecott (1846–1886). The Association for Library Service to Children, a division of the American Library Association, has presented the award annually since 1938 to the artist of the most distinguished picture book written by a citizen of the United States and published in the United States during the preceding calendar year. Young people may find more information about the award, including a list of past award-winning books, at *www.ala.org/alsc/ caldecott.html.*

Reader Response Theory: A theory, set forth by Louise Rosenblatt in *Literature as Exploration*, that a story, which captures a reader's imagination, functions as a blueprint from which the reader constructs his or her own story. Richard Beach in *A Teacher's Introduction to Reader-Response Theories* identified five factors that make any reader's interpretations different from those of other readers: the reader's personal experiences, developmental level, response to the interpretations of other readers, cultural values, and understanding of literary elements and conventions.

Young people may extend their responses to literature, through follow-up activities such as (1) dramatic play, using, for example, Michael Rosen's *We're Going on a Bear Hunt*, (2) book discussion, perhaps after sharing a wordless book such as Tomie de Paola's *Pancakes for Breakfast*, (3) art projects that reinterpret illustrations—for example, after sharing Eric Carle's *The Very Hungry Caterpillar*, (4) readers theatre, using scenes such as the one about lemon pudding in Ann Cameron's *The Stories Julian Tells*. As they respond to stories they will continue to "read" (*i.e.*, interpret) the stories; and, when given the opportunity to interact with other readers, they develop the understanding that a text may be interpreted in many different ways.

Readers Theatre: A method of sharing literature in which, according to Leslie Coger and Melvin White (*Readers Theatre Handbook*), multiple readers use their voices, gestures, and facial expressions to cause an audience to see and hear characters in such a way that the literature becomes a living experience. The participants remain seated, read a script, and utilize voice rather than acting to present the work. It is also referred to as story theatre, interpreters theatre, or play reading.

In children's literature, short stories, poetry, plays, and scenes from fiction or biography can be adapted for readers theatre. If scenes from stories are used, a narrator usually presents the background needed for the audience to understand the scene. The narrator also summarizes needed descriptive passages as the reading progresses and identifies passage of time or any change of scene involved.

Sources for scripts must be selected carefully. The script must compel audience involvement through uniqueness of characterization and through dialogue that shows evidence of emotional conflict. If a scene from a book is selected, it should be a complete episode so the audience has a meaningful experience even though the entire book is never read. Readers theatre scripts that meet the above criteria and that are adapted from well-known children's works may be found in Laughlin and Latrobe's *Readers Theatre for Children*. In this work, suggestions are also given to prepare children for adapting their own readers theatre scripts from dialogue in the books they read.

Reading Aloud: One individual's reading to one other individual or to a group. It is a common and sometimes entertaining way to share literature with others. Reading aloud offers a variety of positive impacts for the listener including: development of a sense of story; an oral introduction to the variety of forms and styles of language; and motivation for independent reading. Listeners are also introduced to stories they might not have read on their own, and they are presented with a model of a good reader. In addition, younger children learn book manipulation concepts such as page turning, relationship of pictures to words in a story, and reading left to right.

Suggestions for reading aloud include: being familiar with the book before reading it aloud; discussing the book with listeners prior to reading; reading slowly and clearly with voice projection; and looking from the book to the audience frequently.

Margaret Mary Kimmel and Elizabeth Segel's *For Reading Out Loud!* report that reading aloud from literature meaningful to children is widely acknowledged to be the most effective way to foster a lifelong love of books and reading. Jim Trelease, author of *The Read-Aloud Handbook*, fourth edition, has noted that "reading is not inborn, it is fostered."

Selected titles to read aloud are:

- Primary:
  Tomie de Paola's *26 Fairmount Avenue*
  Patricia McKissack's *Flossie and the Fox*
  Laura Joffe Numeroff's *If You Give a Mouse a Cookie*
  Cynthia Rylant's *The Relatives Came*
  Bernard Waber's *Ira Sleeps Over*
- Intermediate:
  Christopher Paul Curtis' *Bud, Not Buddy*
  Roald Dahl's *James and the Giant Peach*
  Louis Sachar's *Sideways Stories from Wayside School*
  E. B. White's *Charlotte's Web*
- Advanced:
  Avi's *The True Confessions of Charlotte Doyle*
  Karen Hesse's *Out of the Dust*

- All ages:
  Shel Silverstein's *Where the Sidewalk Ends*

Professional resources that identify numerous books to read aloud to children are Judy Freeman's *More Books Kids Will Sit Still For: A Read Aloud Guide;* Jim Trelease's *The New Read-Aloud Handbook,* fourth edition; and *Trelease on Reading* at *www.trelease-on-reading.com.* Trelease has also edited two collections of stories to read aloud: *Hey, Listen to This! Stories to Read Aloud* and *Read All about It: Great Read-Aloud Stories, Poems and Newspaper Articles for Preteens and Teens.*

Realistic Art: An artistic style that depicts people, places, and things as they are seen in the real life; representational art. In children's picture books, realism allows children to connect visually with illustrations that represent the world as the eye sees it. Children's book illustrators known for this artistic style include Barry Moser, James Ransome, Allen Say, and Mike Wimmer. Excellent examples of realistic art in children's picture books include: Mary Hoffman's *Amazing Grace,* illustrated by Caroline Binch; Allen Say's *Grandfather's Journey;* Margaree King Mitchell's *Uncle Jed's Barbershop,* illustrated by James Ransome; Isabelle Harper's *My Dog Rosie,* illustrated by Barry Moser; Patricia MacLachlan's *All the Places to Love,* illustrated by Mike Wimmer; and Marsha Wilson Chall's *Sugarbush Spring,* illustrated by Jim Daly.

Some representational art is interpreted with the aid of photographs for accuracy and detail. Young people may enjoy creating their own artwork using photographs for assistance. They may also listen to the children's picture storybooks listed above while examining the illustrations. And, they may look for other examples of realism in their own school library media center or public library collection.

Realistic Fiction: Stories and novels that mimic the real world. Realistic fiction includes both historical fiction and contemporary realistic fiction. The term may challenge young readers who can differentiate nonfiction from fiction but be confused by the fact that all fiction is imaginative. They can be encouraged to distinguish realistic fiction from fantasy and science fiction by considering the question: could a novel like Jerry Spinelli's *Maniac McGee* (contemporary realistic fiction) or a picture book like Eve Bunting's *Train to Somewhere* (historical fiction) have happened in the real world?

Rebus: A representation of words, phrases, or syllables through the use of pictures or symbols. Examples of rebus books include Jean Marzollo's *I Love You: A Rebus Poem*; Alyssa Capucilli's *Inside a Barn in the Country: A Rebus Read Along Story*; Shirley Neitzel's *The Jacket I Wear in the Snow*, illustrated by Nancy Winslow Parker; and Shirley Neitzel's Greenwillow publications, illustrated by Nancy Winslow Parker, *The Bag I'm Taking to Grandma, The Jacket I Wear to the Party* (1992), and *We're Making Breakfast for Mother*. These like most rebus books are for young children who enjoy sharing them with an adult who reads along with them. However, older readers, with an interest in adapting a rhyme or fable into a rebus to share with younger children, can enjoy them, too.

Refrain: A word, line, or group of lines that repeat periodically in a poem, folktale, or other literature. This term is most often associated with poetry. The refrain may stay the same throughout a work, or it may vary slightly. In music a refrain is called the chorus and often involves a group of repeated lines. Young children naturally participate in repeating the lines in a poem. Jane Yolen's *Ballad of the Pirate Queen* offers readers an opportunity to hear examples of a refrain. The refrain is identified in many works by its format, which may use indention, as well as a different typeface.

Regional Literature: A body of literature or a type of literature that is closely related to a particular area or region. Usually realistic, this literature tends to focus on rural areas that are descriptively presented. A body of regional literature may be created by one individual or a group of writers. A related term is *regionalism*, the representation of the speech forms and customs of a particular geographical area. A defining characteristic of regional literature is an emphasis on characterizations and setting.

Regional stories about children of minority groups began to appear with more frequency in the 1940s. The 1946 Newbery Medal was awarded to Lois Lenski's *Strawberry Girl;* the story of Birdie growing up in Florida is told with a strong Southern accent. Arkansas is the setting for another Southern story by Lenski: *Cotton in My Sack*. Set in the Central Valley in California, Doris Gates' *Blue Willow* revolves around a young girl, Janey, and her family who depend on seasonal farm work for a living.

Beginning in the 1980s, Cynthia Rylant created a number of children's books set in her own native Appalachia. These regional stories include two which were named Caldecott Honor books for the illustrators: *When I Was Young in the Mountains*, illustrated by Diane Goode, and *The Relatives Came,* illustrated by Stephen

Gammell. Rylant received the 1993 Newbery Award for *Missing May*, which was also set in the Southern mountains. And, Virginia Hamilton's *Appalachia: The Voices of Sleeping Birds*, illustrated by Barry Moser, was named the Boston Globe–Horn Book Award for Non-fiction in 1991.

Young people may participate in a regional study, such as one on Appalachia, which includes a study of the literature, customs, food, and music. They could identify additional stories set in the Appalachian region and plot their locations on a map of the area. For background information, young people could consult Raymond Bial's *Mist Over the Mountains: Appalachia and Its People*. They may also try recipes selected from Joseph Earl Dabney's *Smokehouse Ham, Spoon Bread & Scuppernog Wine: The Folklore and Art of Southern Appalachian Cooking*; listen to recordings of dulcimer music, or share selections about Appalachian history of life, customs, and traditions from the *Foxfire* eleven-volume series, created by Eliot Wigginton and his students from the Appalachian Mountains of Northwest Georgia. After becoming thoroughly familiar with this social study, they may decide whether characters in their selected books could be placed in another setting and still maintain the same character traits they had in their original Appalachian environment.

Resolution: See *Denouement* and *Progressive Plot*.

Retelling: An adaptation. In children's literature, respected adaptations or retellings are often stories from the oral tradition or from a literary tale that is recreated in a picture book or picture storybook format. Ideally, the retelling will be more easily understood by contemporary children; however, the retelling should not diminish the meaning and beauty of the original story.

Successfully retelling a literary tale was Jerry Pinkney who won a 2000 Caldecott Honor for illustrating his adaptation of Hans Christian Andersen's *The Ugly Duckling*. Among the retellings of folklore that have been recognized by a Caldecott Committee are Simms Taback's *There Was an Old Lady Who Swallowed a Fly*; Janet Stevens' *Tops & Bottoms*; Julius Lester's *John Henry*, illustrated by Jerry Pinkney; Ed Young's *Seven Blind Mice* and *Lon Po Po*; and Fred Marcellino's *Puss in Boots*.

Young people may explore the nature of retellings by comparing multiple versions of the same tale. They may compare and contrast such issues as word choice, plot, refrains, and settings (especially in illustrated versions). Older children who include in their comparisons the earliest versions (*e.g.*, the collected tales by the Grimms or Perrault) will find the widest diversity of versions.

Rhyme: A similar sound between words at the end of two or more lines at the end of a sentence or the end of a line of verse. When there is repetition of initial consonant sounds in two or more nearby words in a line, it is known as initial rhyme.

Maurice Sendak illustrated a collection of 170 schoolyard rhymes originally published in 1947, *I Saw Esau: The School Child's Pocket Book*, edited by Iona and Peter Opie. Several hundred examples of a rhyming text in picture storybooks are listed in Carolyn W. Lima and John A. Lima's *A to Zoo: Subject Access to Children's Picture Books*, fifth edition.

Young people may enjoy locating rhyme in the poetry books they read. They may explore the picture storybook section of the library media center for rhyming books. They may also create their own rhyming poetry and stories using Sue Young's *The Scholastic Rhyming Dictionary* for groups of words that rhyme.

Riddle: A form of literature that may imply or ask a deliberately perplexing question to be deciphered or guessed. The riddle is universal, being a part of the folklore of most cultures since ancient times.

Examples of folklore riddles familiar to young Americans may be found in Carl Withers' *A Rocket in My Pocket*:

> Railroad crossing, look out for the cars!
> Can you spell that without any r's?
> —T-H-A-T (1988: 95)

and

> I washed my hands in water
> That never rained nor run;
> I dried them with a towel
> That was never wove nor spun.
> —*Dew and Sun* (1988: 93)

The first of the two is an example of the riddle as a direct question, and the second that of an implied question. Literary scholars categorize the two types as the clever question and the descriptive riddle.

The descriptive riddle is not only a guessing game; it is pure imagery. A riddle from *Lightning Inside You and Other Native American Riddles*, edited by John Bierhorst (Beechtree, 1992: 19), also illustrates the metaphorical nature of the riddle, "Threads of seven colors are stretched on the great prairie. Thunder. *Oklahoma Comanche.*"

As children enjoy reading and sharing traditional and contemporary riddles, they are exploring the essence of poetry. An excellent contemporary work that lets young children experience the metaphorical nature of riddles is Myra Cohn Livingston's *My Head Is Red and Other Riddle Rhymes*. Older children may consider the analogy of the riddle to the imagery within various collections of poems. And, young people always enjoy the fun of sharing riddles from collections such as J. Patrick Lewis' *Riddle-icious*, illustrated by Deborah Tilley.

Rising Action: The part of a dramatic plot that precedes the crisis. It typically begins after the exposition with an inciting incident and then includes a series of complications and conflict that culminate in the crisis. Young people could use *Freytag's Pyramid* to chart the rising action of a favorite folktale. (See *Progressive Plot*.) After they have had success at identifying inciting incidents and complications in folktales, they may identify the events in the rising action of a linear novel, such as Will Hobbs' *Far North*, the story of Gabe's struggle in Canada's Northwest Territories. If young people experience this novel read aloud, they could chart on butcher paper the complicating events as they unfold.

Robert F. Sibert Informational Book Award: A children's book award administered and presented by the Association for Library Service to Children, a division of the American Library Association, to the author of the most distinguished informational book published during the preceding year. The award is named in honor of Robert F. Sibert, the long-time President of Bound to Stay Bound Books, Inc. of Jacksonville, Illinois, and is sponsored by the company. The first presentation was made in 2001 for Marc Aronson's *Sir Walter Raleigh and the Quest for El Dorado*. Young people may find more information about the Sibert Award on the Web (*www.ala.org/alsc/sibert/html*).

Romance: Generally, a work, such as an adventure story, which emphasizes plot rather than character; however, critically, one of the four modes or fundamental stories identified by Northrop Frye in *Anatomy of Criticism: Four Essays*. Characteristics of works in this mode may include a triumph of good over evil; a happy ending; a quest with a journey, a struggle, and a return; a young and admirable hero who has mysterious origins, who is above the ordinary, and who moves from innocence toward understanding and experience; or a villain who is often associated with darkness and old age. Characteristics of the mode can be found in such diverse works as Lloyd Alexander's *The High King*, Beatrix Potter's *The Tale of*

Peter Rabbit, Maurice Sendak's *Where the Wild Things Are*, Christopher Paul Curtis' *Bud, Not Buddy*, and William Steig's *Abel's Island*. Young people may develop an understanding of the fundamental romance story by comparing the similarities of romances in different formats and genres. See *Mode*.

Roughs: See *Editor*.

Round Character: A fictional character that has a fully developed, multi-faceted personality. Although round characters are never expected in certain genres (*e.g.*, folktales) or in all roles (minor characters), they are critical in others. For example, a reader of a contemporary realistic fiction novel expects the main character to be portrayed honestly, with the positive and negative qualities of a real human being. Young people may discuss the issue of round character by considering how novels' main characters determine and are determined by conflicts in the story. For example, they may consider: How does Karana's character interact with challenges of an isolated life in Scott O'Dell's *Island of the Blue Dolphins*? In Katherine Paterson's *Bridge to Terabithia*, how is Jess Aarons' round character revealed in his interactions with the energetic and adventurous Leslie Burke? How does he cope with the sudden loss of that friend? In Phyllis Naylor's *Shiloh*, what aspects of Marty's personality cause him to react as he does, to Shiloh, his parents, and Judd?

Satire: A form of literature in which humor is used to ridicule a person, a group or society, or an idea. Satire attempts to benefit humankind by pointing out foibles and frailties like arrogance and self-deceit. It differs from comedy, which uses humor to entertain, and sarcasm, which uses humor to abuse. Originating from Latin for *a dish of mixed ingredients*, satire has existed since ancient times. Although most satire is beyond the understanding of young children, two stories that can introduce the concept are Hans Christian Andersen's "The Ugly Duckling" and "The Emperor's New Clothes." After reading *The Ugly Duckling*, retold and illustrated by Jerry Pinkney, or *The Emperor's New Clothes*, retold and illustrated by Demi, young people may identify and consider the human qualities that cause the reader to smile and yet that Andersen found troublesome. Contemporary novels, such as Mary Rodgers' *Freaky Friday*, also offer young people opportunities to experience satire. See *Mode* and *Irony/Satire*.

Science Fiction: A narrative form, ranging in length from a short story to a novel, that presents and describes a world functioning by scientific laws or variants of scientific laws. Although science fiction has been described as a form of fantasy, it is actually a distinct genre that suggests the future for humankind and the universe.

G. Robert Carlsen, seeing fantasy and science fiction as distinct but not mutually exclusive genres, compared the two to the opposite ends of a continuum: "At the fantasy end are such books as J.R.R. Tolkien's *The Lord of the Rings* trilogy and at the science fiction end, Isaac Asimov's *The Fantastic Voyage*. But a book like Madeleine L'Engle's *A Wrinkle in Time* has affinities with both genres" (1980: 254). The term science fantasy is sometimes used to describe those works that demonstrate characteristics of both genres.

Characteristics of well-written science fiction include: (1) information that is accurate or is a plausible extension of scientific fact; (2) the capacity to encourage critical examination of technology on social change and on human values; (3) scientific explanations that are understandable yet not a distraction from the story; (4) the consistency with which the premise is followed. Largely lacking these characteristics, early science fiction was not considered literature, but rather subliterature "appropriate only for comic books and pulp magazines" (Carlsen, 1980: 254). Since 1970 science fiction has made remarkable gains in both popularity and respectability. It has come to be valued for its potential in helping young people develop both imagination and new perspectives of their world. Authors of science fiction for young people include Bruce Brooks' *No Kidding*, Bruce Coville's *Aliens Ate My Homework*, Nancy Farmer's *The Ear, the Eye, and the Arm: A Novel*, H. M. Hoover's *Orvis*, Madeleine L'Engle's *A Wrinkle in Time*, Lois Lowry's *The Giver*, Margaret Mahy's *Aliens in the Family*, Daniel Pinkwater's *Alan Mendelsohn, the Boy from Mars*, Pamela Service's *Stinker From Space*, and Alfred Slote *My Trip to Alpha I*.

Young people may test the credibility of the science in this genre by doing library research on science facts and hypotheses addressed in their favorite novel.

Scott O'Dell Award for Historical Fiction: A children's book award established in 1981 by Mr. Scott O'Dell to recognize an outstanding work of historical fiction, written by a citizen of the United States, set in the New World, and published the previous calendar year by a U.S. publisher. The award is typically given annually; however, there may be years when no award is given. As stipulated in Scott O'Dell's will, the award is administered by the Scott O'Dell Committee, Zena Sutherland, chair.

Scratch Board: A drawing board that is first covered with white clay (or another colored substance) then with a layer of black ink coating, which is scratched away to produce an illustration; also known as *scraperboard*. The boards may come in other combinations of two colors, such as white on black or black on a metallic surface. A steel scratch knife or other sharp art instrument is used to scratch off the top coating so that the color beneath shows through to produce an effect similar to etching. Artists often use some combinations of scratched dots, lines, hatching, or cross-hatching to create the illustration. The resulting illustration may be colored with oil pastels, watercolors, or other media.

Brian Pinkney's name is synonymous with award-winning scratchboard illustrations in children's picture books. Young people may find examples of his work in *In the Time of the Drums*, written by Kim L. Siegelson, *Duke Ellington: The Piano Prince and the Orchestra*, written by Andrea Davis Pinkney, and *The Faithful Friend*, written by Robert D. San Souci. The scratchboard technique was also used by Michael McCurdy in *The Seasons Sewn: A Year in Patchwork*, written by Ann Whitford Paul.

Young people may experiment with the scratchboard technique by painting a surface with crayon and scratching an illustration into it.

Sepia: A brownish color associated with a semi-transparent pigment that was once widely used in ink, watercolor, and photographs. The original dark brown pigment (prepared from the natural secretion of the cuttlefish) tended to lose color under strong light and, thus, was not popular as an artistic medium.

A number of examples of sepia-toned photographs are included in Walter Dean Myers' *Brown Angels: An Album of Pictures and Verse* that features African American children from the early 1900s, and sepia-colored photographs and illustrations were used in Jim Murphy's *Blizzard! The Storm That Changed America*. One of the best well-known children's books that features sepia-toned illustrations is the 1942 Caldecott Award book, Robert McClosky's *Make Way for Ducklings*. And, Ken Mochizuki's *Passage to Freedom: The Sugihara Story*, illustrated by Dom Lee, uses sepia-toned art to set a somber mood for this personal history about a Japanese diplomat who in 1940 defied his government to save thousands of Lithuanian Jews. Young people may create their own "sepia-colored" illustrations by using only a brown crayon or brown paint to depict their scene of choice.

Sequel: Refers to the later book that continues the same characters, setting, and storyline as the preceding one. The 1986 Newbery Award book, Patricia MacLachlan's *Sarah Plain and Tall*, illustrated by Marcia Sewall, was followed six years later by the sequel *Skylark*.

Gary Paulsen's popular *Hatchet*, which relates thirteen-year-old Brian's survival in the Canadian wilderness after a fateful plane crash, was followed with a sequel *The River* in which Brian returns to the same place to help scientists learn more about the psychology of his survival in the wilderness for fifty-four days. Paulsen continued this story with *Brian's Return*, in which Brian, unable to live in the city, returns to the wilderness where he believes he belongs. An interesting twist to these three titles is that Paulsen's *Brian's Winter* is a companion book, not a sequel. Providing a new storyline, it portrays what would have happened if Brian had originally been forced to survive an entire winter in the wilderness.

Also of note, the 1999 Newbery Honor book, Richard Peck's *A Long Way from Chicago: A Novel in Stories* was followed with the sequel *A Year Down Yonder*, which won the 2001 Newbery Award.

Young people, interested in reading books that have a sequel or in finding a sequel to a book they have read, may find helpful reading advice from Vicki Anderson's *Sequels in Children's Literature: An Annotated Bibliography of Books in Succession, K–6.* They may also be challenged to write a sequel for a book that does not have one.

Series: A group of works centering on a single subject, author, format, or character. Developed in the nineteenth century, series fiction has often been based on formulas yielding superficial characters and predictable plots. However, young readers who like to return to the familiar can find round characters and fresh plots in series such as Lois Lowry's *Anastasia Series,* Phyllis Naylor's *Alice Series,* and J. K. Rowling's *Harry Potter Series.* Like Lucy Maud Montgomery's *Anne of Green Gables Series* of another era, series books thrive on peer recommendations, and effective ways to increase young people's awareness may include occasional displays, the inclusion of paperback editions in library collections, and providing opportunities for young people to trade personal copies with each other. Professional resources on series books are Catherine Barr's *Reading in Series: A Selection Guide to Books for Children;* Philip Young's *Children's Fiction Series: A Bibliography, 1850–1950;* and Bridget Dealy Volz's *Junior Genreflecting: A Guide to Good Reads and Series Fiction for Children.*

Setting: In literature, the time and place of a story. Setting also refers to the background, surroundings, environment, and context of a story. The setting may be broadly defined as in a country or city or as narrowly defined as in a school classroom or home. A story may take place over several years or over a brief period, such as one day.

An integral setting refers to an essential time and place for the story to take place, as is required in biography or historical fiction. For example, a children's book that could not be placed in another time or place is Karen Hesse's *Stowaway,* which is a fictionalized journal set from 1768–1771 aboard the *Endeavor,* a sailing ship under the direction of Captain James Cook. Another example is the 2000 National Book Award for Young People, Gloria Whelan's *Homeless Bird,* which shares the plight of thirteen-year-old Koly who must enter an arranged marriage as dictated by the traditions of her native India.

A backdrop setting merely sets the stage and the mood for a story. Backdrop settings are often used in folklore as in Mary Pope Osborne's *Kate and the*

Beanstalk, illustrated by Giselle Potter, which begins with "Long ago, a girl named Kate lived with her mother in a humble cottage. One day, after a hard winter, Kate's mother was in despair."

Examples of picture storybooks with important settings include Barbara Cooney's *Miss Rumphius* and Jane Yolen's *Owl Moon*, illustrated by John Schoenherr. Two Newbery Award books with integral settings are Sharon Creech's *Walk Two Moons* and Karen Hesse's *Out of the Dust*.

Young people may look through the last five years of the Newbery Medal books and Honor books and discuss whether the setting is important to the story. A complete listing of the books can be found on the Web (*www.ala.org/alsc/ newbpast.html*). Students may also choose to write their own stories and define a particular time and place. They may also select favorite books with well-known settings and try to fit the characters into another time and place.

Short Story: A brief prose narrative in which an author does not develop characters fully but typically emphasizes one aspect of one character's personality as it is involved in limited conflict. Edgar Allan Poe (United States, 1809–1849) developed the structure of the short story and established it as a literary form that strives for a single effect and can be read in a single sitting. Structure in the short story is like that in the novel but shorter. "It is," says short story author Tim Wynne-Jones, "just the big game, not the whole season, and read in twenty minutes, max," quoted in Alleen Nilsen and Kenneth Donelson's *Literature for Today's Young Adults* (2001: 364).

Short story collections are well suited to older readers who typically spend less time reading than in years past. Among young adult short story collections worthy as first introductions to older readers are Lois Duncan's *On the Edge: Stories on the Brink*, Chris Crutcher's *Athletic Shorts*, and Donald Gallo's *Short Circuits: Thirteen Shocking Stories by Outstanding Writers for Young Adults*. Preteens also enjoy short stories, and among those that would make a good introduction are Gary Soto's *Baseball in April*, Johanna Hurwitz's *Birthday Surprises: Ten Great Stories to Unwrap*, Cynthia Rylant's *Every Living Thing*, and Robert D. San Souci's *Short and Shivery: Thirty Chilling Tales*.

Short stories are easily introduced to young people by reading them aloud, and their brevity allows thematic pairings with other short genres. Young people's discussions of short stories could focus on ways authors quickly draw aspects of short story personalities into meaningful conflicts. Young people who are interested in short stories may search the library catalog to find one by a favorite author.

Simile: A figure of speech in which two unlike things are compared in such a way as to assist the reader in developing a meaningful image. Usually the comparison utilizes the words "like" or "as."

For the intermediate level child, an excellent introduction to the simile is Norman Juster's *A Surfeit of Similes*. As the book is read aloud, the children may be invited to complete selected examples before the author's comparison is read (*i.e.*, "as soft as a _____" or "as hungry as a _____").

Sociological Criticism: A type of criticism that considers how society is reflected in literature. It is a term applied to the criticism of children's literature by Mary Lou White in her 1976 work *Children's Literature: Criticism and Response*. White explains that the critic analyzes, interprets, and evaluates literature through social, economic, and political views of its time; thus, the approach enables a reader to consider a work "in the context with which it was written" (1976: 51), focusing on issues of honesty and reality. Sociological criticism includes aspects of cultural and gender studies. Young people may engage in sociological criticism by:

- reading contemporary works, such as Jack Gantos' *Joey Pigza Swallowed the Key*, and discussing what they reveal about life in the United States;
- reading a work of historical fiction with a female main character, like Avi's *The True Confessions of Charlotte Doyle*, and considering whether the character behaved in a way realistic for females in her time;
- reading a work of historical fiction with central characters who represent a minority group, for example, William Armstrong's *Sounder*, and evaluating whether the Black characters behaved in believable ways for the group at the turn of the twentieth century;
- reading a work, such as Karen Hesse's *Out of the Dust*, and considering the influence economic conditions on the way of life of families caught up in the Dust Bowl.

Spiritual: A deeply emotional religious song that developed anonymously among African Americans in the southern United States. Critics, such as M. H. Abrams in *A Glossary of Literary Terms*, seventh edition, have described spirituals as the greatest American devotional songs. Young people may be introduced to twenty spirituals in Ashley Bryan's *All Night, All Day—A Child's First Book of African-American Spirituals*, which includes piano accompaniments and guitar chords.

Stanza: Within a poem, a grouping of lines equivalent to a paragraph and set apart by a blank line in the text. Conventionally, a stanza pattern will have a set number of lines and feet per line, defined meter, and a rhyme scheme. The term originated from the Italian word for *room*; hence, a stanza is a small unit of a larger structure.

Young people may examine a variety of edited anthologies, such as Jack Prelutsky's *The Twentieth Century Children's Poetry Treasury*, Alvin Schwartz's *And the Green Grass Grew All Around: Folk Poetry from Everyone*, and Donald Hall's *The Oxford Book of Children's Verses in America*. Browsing in small groups, they may consider the variations in the number of lines or the pattern of rhymes recurring in poems' stanzas. They may share a favorite stanza with the larger group.

Static Character: Character who remains fundamentally the same throughout the story. This is in opposition to a main character that changes, grows, and develops during the story. In E.L. Konigsburg's *A View from Saturday*, the villainous Hamilton Knapp does not change nor does the horrible grandmother in Jennifer L. Holm's Newbery Honor book, *Our Only May Amelia*. In order to introduce children to the range and depth of characters in a book, take a book familiar to most children, such as *Charlotte's Web*, review the story, list characters, and discuss in terms of the rounded (Charlotte and Wilbur), flat (Mr. Arable), dynamic (Wilbur), and static character (Templeton). Discuss the difference and why it is important to not have all dynamic characters, but to also have the foil or backdrop of flat and static characters. Young people may consider John Steptoe's *Mufaro's Beautiful Daughters* and discuss in terms of character types.

Stereotype: A flat character lacking individual traits and representing an uncritical assessment of the attributes of a social, cultural, or other group. *Stereotype* originated in the nineteenth century as a French printing term for a plate cast from a printing surface; thus, a stereotype plate could repeatedly and unvaryingly reproduce the original surface. The meaning of *stereotype* became synonymous with *any standard pattern*, including an oversimplified mental image shaped by generally held attitudes and opinions. In literature, stereotype is typically a negative term that describes trite, hackneyed characters that can perpetuate thoughtless generalizations about groups (*e.g.*, spoiled children and nagging wives). Older readers who are developmentally ready to consider the negative social (*e.g.*, racism) as well as negative literary aspects of stereotypes will find many examples that still remain in children's library collections, including such unfortunate ones as Robert Louis Stevenson's poem "Foreign Children" in one of the many editions of *A Child's Garden of Verses*, first published as *Penny Whistles* in 1885 in the United Kingdom, and the treatment of minority groups in Harold Keith's Newbery-winning novel *Rifles for Waite*. Older collections may also allow the comparisons of later editions of some works that have been edited to remove the negative portrayal of minority groups. For example, Pamela Travers' chapter "Bad Tuesday" in *Mary Poppins* can be compared to later editions (beginning with the 1971 paperback edition) in which Travers changed the language of the Africans. A folktale that has been the center of discussions on stereotyping is "The Five Chinese Brothers," the story of Chinese brothers who elude execution by virtue of their extraordinary individual qualities. Claire Huchet Bishop's *The Five Chinese Brothers* portrayed the brothers stereotypically without individual characteristics. However, they were individuals in Margaret Mahy's retelling *The Seven Chinese Brothers*, illustrated by Jean and Mou-Sien Tseng.

Stock Character: A flat, conventional character type often associated with a particular literary genre. In children's literature, folktales provide a familiar source of such universally recognizable types as the simple peasant boy (*e.g.*, "Jack and the Beanstalk"), the fairy godmother (*e.g.*, "Cinderella"), the wicked witch (*e.g.*, Baba Yaga in "Maria Morevna"), and the heartless stepmother (*e.g.*, "Hansel and Gretel"). Young people may begin to develop an understanding of the use of stock characters by comparing the qualities of a single stock character (such as the wicked witch) across a set of tales that include such a character type.

Storyboard: A panel or a series of drawings that show the consecutive order of the images for a picture book, film, animated cartoon, advertisement, or television show. They are useful in planning the finished product because of the ease of editing the project at this early stage. Janet Stevens' *From Picture Books to Words: A Book about Making a Book* includes a sample storyboard in a double-page spread. Stevens defines a storyboard as "a map of the book—like a comic strip—that shows all thirty-two pages on a single piece of paper." A storyboard is also illustrated in Eileen Christelow's *What Do Illustrators Do?*

Young people may follow the creative process outlined in Stevens' *From Picture Books to Words*. They may use a duplicated long piece of paper that features thirty-two storyboard boxes similar to the Stevens' sample and work out an idea for an original children's picture book. Some students may feel more comfortable writing the story first and then completing the storyboard. For an interesting assignment, students might follow the process used for creating many children's books by having one person write the story and another create the storyboard and illustrations for the book dummy.

Structural Criticism: A critical approach that analyzes a work according to the relationships among its literary elements. Incorporating concepts of structural linguistics and structural anthropology into literary criticism, structuralism became prominent in the 1960s, having developed from the writings of the Swiss linguist Ferdinand de Saussure, author of *Cours de Linguistique Generale* (second edition, with Eisuke Komatsu and George Wolf), first published in 1913 from lecture notes he gave in 1908–09. Mary Lou White, author of *Children's Literature: Criticism and Response* advocated its application to children's literature, suggesting such activities as considering how meaning is communicated through illustrations that complement the text, the subtle differences in similar words, and the repetition of literary elements.

Young people could be encouraged to consider some aspects of structuralism in a folktale such as "Jack and the Bean Tree," included in *The Jack Tales*, retold by Richard Chase (1943: 39). A dominant feature in "Jack and the Bean Tree" is the use of repetition. On three different occasions, Jack checks on his tree in the morning; his mother punishes him for lying; he climbs up the tree; he encounters the giant's wife; she hides him; the giant arrives home and searches for Jack; Jack steals an object from the giant; and Jack descends the bean tree. Each repetition emphasizes a consistency of character as well as an escalating intensity of the characters' responses. For example, the first time that Jack's mother thought he had lied, she told him he should not do that; the second time, she "slapped him pretty keen"; and the third time she "slapped his jaws real hard." And, the first time the giant's wife saw Jack, she said, "Law, stranger. What you a-doin up here?"; the second time, she said, "Why, you little scamp!"; and the third time, she said, "Why, buddy, what in the world you doin' up here again?" Also, the illustrations define an Appalachian setting where the giant's rifle-gun and skinnin' knife would be as common as the corn pones in his refrain and the bread bowl that hides him. When young people discover these repetitions, subtle differences in word choice, and the contributions of illustrations, they are able to consider how a work's structure creates meaning for the reader.

Style: Manner of expression. Devices of style include figurative language (*e.g.*, similes and metaphors), symbols, allusions, wordplay, understatement, hyperbole, imagery, rhythm, connotation, and repetition. Emphasizing that a work's style should be suitable for both its audience and its subject matter, Jonathan Swift described it as "proper words in proper places" (in Kathleen Morner and Ralph Rausch's *NTC's Dictionary of Literary Terms* [1991: 214]). Young people may explore the concept of style by considering alternatives to the devices that they encounter in literary works. For example, they could suggest objects that could be symbols of friendship, such as the necklace that Karana gave to Tutok in *Island of the Blue Dolphins* by Scott O'Dell or the one that best friends gave each other in Karen Ackerman's *The Tin Heart*, as well as the teas served in Elaine Konigsburg's *The View from Saturday*.

Subplot: A sequence of events minor to the main story in a work of fiction. Protagonists in subplots are often the minor characters of the main plot; however, they are involved in events that are not necessarily a part of the main story. When used with skill, a subplot can make a work more interesting, add complications to the main story, and reflect the theme of the main story. For example, in Sharon Creech's *Walk Two Moons* the main plot centers around a journey. Salamanca Hiddle and her grandparents are driving to Idaho to find Salamanca's missing mother; however, Salamanca introduces a subplot as she relates the amazing story of her friend Phoebe Winterbottom whose mother has also disappeared. Salamanca's story fascinates the reader (as well as Salamanca's grandparents) as she relates the activities of Phoebe, a lunatic, and Mrs. Cadaver. However, more than a digression, Phoebe's story is a subplot that functions as a shadow of Salamanca's real life and, thus, reflects and reinforces the theme of the major plot. Young people may discuss the use of the subplot in *Walk Two Moons* or find other subplots in the novels they are reading.

Subtitle: Secondary part of a title that generally follows a colon. The subtitle, referred to by catalogers as "other title information," is descriptive or adds more details to the title (title proper). Newbery Medal and Honor books since 1990 with a subtitle include Russell Freedman's *Eleanor Roosevelt: A Life of Discovery*, Patricia C. McKissack's *The Dark-thirty: Southern Tales of the Supernatural*, Avi's *Nothing But the Truth: A Documentary Novel*, and Russell Freedman's *The Wright Brothers: How They Invented the Airplane*.

Young people can learn the value of subtitles by attempting to match pairs of titles proper and subtitles that have been placed separately on story strips. The examples could be taken from the titles and subtitles of the above books, or of any set of books. Young people may be challenged to write imaginary titles and subtitles for a period of history they are studying. Or, using a book or an online source (*www.ala.org/alsc/*) that gives complete title information on the Newbery, Caldecott, Coretta Scott King, and Batchelder awards, young people could analyze why books for older readers are more likely to have subtitles.

Surrealism: Artwork that depicts incongruous dream and fantasy images that often juxtapose unlikely objects in unreal scenes that are somewhat believable. Surrealistic art is usually meticulous in detail. Examples of surrealism in children's book illustration include: Molly Bang's *The Grey Lady and the Strawberry Snatcher*; Anthony Browne's *Voices in the Park*; Michael Garland's *Dinner at Margritte's*; Dav Pilkey's *When Cats Dream*; and Chris Van Allsburg's *Jumanji* and *The Mysteries of Harris Burdick*.

Young people may locate several of the books listed and discuss the surrealistic elements they find in each. Van Allsburg's *The Mysteries of Harris Burdick* offers young people fourteen illustrations that can serve as story starters in either written or oral forms.

Survival Story: A realistic story that tells of the protagonist's struggle to survive physically or emotionally. The hallmark of an excellent survival story is dynamic characterization. Having survived a life-threatening challenge, the protagonist emerges knowing that he or she is fundamentally changed. The stories also involve the development of problem-solving skills that prove necessary for survival. Without exception, characters must consider the consequences of their actions because the decisions they make are often a matter of life and death. A well-developed character is created through the author's choice of point of view, which is often first person or limited omniscient. A consistent point of view allows readers to identify with the protagonist, making the story more plausible.

Survival stories can have varied settings. Will Hobbs' *Jason's Gold* and Sherry Shahan's *Frozen Stiff* are examples of the struggle to survive in a harsh or alien wilderness. Some survival stories have an urban setting in which the main character must overcome adversity such as homelessness or poverty. For example, Felice Holman's *Slake's Limbo* depicts a boy's survival in a New York subway. Other survival stories are set in the milieu of war, terrorism, hostage situations, and political persecution. For example, Maxine Schur's *Circlemaker* and Felice Holman's *Wild Children* are set in the turmoil of twentieth century Russia.

For any well-written survival story, young people can explore/discuss the fundamental changes that occur in the protagonist's life. Readers may also imagine or develop plausible scenes or alternate endings that require different decisions and actions from the protagonist.

Suspension of Disbelief: The reader's willingness to accept supernatural premises in science fiction, fantasy, or other imaginative work. In explaining the creation of a "semblance of truth" in works of the supernatural, "or at least the romantic," Samuel Taylor Coleridge introduced the term in *Biographia Literaria* by explaining the need for "that willing suspension of disbelief for the moment, which constitutes poetic faith" *(www.english.upenn.edu/~Romantic/biographica.html).*

Authors can use several techniques to encourage the suspension of disbelief. For example, the author might begin the fantasy in the real world and then use small events to ease the reader into accepting that the inexplicable is occurring. Susan Cooper's *The Dark Is Rising* begins on an ordinary day, but Will begins to notice unexpected occurrences: The radio has unusual static and birds are behaving unpredictably. Slowly the reader is prepared to accept the fantasy into which Will awakens the next morning. Sometimes artifacts are left behind after the story's magical elements have concluded. For example, in E. B. White's *Charlotte's Web,* Charlotte's egg sac remains after Charlotte is gone, and in Natalie Babbitt's *Tuck Everlasting* magical spring water remains after the Tuck family has left. Another technique authors can use to encourage the suspension of disbelief is the inclusion of rich details about the fantastic elements. Jane Langton's *The Fledgling* has detailed descriptions, such as those of the Goose's feathers and the shape of his back where Georgie flies, which make him more imaginable and, therefore, believable. To explore the concept, young people may identify techniques that encourage their suspension of disbelief in fantasies they read, considering what makes the story seem real.

Symbol: An object, a place, a character, event, or action that has an abstract, figurative meaning as well as a concrete meaning. Symbols are more than signs, which, like a railroad crossing sign, can mean only one thing. In Elaine Konigsburg's *A View from Saturday,* the cups of tea served on Saturday were concrete objects with a literal meaning; however, the cup of tea, when served, also functions figuratively and universally as a symbol of friendship and sharing. An example of symbol that is specific to a story is the use of setting in Katherine Paterson's *Jacob Have I Loved.* Rass Island is not only the setting of the novel; as storms and waves literally wash it away, it is also a symbol of an isolated way of life that cannot be sustained.

Young people may begin to consider the use of symbols by finding and interpreting universal symbols (*e.g.,* a circle for eternity or a dove for peace). And, they may discuss what objects, like a cup of tea, or settings, like an eroding island, also suggest.

Synonym: A word or expression with the same or close to the same meaning or concept as another word or expression. Two reference sources that list synonyms include J. I. Rodale's *Synonym Finder* and Barbara Ann Kipfer's *21st Century Synonym and Antonym Finder*. Young people may make a list of synonyms that they have encountered in their reading.

Tall Tale: A humorous tale that depends on blatant exaggeration for its effect. The exaggeration is focused on the superhuman abilities of a character and is emphasized with the use of precise details, a literal and reasonable manner, and the use of everyday language. Often the present tense is used to achieve a sense of immediacy. Although many countries have tall tales in their folklore, it often has been associated with America and especially the American frontier.

Among famous American tall tale characters are Johnny Appleseed, Pecos Bill, Stormalong, Paul Bunyan, Davy Crockett, Joe Magarac, John Henry, and Mike Fink, thus evidencing folk heroes both real and imaginary. The nature of the tall tale appeals to children and offers them a variety of extended literature activities (*e.g.*, adding a new episode to the lore of an existing hero or creating a new hero). A useful geography activity is to locate on a United States map the states identified with each tall tale character. A more in-depth project could be developed by presenting Steven Kellogg's *Johnny Appleseed* to children and encouraging them to discover which details in illustrations or text can be historically substantiated in an encyclopedia.

Tangram: A Chinese toy made by cutting a square of thin material into seven pieces (a rhomboid, a square, and five triangles) that can be arranged in many different figures. Each separate piece is a *tan*, and the entire set of tans must be used in constructing a picture. Each tan must touch an adjacent tan, but one may not be placed over another. Chinese storytellers often use the tangram to illustrate characters, changing the shapes as the characters change. A professional resource on the tangram is Valerie Marsh's *Story Puzzles: Tales in the Tangram Tradition.*

The tangram may be introduced to children by sharing Ann Tompert's picture book *Grandfather Tang's Story*. After listening to the book and viewing the illustrations, children may cut out their own tangrams or use tangram pieces in the *Tangram Discovery Box*, which illustrates the construction of a variety of tangram designs. They may practice reproducing the pictures in the story and create new pictures of their own to use in illustrating stories they choose to write or tell.

Tempera: A traditional painting technique involving the mixture of colored pigments with a binding emulsion of water and pure egg yolk or a mixture of egg and oil, sometimes called egg tempera. Tempera is quick drying and has a lean film-forming property. Its opaqueness can be increased or decreased, and the brightness or dullness can be controlled. Selected children's books created with this artistic medium include the 1950 Caldecott Award book, Leo Politi's *Song of the Swallows*; 1951 Caldecott Award book, Katherine Milhous' *The Egg Tree*; and the 1964 Caldecott Award-winning illustrations of Maurice Sendak's *Where the Wild Things Are*. Nicolas Sidajakov's 1961 Caldecott Award book *Baboushka and the Three Kings* used both tempera and felt-tip pens.

Using the medium of tempera paints, young people may illustrate what they believe is the most important scene or idea from one of the books listed above or another picture book. If using a picture book in a different medium, they may compare their own tempera painting to that of other known artistic renderings.

Tercet: Triplet; stanzas of three lines of verse; usually the lines in the stanza rhyme with each other or with an adjoining tercet. However, there are arrangements of unrhyming tercets, and sometimes rhyme schemes vary. A poem may be entirely in the tercet structure or include a few stanzas of tercet. Two examples of a tercet, or triplet, are William Jay Smith's "Butterfly," from May Hill Arbuthnot's *A Time for Poetry*, third edition, and David McCord's "Mr. Bidery's Spidery Garden," from Jack Prelutsky's *The Random House Book of Poetry for Children*, illustrated by Arnold Lobel.

Young people may select a favorite animal or season and write a poem comprised of a tercet. They will find Sue Young's *The Scholastic Rhyming Dictionary* useful to locate rhyming words.

Terse Verse: A rhyming verse that consists of two one-syllable words. Among collections of terse verse are Bruce McMillan's *One Sun: A Book of Terse Verse* and *Play Day: A Book of Terse Verse*, as well as George Ella Lyon's *Day at Damp*

Camp. Day at Damp Camp, illustrated by Peter Catalanotto, is a collection of terse verse about summer camp experiences (*e.g.*, "HOT COT" and "COOL POOL"). After being introduced to terse verse and a rhyming dictionary, a group of young people could produce a joint collection of terse verses created around a shared experience such as a holiday, a field trip, or a topic interest.

Theme: As it relates to literature, the basic idea or underlying meaning of a work. It represents the discovery of a universal truth that may be applied to many stories. Theme is not the didactic presentation of a moral. If the reader finds within the work a statement made by the author that identifies clearly the central idea of the story, that statement is an explicit theme, such as "Nothing you love is lost," from Bruce Coville's *Jeremy Thatcher, Dragon Hatcher*. If, after completing the story, the reader derives the meaning from a consideration of the characters' thoughts and actions as they cope with the conflict of the plot, the theme is implicit. An example of an implicit theme from E. B. White's *Charlotte's Web* is: life has a natural inevitability that includes birth and death. *Charlotte's Web*, like other enduring works, has several themes for readers to explore.

If young people learn to state themes as complete sentences about a universal truth, they will avoid merely identifying topics or subjects (*e.g.*, friendship or peace). For example, the title of Byrd Baylor's *The Best Town in the World* may be identified loosely as a theme; but, as such, it evidences no serious contemplation until the reader decides the implicit theme may be that the best town in the world is the one that holds pleasant memories. Young people develop the ability to state themes in universal terms when they do not include references to specific characters and events of the story.

Tone: A term that reflects the author's attitude toward the subject or the reader of a literary work. The writer reveals tone through the choice of descriptive words or by the actions and conversations of the characters. Stories and poems for children may have a tone that is humorous, serious, informative, playful, or any of many other attitudes. However, in children's works a didactic, nostalgic, or condescending tone should be avoided in order to allow a pleasurable reading experience. Tone may shift within a book. For example, in a very serious work the author may insert a humorous scene or light conversation in order to avoid undue reader tension.

To introduce tone to children in the upper grades, one might read Tomie de Paola's *The Popcorn Book*. In a discussion of tone, the children may determine that it is humorous. Yet, with further discussion of the many facets of popcorn that are included, the children may decide it is meant to be informative. The title alone in Alvin Schwartz's *Scary Stories to Tell in the Dark* indicates a scary tone, but if "The Viper" from that collection were read to the children, they would find that tale to be humorous. Young people may explore the concept of tone in picture books because the visual message often creates a more immediate impression. For example, they may consider Myra Cohn Livingston's *Celebrations*, a collection of poems about holidays. Leonard Everett Fisher's dramatic paintings enhance the reaction of the reader to each celebrated day. Reflecting on the poems and illustrations, young people may decide that "April Fool" is funny, "Halloween" scary, "Memorial Day" serious, and that "Fourth of July" is exciting.

Tongue Twister: Phrase or sentence created by repetition of the same words or sounds in words. Tongue twisters are often associated with nonsense verse, nursery rhymes, and pattern songs. The sequence of words or sounds, often alliterative, is difficult (and fun) to read aloud quickly. Sometimes called tongue-trippers, tongue twisters have been used effectively in speech therapy and for changing an individual's accent. Occasionally, the story line of a rhyming picture book will incorporate tongue twister sentence structures, as in Nancy Shaw's *Sheep on a Ship* and *Sheep in a Jeep*. Young people may enjoy listening to and reading tongue twisters from Joanna Cole's *Six Sick Sheep: 101 Tongue Twisters* or Joseph Rosenbloom's *World's Toughest Tongue Twisters*. A Web resource for tongue twisters is *www.geocities.com/Athens/8136/tongtwisters.html*.

Touchstone: A criterion or standard through which the merit of a work may be judged. The term is derived from the testing of the purity of gold or silver by rubbing it against a fine-grained stone. Matthew Arnold used the term in his essay "The Study of Poetry" in *The Complete Prose Works of Matthew Arnold*, edited by P. H. Super, in which he suggested that, in order to discover what is truly excellent, it is wise to consider the works of the great masters and to apply them as a touchstone to other poetry.

Rebecca J. Lukens, in her sixth edition of *A Critical Handbook of Children's Literature* uses *Charlotte's Web* by E. B. White as a literary standard against which to evaluate character, plot, setting, theme, point of view, style, and tone in other works of fiction. Young people have opportunities to evaluate books by literary standards when they participate in readers' choice awards.

Toy Book or **Pop-up Book** or **Movable Book:** A book in which parts of the pages pop up, pull out, or extend by lifting a flap. Toy books are designed to invite interaction with the text. The major negative aspect is that they tear with extended use. The term toy books was used by Walter Crane between 1867 and 1876 to distinguish over thirty of his books published by Routledge that were intended for the nursery child. However, they did not have movable parts.

Robert Sabuda has elevated pop-up/movable books to incredible feats of paper engineering. Some excellent examples of his work include Frank Baum's *The Wonderful Wizard of Oz: A Commemorative Pop-up*; *Cookie Count*; *The Twelve Days of Christmas: A Pop-up*; and *The Christmas Alphabet.*

Examples of books that are more like toys include Lucy Cousins' *Maisy's Pop-up Playhouse*, which is tied on the right side of the cover with red ribbons and opens out fully to provide Maisy's domain as a circular playhouse with some removable pieces, and Stephen A. Johnson's *My Little Red Toolbox*, which is shaped like a toolbox and has several removable cardboard tools inside, including a hammer, wrench, screwdriver, and saw.

Young people may be interested in learning how pop-up books work by exploring David A. Carter and James Diaz's *Elements of Pop-up*, which includes the elements and dimensions of pop-up and movable books by including many manipulative examples. Young people may also enjoy making their own pop-ups using the books of Joan Irvine, including *How to Make Pop-ups*, *How to Make Super Pop-ups*, and *How to Make Holiday Pop-ups.*

For kindergarten children Margaret W. Brown's *Goodnight Moon: A Pop-Up Book* demands participation in order to reveal recognizable settings from fiction. Older children will enjoy exploring Jan Pienkowski's *Haunted House* in which details are portrayed through pop-ups and movable flaps. Ann R. Montanaro's *Pop-up and Movable: A Bibliography, Supplement 1, 1991–1997* is a record of over 1,600 examples of nineteenth and twentieth century works.

Tragedy: A serious literary work in which a protagonist, who is neither all good nor all evil, moves from happiness to disaster that is not deserved; critically, one of the four modes or fundamental stories identified by Northrop Frye in *Anatomy of Criticism: Four Essays.* The term comes from the Greek *tragoidia*, which means goat song; and *tragedy* is probably associated with a sacrificial ritual. A reader of tragedy feels that the destruction of what is good, innocent, heroic, or beautiful should not happen; yet, the reader recognizes that events in life are not always reasonable or fair.

Tragedies range from the romantic to the ironic. A romantic tragedy presents the downfall of an innocent hero, such as in Hans Christian Andersen's "The Tin Soldier" or a biography of John F. Kennedy. Another kind of tragedy is a story of innocence confronting death as in Katherine Paterson's *Bridge to*

Terabithia in which Jess Aarons' best friend, Leslie, drowns. William Armstrong's *Sounder* presents a different kind of tragic hero in the character of a sharecropper who suffers an unjust and cruel imprisonment but never loses his human dignity.

Young people reading tragic stories may be encouraged to consider the importance of characterization over other literary elements. They may evaluate how the main character reacted to an unhappy or unfair outcome and how the character came to accept the inevitable.

Translation: The rewriting of a literary work from one language to another. The difficulties for any translator involve vocabulary, idiom, and syntax; and, therefore, works that are more poetic present the greater challenges. Translations may be literal (exactly word for word, including idioms, without regard for the emotional intent) or loose (spirit and tone emphasized rather than precision). An adaptation is a version that might incorporate major elements, such as setting, plot, and character, and that might retain the spirit of the original but that does not reflect the original language in any way.

In literature for young people, the best-known book translations into English are often those that have received the Batchelder Award, given annually by the Association for Library Service to Children to an American publisher for the outstanding book translated from another language into English. Details about the Batchelder Award and lists of award winners, as well as Batchelder Honor books, are at the American Library Association Web site (*www.ala.org/alsc/batch.html*). Recognition of translations is especially important in the United States where young people typically read only English.

A bilingual book has text in two languages within the same book. Bilingual books have become more numerous and popular in recent years, especially Spanish/English editions. Bilingual books in Spanish and English are eligible for the Pura Belpré Award, an example being Francisco X. Alarcón's *From the Bellybutton of the Moon and Other Summer Poems/Del Ombligo de la Luna y Otros poemas de verano*. Other Pura Belpré Award books are translations from English into another language; for example, the 2000 Honor Book for illustration, George Ancona's *Barrio: José's Neighborhood*. See *www.ala.org/alsc/belpre.html* for a complete listing of Pura Belpré Award books.

Young people will enjoy hearing and seeing the beauty of a translated book, read in both languages. The 1998 Pura Belpré Honor book by Silva Simón, *Gathering the Sun: an Alphabet in Spanish and English* is suitable for young children, and older children will relate to poetry from Juan Felipe Herrera's 2000 Pura Belpré Honor book *Laughing out Loud, I Fly: Poems in English and Spanish*.

Trickster Tale: A tale that features a rascal or rogue who plays tricks and outwits others. Tricksters familiar to most children include Brer Rabbit (African American), Jack (English and Appalachian), and Anansi the spider (West African, Gullah region of U.S., and Caribbean). First collected and published as Uncle Remus stories by Joel Chandler Harris (United States, 1848–1909), Brer Rabbit retellings and adaptations include *Jump! The Adventures of Brer Rabbit*, illustrated by Barry Moser; *Jump Again! More Adventures of Brer Rabbit*, illustrated by Barry Moser; *Jump on Over! The Adventures of Brer Rabbit and His Family*, illustrated by Barry Moser; and Julius Lester's *The Tales of Uncle Remus*, illustrated by Jerry Pinkney. The 1996 Caldecott Honor book, Janet Stevens' *Tops and Bottoms*, was based on Brer Rabbit and Jack tales. As is often found in trickster tales, the basic story, in this case "The Crop Division" tale, is adapted to different regions. Anansi tales include Eric A. Kimmel's retellings of *Anansi and the Talking Melon* and *Anansi and the Moss-Covered Rock*. Native Americans also have their trickster tales, and Gerald McDermott has retold and illustrated *Coyote: A Trickster Tale from the American Southwest* and *Raven: A Trickster Tale from the Pacific Northwest*. A professional resource is Ann Kraus' *Folktales Themes and Activities for Children*.

Young people enjoy reinterpreting trickster tales with creative dramatics, readers theatre, puppets, and storytelling activities. After a diverse sampling of trickster tales, young people may be encouraged to identify common elements shared across cultures.

Trilogy: A series of three literary works that are usually closely related with characters, setting, and theme; three connected dramas or musical compositions that are similar in subject.

A recent popular trilogy for older children is Phillip Pullman's "His Dark Materials" series. The first is *The Golden Compass*, which was followed by *The Subtle Knife* and *The Amber Spyglass*. Young people may listen to the Association for Library Service to Children's Notable Recording of *The Golden Compass*, narrated by the author with support from actors from the London stage. The recording is packaged in a set of eight audiocassettes (eleven hours).

Trochee: See *Meter*.

Typeface: Style of printed characters in the text, also referred to as type style in book publication. Word processing documents use the term *font*. In preparing a book for publication, the art editor or designer usually selects the typeface for the space allocated and for the appropriate look of the book. Typeface size is important in children's books and depends on the age level of the intended audience. "Children are surprisingly sensitive to typeface" (Horning, 1997: 6). They do not like a type that is too large, which implies "babyish," or too small, which looks "too hard." A special typeface was designed for use in *October 45: Childhood Memories of the War* by Jean-Louis Besson. Picture books often provide the style of typeface used on the title page verso or copyright page of the book.

Young people can be introduced to the concept of typeface with Roberto deVicq de Cumptich's *Bembo's Zoo: An Animal ABC Book*, an alphabet book that uses Bembo font style to create the illustrations. Young people can better understand the need for the typeface to be compatible with the story, the art medium, and style of illustrations by comparing the Caldecott Honor books of a given year (*e.g.*, Andrea Davis Pinkney's *Duke Ellington*, illustrated by Brian Pinkney; David Shannon's *No, David!*; Uri Shulevitz's *Snow;* and Peter Sís' *Tibet: Through the Red Box.* They may discuss the differences, and analyze and synthesize why each typeface was chosen.

Typography: The design, arrangement, and layout of type letter forms on a page. The term can also refer to the appearance, spacing, style, and size of the type fonts. The words on a printed page are important in children's books because their size often denotes reading level, *i.e.*, large size type is usually for younger children. Readability of the text is crucial. There should be enough space between lines, and the style of the font should not detract from the story.

Typography is a structural element that can impart shades of meaning to a story. For example, in the opening page of the 1943 Caldecott Award-winner Virginia Lee Burton's *The Little House*, the arrangement of the type is on a road up to the little house, and many of the other pages show the typeface sweeping toward the right. And, in Donald Crews' *Bigmama's* most of the type on the pages is flush left, but when the children return to Bigmama's house for the summer, the type on the page is placed with a graduated left margin to indicate movement of the children down the hallway. On a later page when the children are looking down a well to get a dipper full of water the typeface moves toward the right.

Word processing programs usually feature a variety of fonts, the ability to manipulate the font size, and special features to change the appearance of fonts (boldface and italics). Young people may be interested in experimenting with several font variations and their spacing of words on a page.

Understatement: A form of verbal irony in which the literal meaning falls short of the significance of what really is being said or is happening. The irony of minimizing the reality serves to accentuate it. A rich source of this figure of speech is Richard Peck's *A Long Way from Chicago* (Dial, 1998). In the first chapter, for example, Grandma uses a shotgun to blast the lid off a coffin in her living room as Effie flees for her life and the reporter dives out a window. Mary Alice thinks she has been killed, and, rather than acknowledge these events, Grandma turns around and matter-of-factly announces, "It's time you kids were in bed." Young people can appreciate the wit in Grandma's statement, and they can be encouraged to consider why the comment makes the scene even more humorous.

Video/Videotape: Recorded images on tape or an optical disc that can be viewed on either a television screen or with the assistance of a video projector. The Association for Library Service to Children (ALSC) denotes an award-winning list of children's videos each year. The ALSC evaluative criteria for selection of these videos appropriate for children through age 14 years old includes: (1) utilization of media; (2) technicality; (3) organization and appropriate treatment of material; (4) authenticity; and (5) subject matter of interest and value to children. Additional information can be found at *www.ala.org/alsc/notablevideo_terms.html*. A listing of the most recent Notable Children's Videos is located at *www.ala.org/alsc/awards.html#notable*. The ALSC also recognizes outstanding video production for children through the Andrew Carnegie Medal for Excellence in Children's Videos. Popular picture books are often adapted to video through techniques such as live action, puppets, animation, and iconography (the use of videotaped illustrations). An example of a successful adaptation is the 2001 Carnegie Award-winning production, *Antarctic Antics*, an animated rendering of Judy Sierra's children's poetry book of the same title. Young people may find more information about this award at *www.ala.org/alsc/carnegie.html*.

Activities for young people could involve comparisons of picture books with their video adaptations, analysis of the technique used in an adaptation, and discussion of how titles on the ALSC Notable Children's Video list meet selection criteria.

Visual Literacy: The skill that through combining vision competencies allows an individual to comprehend visual messages in a variety of forms *and* to creatively communicate images to others. The spectrum of visual skills needed both to understand and communicate visually correlates well with reading and writing abilities. Many aspects of visual awareness can be incorporated into children's literature experiences with picture books. For example: (1) Meaningful translation from the visual to the verbal can occur during a group discussion of the structural aspects of Lynd Ward's textless story *The Silver Pony*. The difficulties of translating visual to verbal are highlighted by Gerald McDermott in *Evolution of a Graphic Concept: The Stonecutter*. He first created this Japanese folktale as an animated film, then illustrated the book of *The Stonecutter*. Utilizing both sound filmstrip and book versions with upper grade children will also extend appreciation of symbolism in delivering a visual message. (2) Translation from verbal (book) to visual (video) occurs each time children are asked to illustrate a nursery rhyme or their favorite scene from a story. Young people may view a video production of a favorite folktale or novel and evaluate the translation from book to video. (3) Creating a new visual product may be stimulated by sharing William Steig's *CDB!*, second edition, and urging children to devise new rebus messages. A creative dramatics activity can follow the reading of Marie Hall Ets' *Play with Me* or improvised dance can be stimulated by George Shannon's *Dance Away*. (4) Developing environmental vision in order to understand and appreciate the beauties of nature can be assisted by sharing the photography of Henri Silberman in *Stone Bench in an Empty Park*, collected by Paul B. Janeczko, which should inspire child photographers to interpret their observations of natural beauty. They may also communicate further through original haiku. (5) The appreciation of masterworks of art may begin by sharing the variety of styles and techniques apparent in Caldecott Medal books.

Achieving visual literacy comes through many small steps in which children are provided opportunities for interpreting and communicating images.

Wash: A thin, translucent layer of pigment, usually watercolor, India ink or oil. Washes are often used as the background color for an illustration and are applied with large brush strokes as in a whitewash. This thin paint can also be used in soft applications of color daubed onto the surface. Maurice Sendak used watercolor wash and line drawings for the illustrations in his 1971 Caldecott Honor book, *In the Night Kitchen*. Rosemary Wells sometimes uses watercolor wash; a fine example is *Max's Dragon Shirt*. Don Freeman used pen and wash illustrations in full color for *A Pocket for Corduroy*; Sam McBratney used pen-and-ink line sketches filled in with full color watercolor wash in *Guess How Much I Love You*, illustrated by Anita Jeram; and True Kelley created the illustrations for *I've Got Chicken Pox* with cartoon style lines and watercolor-wash illustrations. Helen Oxenbury's set of board books: *All Fall Down, Clap Hands, Playing, Say Goodnight and Tickle, Tickle* incorporate line-and-wash illustrations. Oil washes comprised of transparent layers of paint were used by Floyd Cooper in *Coming Home: From the Life of Langston Hughes*. Betsy Lewin applied watercolor wash to black outline watercolor drawings that had been photographed for the illustrations in her 2001 Caldecott Honor book, *Click, Clack, Moo: Cows That Type*, by Doreen Cronin.

Young people may look at the illustrations in some of the children's books listed above and note the use of wash. Then they may create their own illustrations that incorporate this technique.

Watercolor: Paint made from pulverized pigment mixed in a water-soluble gum binder to which is added water. Being transparent, watercolor allows the paper to give highlights to a painting. A watercolor wash uses more water and is spread across the paper to create a thin translucent film. Watercolor is difficult to use and cannot be corrected as in oil painting, yet it is commonly used by illustrators because it can portray atmosphere, activities, people, landscapes, and animals. Watercolors are versatile, being light and airy or rich and vibrant. Watercolor has been the medium of choice for a number of picture book illustrators, including Judith St. George's *So You Want to Be President?*, illustrated by David Small; Kevin Henkes' *Wemberly Worried;* Elizabeth Howard's *Virgie Goes to School with Us Boys*, illustrated by E. B. Lewis; Simon James' *Days Like This. A Collection of Small Poems;* David Wiesner's *Sector 7;* Uri Shulevitz's *Snow;* Peggy Rathmann's *Officer Buckle and Gloria;* Allen Say's *Grandfather's Journey;* David Wiesner's *Tuesday;* and Jane Yolen's *Owl Moon*, illustrated by John Schoenherr.

Young people may be introduced to these examples of watercolor illustrations through a book display and by examining carefully one that appeals most to them. Those activities may be followed by a demonstration of watercolor painting by a local artist.

Wit and Humor: Elements of literature designed to amuse or evoke laughter. Wit, more specifically, is written or spoken language that is crafted to reveal the similarities in apparently dissimilar things. Calculated by its author to amuse and surprise, wit uses puns, paradoxes, clever wording, epigrams, and other literary devices. The laughter resulting from wit is intellectual and may be derisive. An example of wit in E. B. White's *Charlotte's Web,* is the sheep's observation that Templeton shares Wilbur's fate: "If Wilbur is killed and his trough stands empty day after day, you'll grow so thin we can look right through your stomach and see objects on the other side" (White, 1952: 99).

Humor, on the other hand, is expressed in appearances, behaviors, and comic words, which differ from the comic words in wit in that they are not necessarily recognized as amusing by the speaker. The amusement in humor results from a good-natured focus on human foibles. Often the human foible involves the reader's or one character's feelings of superiority over another character. For example, a reader, who assumes superiority, can laugh at the embarrassments that befall Betsy Byars' series character Bingo Brown. Summing up the essence of wit, Michael Cart quotes Lloyd Alexander: "Wit deals with ideas and humor deals with humanity. Wit is laughter of the mind; humor is laughter of the heart" in *What's So Funny?* (1995: 8).

Michael Cart's organizational approach (hyperbole and tall tale, family comedy, and talking animals) in *What's So Funny?* would be appropriate for the introduction of humor to young people. Hyperbole and tall tales could be introduced with works like Steven Kellogg's *Paul Bunyan, Johnny Appleseed, Pecos Bill,* and *Sally Ann Thunder Ann Whirlwind Crockett.* Family comedies could include those about series characters like Lois Lowry's Sam, Phyllis Reynolds Naylor's Alice, and Beverly Cleary's Ramona. Humorous stories to share about talking animals are Robert Lawson's *Rabbit Hill*; Tony Johnston's *The Iguana Brothers: A Tale of Two Lizards*, illustrated by Mark Teague; and Arnold Lobel's *Frog and Toad Are Friends*.

Woodcut: Block prepared for printing by carving a reverse image into an end of a block of hard wood. After the block is rolled with paint, it is pressed onto paper. The effect is rustic and seems old-fashioned. Comenius' *Orbis Pictus,* generally considered the first picture book for children, used woodcuts. In the early days of printing, woodcuts were generic and could be applied to multiple stories. Most early woodcut illustrations were not well done. However, Thomas Bewick (1753–1828) was considered a master of this art form (*The New Lottery Book of Birds and Beasts*).

Although not many illustrators use this method today, there are notable exceptions, including the 1999 Caldecott Medal-winner, Mary Azarian for Jacqueline Briggs' *Snowflake Bentley*. Mary Azarian's woodcuts have also been the illustration medium in Carol P. Saul's *Barn Cat* and *A Farmer's Alphabet*. Other excellent examples include the illustrations of Chris Manson in J. Patrick Lewis' *Black Swan White Crow*, of Arthur Geisert in *After the Flood*, of Keizaburo Tejima in *Fox's Dream*, of Ed Emberley in Barbara Emberley's *Drummer Hoff,* and of Marcia Brown in her classic *Once a Mouse*.

Children can enjoy the many picture books illustrated using this technique. Young people may experience the process by transposing a previously drawn design onto a sponge, cutting away the unnecessary parts, dipping the sponge lightly into tempera, pressing the design onto paper, and repeating the operation.

Wordless Book: A book format that tells a story through illustrations, not text. Stories for younger children make greater use of this genre in picture book format. For example, Jan Ormerod's *Moonlight* and *Sunshine* and Emily Arnold McCully's *School* and *Picnic* have made their stories a special treat for preschool and primary readers. Occasionally picture books will be nearly wordless, as is the case of David Wiesner's *Tuesday* and Peter Spier's *Noah's Ark*. Wiesner also won the 1989 Caldecott for his wordless book, *Free Fall*. Tomie de Paola's *Pancakes for Breakfast* and Pat Hutchins' *Changes, Changes* continue to be enjoyed by children. Tana Hoban is the master of the wordless concept book, such as *Colors Everywhere*. Mercer Mayer was one of the first to make use of the wordless book format in such works as *A Boy, A Dog, and a Frog*. Wordless books may also be intended for older readers, examples including books such as Lynn Ward's 175-page book *The Silver Pony*, Mitsumasa Anno's *Anno's Journey*, and Tom Feelings' *The Middle Passage: White Ships, Black Cargo*, which narrates through illustrations the horrific plight of Africans brought on slave ships to North America. A professional resource on wordless picture books is Katharyn Tuten-Puckett and Virginia H. Richey's *Using Wordless Picture Books: Authors and Activities*.

Young people may engage in verbal activities by telling aloud, taping, or writing their interpretations of wordless stories. Young people who may be challenged by a printed text can sometimes have special skills in reading pictures, and these books give them an opportunity to excel as they share insights and discuss interpretations.

Reference List

Adoff, Arnold. 1997. *Love Letters*. New York: Scholastic/Blue Sky Press.

Aliki. 1986. *How a Book Is Made*. New York: Crowell.

American Library Association. 2001. Caldecott Medal Home Page [Online]. Available: www.ala.org/alsc/caldecott.html [14 August 2001].

Babbitt, Natalie. 1975. *Tuck Everlasting*. New York: Farrar, Straus and Giroux.

Bierhorst, John. 1992. *Lightning Inside You and Other Native American Riddles*. New York: Beechtree.

Brooks, Cleanth, and Robert Penn Warren. 1959. *Understanding Fiction*. 2nd ed. New York: Appleton.

Byars, Betsy. 1968. *The Midnight Fox*. New York: Viking.

Campbell, Joseph, ed. 1976. *The Portable Jung*. New York: Viking Penguin.

Carlsen, G. Robert. 1980. *Books and the Teenage Reader: A Guide for Teachers, Librarians, and Parents*. New York: Harper & Row.

Cart, Michael. 1995. *What's So Funny? Wit and Humor in American Children's Literature*. New York: HarperCollins.

Chase, Richard. 1943. *The Jack Tales*. Boston: Houghton Mifflin.

The Chicago Manual of Style. 1993. Chicago: University of Chicago Press.

Dresang, Eliza T. 1999. *Radical Changes: Literature for Youth in an Electronic Age*. New York: H. W. Wilson.

Duvoisin, Roger. 1965. "Children's Book Illustration: The Pleasures and Problems." *Top of the News* 22 (November):22-23.

Harmon, William, and C. Hugh Holman. 2000. *A Handbook to Literature*. 8th ed. Upper Saddle River, N.J.: Prentice Hall.

Horning, Kathleen T. 1997. *From Cover to Cover: Evaluating and Reviewing Children's Books*. New York: HarperCollins.

Huck, Charlotte, Susan Hepler, Janet Hickman, and Barbara Z. Kiefer. 2001.

Children's Literature in the Elementary School. 7th ed. Dubuque, Iowa: McGraw Hill.

Lester, Julius. 2001. *Ackamarackus.* New York: Scholastic.

Lowry, Lois. 1989. *Number the Stars.* New York: Houghton Mifflin.

Lowry, Lois. 1997. *Stay!: Keepers Story.* New York: Houghton Mifflin.

McMillan, Bruce. 1996. *Jelly Beans for Sale.* New York: Scholastic.

Merriam, Eve. 1966. "I, Says the Poem." In *It Doesn't Always Have to Rhyme.* New York: Atheneneum.

Morner, Kathleen, and Ralph Rausch. 1991. *National Textbook Company's Dictionary of Literary Terms.* Lincolnwood, Ill.: NTC Publishing Group.

NCTE. 2000. Orbis Pictus Award Home Page [Online]. Available: www.ala.org/alsc/caldecott.html [14 August 2001].

Nilsen, Alleen Pace, and Kenneth L. Donelson. 2000. *Literature for Today's Young Adults.* 6th ed. New York: Longman.

Paulsen, Gary. 1989. *The Winter Room.* New York: Orchard.

Peck, Richard. 1998. *A Long Way from Chicago.* New York: Dial.

Rowling, J. K. 2000. *Harry Potter and the Goblet of Fire.* New York: Scholastic.

Sandburg, Carl. 1984. *Rainbows Are Made.* San Diego: Harcourt Brace.

Stevenson, Robert Louis. 1885. "Good and Bad Children." In *A Child's Garden of Verses.* n.p.

Stewig, John W. 1995. *Looking at Picture Books.* Fort Atkinson, Wisc.: Highsmith Press.

White, E.B. 1952. *Charlotte's Web.* New York: Harper & Row.

White, Mary Lou. 1976. *Children's Literature: Criticism and Response.* Columbus, Ohio: Merrill.

White, Ruth. 1996. *Belle Prater's Boy.* New York: Farrar, Straus and Giruox.

Withers, Carl. 1988. *A Rocket in My Pocket.* New York: Owlet.

Bibliography

Abrams, M. H. 1999. *A Glossary of Literary Terms.* 7th ed. Fort Worth, Tex.: Harcourt Brace.

Anderson, Vicki. 1998. *Sequels in Children's Literature: An Annotated Bibliography of Books in Succession, K-6.* Jefferson, N.C.: McFarland.

Arbuthnot, May Hill. 1976. *The Arbuthnot Anthology of Children's Literature.* 4th ed. Glenview, Ill.: Scott, Foresman.

Arbuthnot, May Hill. 1951. *Time for Poetry.* Chicago: Scott, Foresman.

Arnold, Matthew. 1977. "The Study of Poetry." In *Complete Prose Works,* B.H. Super, ed. Ann Arbor, Mich.: University of Michigan Press.

Asher, Sandy. 1996. *But That's Another Story: Favorite Authors Introduce Popular Genres.* New York: Walker.

Bader, Barbara. 1976. *American Picturebooks from Noah's Ark to the Beast Within.* New York: Macmillan.

Bader, Barbara. 2001. *The World in 32 Pages: One Hundred Years of American Picturebooks.* Delray Beach, Fla.: Winslow Press.

Barr, Catherine, ed. 1999. *Reading in Series: A Selection Guide to Books for Children.* New York: Bowker.

Beach, Richard. 1993. *A Teacher's Introduction to Reader Response Theories.* Urbana, Ill.: National Council of Teachers of English.

Beckman, Karl, and Arthur Ganz. 1989. *Literary Terms: A Dictionary.* New York: Noonday Press.

Berman, Art. 1988. *From the New Criticism to Deconstruction: The Reception of Structuralism and Post-Structuralism.* Urbana: University of Illinois Press.

Bodart, Joni. 1980. *Booktalk! Booktalking and School Visits for Young Adult Audiences.* New York: H.W. Wilson.

Bodart, Joni. *Booktalking with Joni Bodart.* Produced by Visual Education Corp. for H.W. Wilson. 25 min. H.W. Wilson, 1985. Videocassette.

Bodart, Joni. 2000. *The World's Best Thin Books: What to Read if Your Book Report Is Due Tomorrow.* Lanham, Md.: Scarecrow.

Brooks, Cleanth, and Robert Penn Warren. *Understanding Fiction.* 1959. New York: Appleton.

Campbell, Joseph. 1968. *The Hero with a Thousand Faces.* 2nd ed. Princeton, N.J.: Princeton University Press.

Campbell, Joseph, ed. 1976. *The Portable Jung.* New York: Viking Penguin.

Campbell, Joseph, and Bill Moyers. 1988. *The Power of Myth.* New York: Doubleday.

Carlsen, G. Robert. 1980. *Books and the Teenage Reader: A Guide for Teachers, Librarians, and Parents.* New York: Harper & Row.

Carpenter, Humphrey, and Mari Prichard. 1999. *The Oxford Companion to Children's Literature.* New York: Oxford University Press.

Cart, Michael. 1995. *What's So Funny? Wit and Humor in American Children's Literature.* New York: HarperCollins.

Carter, Betty, and Richard F. Abrahamson. 1990. *Nonfiction for Young Adults: From Delight to Wisdom.* Phoenix, Ariz.: Oryx.

Chase, Richard. 1943. *The Jack Tales.* Boston: Houghton Mifflin.

Cianciolo, Patricia J. 2000. *Informational Picture Books for Children.* Chicago: American Library Association.

Cianciolo, Patricia J. 1997. *Picture Books for Children.* 4th ed. Chicago: American Library Association.

Clarkson, Atelia, and Gilbert B. Cross, eds. 1980. *World Folktales.* New York: Scribner.

Coger, Leslie I., and Melvin R. White. 1982. *Readers Theatre Handbook: A Dramatic Approach to Literature.* Glenview, Ill.: Scott, Foresman.

Cooper, Cathie Hilterbran. 1996. *ABC Books and Activities: From Preschool to High School.* Lanham, Md.: Scarecrow.

Cooper, Cathie Hilterbran. 1997. *Counting Your Way Through 1-2-3: Books and Activities.* Lanham, Md.: Scarecrow.

Cuddon, J. A. 1998. *A Dictionary of Literary Terms and Literary Theory.* 4th ed. Malden, Mass.: Blackwell.

Cullinan, Bernice E., and Lee Galda. 1998. *Literature and the Child.* 4th ed. Fort Worth, Tex.: Harcourt Brace.

Curl, Michael. 1996. *The Anagram Dictionary.* London: Hale.

Davis, Robin. 1999. *Big Books for Little Readers.* Lanham, Md.: Scarecrow.

De Vries, Jan. 1963. *Heroic Song and Heroic Legend.* London: Oxford Press.

Doyle, Robert P. 2000. *Banned Books Resource Guide.* Chicago: American Library Association.

Dresang, Eliza T. 1999. *Radical Changes: Literature for Youth in an Electronic Age.* New York: H. W. Wilson.

Drury, John. 1995. *The Poetry Dictionary.* Cincinnati, Ohio: Story Press.

Duvoisin, Roger. 1965. "Children's Book Illustration: The Pleasures and Problems." *Top of the News* 22 (November):22-23.

Egoff, Sheila. 1988. *Worlds Within: Children's Fantasy from the Middle Ages to Today.* Chicago: American Library Association.

Egoff, Sheila, Gordon Stubbs, Ralph Ashley, and Wendy Sutton, eds. 1996. *Only Connect: Readings on Children's Literature.* 3rd ed. New York: Oxford University Press.

Ehresmann, Julia M. 1979. *The Pocket Dictionary of Art Terms.* 2nd ed. Boston: New York Graphic Society.

Ellis, John M. 1974. *The Theory of Literary Criticism: A Logical Analysis.* Berkeley, Calif.: University of California Press.

Freeman, Judy. 1995. *More Books Kids Will Sit Still For: A Read Aloud Guide.* New York: Bowker.

Frye, Northrop. 1957. *Anatomy of Criticism: Four Essays.* Princeton, N.J.: Princeton University Press.

Frye, Northrop. 1964. *The Educated Imagination.* Bloomington, Ind.: Indiana University Press.

Frye, Northrop, George Perkins, and Sheridan Baker. 1997. *The Harper Handbook to Literature.* New York: Longman.

Gillespie, John Thomas, and Corinne J. Naden. 1993. *Juniorplots 4: A Book Talk Guide for Use with Readers Ages 12-16.* New York: Bowker.

Gillespie, John Thomas, and Corinne J. Naden. 1994. *Middleplots 4: A Book Talk Guide for Use with Readers Ages 8-12.* 4th ed. New York: Bowker.

Gillespie, John Thomas, and Corinne J. Naden. 1989. *Seniorplots: A Book Talk Guide for Use with Readers Ages 15-18.* New York: Bowker.

Grimal, Pierre, ed. 1965. *Larousse World Mythology.* New York: Putnam.

Groden, Michael, and Martin Kreiswirth, eds. 1994. *The Johns Hopkins Guide to Literary Theory & Criticism.* Baltimore: Johns Hopkins University Press.

Guerin, Wilfred, et al. 1992. *A Handbook of Critical Approaches to Literature.* 3rd ed. New York: Oxford University Press.

Haines, Helen. 1950. *Living with Books: The Art of Book Selection.* New York: Columbia University Press.

Hall, Susan. 1990. *Using Picture Storybooks to Teach Literary Devices: Recommended Books for Children and Young Adults.* Phoenix, Ariz.: Oryx.

Hall, Susan. 1994. *Using Picture Storybooks to Teach Literary Devices: Recommended Books for Children and Young Adults.* Vol. 2. Phoenix, Ariz.: Oryx.

Hamilton, Martha, and Mitch Weiss. 2000. *Noodlehead Stories: World Tales Kids Can Learn and Tell*. Little Rock, Ark.: August House.

Harley, Avis. 2000. *Fly With Poetry: An ABC of Poetry*. Honesdale, Pa.: Wordsong/ Boyds Mills Press.

Harmon, William, and C. Hugh Holman. 1996. *Handbook to Literature*. 7th ed. Upper Saddle River, N.J.: Prentice Hall.

Harmon, William, and C. Hugh Holman. 2000. *A Handbook to Literature*. 8th ed. Upper Saddle River, N.J.: Prentice Hall.

Harris, Theodore, and Richard E. Hodges, eds. 1995. *The Literacy Dictionary: The Vocabulary of Reading and Writing*. Newark, Del.: International Reading Association.

Heathcote, Dorothy. 1976. *Drama as a Learning Medium*. Washington, DC: National Educational Association.

Hillman, Judith. 1995. *Discovering Children's Literature*. Englewood Cliffs, N.J.: Merrill.

Horning, Kathleen T. 1997. *From Cover to Cover: Evaluating and Reviewing Children's Books*. New York: HarperCollins.

Huck, Charlotte, Susan Hepler, Janet Hickman, and Barbara Z. Kiefer. 2001. *Children's Literature in the Elementary School*. 7th ed. Dubuque, Iowa: McGraw Hill.

Hunt, Peter.1991. *Criticism, Theory, and Children's Literature*. Cambridge, Mass.: Blackwell.

Hunt, Peter, ed. 1995. *Children's Literature: An Illustrated History*. New York: Oxford University Press.

Jacobs, James S., and Michael O. Tunnell. 1996. *Children's Literature, Briefly*. Englewood Cliffs, N.J.: Merrill.

Johnson, Paul. 1998. *A Book of One's Own: Developing Literacy through Making Books*. 2nd ed. Portsmouth, N.H.: Heinemann.

Jones, Patrick. 1998. *Connecting Young Adults and Libraries*. 2nd ed. New York: Neal-Schuman.

Kennedy, X. J., and Dana Gioia. 1999. *An Introduction to Fiction*. 7th ed. New York: Longman.

Kiefer, Barbara Z. 1995. *The Potential of Picture Books: From Visual Literacy to Artistic Understanding*. Englewood Cliffs, N.J.: Merrill.

Kimmel, Margaret Mary, and Elizabeth Segel. 1988. *For Reading Out Loud!* New York: Delacorte.

Kipfer, Barbara Ann, ed. 1993. *21st Century Synonym and Antonym Finder*. New York: Dell.

Knowles, Elizabeth, and Martha Smith. 1999. *More Reading Connections: Bringing Parents, Teachers and Librarians Together*. Englewood, Colo.: Libraries Unlimited.

Knowles, Elizabeth, and Martha Smith. 1997. *The Reading Connection: Bringing Parents, Teachers and Librarians Together.* Englewood, Colo.: Libraries Unlimited.

Kobrin, Beverly. 1995. *Eyeopeners II: Children's Books to Answer Children's Questions About the World Around Them.* New York: Scholastic.

Landow, George P., ed. 1994. *Hyper/Text/Theory/.* Baltimore: Johns Hopkins.

Langer, Judith A., ed. 1992. *Literature Instruction: A Focus on Student Response.* Urbana, Ill.: National Council of Teachers of English.

Latrobe, Kathy Howard, and Mildred Knight Laughlin. 1989. *Readers Theatre for Young Adults: Scripts and Script Development.* Englewood, Colo.: Teacher Ideas Press.

Lima, Carolyn W., and John A. Lima. 1998. *A to Zoo: Subject Access to Children's Picture Books.* 5th ed. New York: Bowker.

Lukens, Rebecca J. 1999. *A Critical Handbook of Children's Literature.* 6th ed. New York: Longman.

Lynch-Brown, Carol, and Carl M. Tomlinson. 1999. *Essentials of Children's Literature.* 3rd ed. Boston: Allyn and Bacon.

MacDonald, Margaret Read, and Brian W. Sturm. 2001. *The Storyteller's Sourcebook: A Subject, Title, and Motif Index to Folklore Collections for Children, 1983-1999.* Detroit: Gale Group.

Manna, Anthony L., and Carolyn S. Brodie, eds. 1997. *Art & Story: The Role of Illustration in Multicultural Literature for Youth.* Fort Atkinson, Wis.: Highsmith Press.

Marantz, Sylvia S., and Kenneth A. Marantz. 1995. *The Art of Children's Picture Books: A Selective Reference Guide.* 2nd ed. New York: Garland Publishing.

Marsh, Valerie. 1996. *Story Puzzles: Tales in the Tangram Tradition.* Fort Atkinson, Wis.: Alleyside.

May, Jill P. 1995. *Children's Literature and Critical Theory: Reading and Writing for Understanding.* New York: Oxford University Press.

McCaslin, Nellie. 1996. *Creative Drama in the Classroom and Beyond.* 6th ed. New York: Longman.

McCord, David. 1970. "Excerpts from 'Write Me Another Verse'." *Horn Book* 46 (August): 367-368.

Montanaro, Ann R. 2000. *Pop-Up and Movable: A Bibliography, Supplement 1, 1991-1997.* Metuchen, N.J.: Scarecrow.

Moore, John Noell. 1997. *Interpreting Young Adult Literature: Literary Theory in the Secondary Classroom.* Portsmouth, N.H.: Boynton/Cook.

Morner, Kathleen, and Ralph Rausch. 1991. *National Textbook Company's Dictionary of Literary Terms.* Lincolnwood, Ill.: NTC Publishing Group.

The Newbery and Caldecott Awards: A Guide to the Medal and Honor Books. 2000 ed. Chicago: Association for Library Service to Children, American Library Association.

Nikolajeva, Maria, and Carole Scott. 2001. *How Picturebooks Work*. New York: Garland.

Nilsen, Alleen Pace, and Kenneth L. Donelson. 2000. *Literature for Today's Young Adults*. 6th ed. New York: Longman.

Nodelman, Perry. 1992. *The Pleasures of Children's Literature*. New York: Longman.

Nodelman, Perry. 1988. *Words About Pictures: The Narrative Art of Children's Picture Books*. Athens, Ga.: University of Georgia Press.

Norton, Donna E. 1995. *Through the Eyes of a Child: An Introduction to Children's Literature*. 4th ed. Englewood Cliffs, N.J.: Merrill.

Opie, Iona, and Peter Opie, eds. 1992, 1947. *I Saw Esau: The School Child's Pocket Book*. Cambridge, Mass.: Candlewick.

Opie, Iona, and Peter Opie, eds. 1977. *The Oxford Dictionary of Nursery Rhymes*. New York: Oxford University Press.

Opie, Iona, and Peter Opie, eds. 1955. *The Oxford Nursery Rhyme Book*. New York: Oxford University Press.

Preminger, Alex, and T.V.F. Brogan, eds. 1993. *The New Princeton Encyclopedia of Poetry and Poetics*. Princeton, N.J.: Princeton University Press.

Ransom, John Crowe. 1979, 1941. *The New Criticism*. Westport, Conn.: Greenwood.

Rodale, J. I. 1986. *Synonym Finder*. New York: Warner.

Rosenblatt, Louise M. 1993. "The Literary Transaction and Response." In *Journeying: Children Responding to Literature*, Kathleen E. Holland, Rachel Hungerford, and Shirley B. Ernst, eds. Portsmouth, N.H.: Heinemann.

Rosenblatt, Louise M. 1938. *Literature as Exploration*. New York: Modern Language Association.

Russell, David L. 2001. *Literature for Children: A Short Introduction*. 4th ed. New York: Longman.

Sadler, Glenn Edward, ed. 1992. *Teaching Children's Literature: Issues, Pedagogy, Resources*. New York: Modern Language Association of America.

Saussure, Ferdinand de. 1997. *Saussure's Second Course of Lectures on General Linguistics (1908-1909): From the Notebooks of Albert Riedlinger and Charles Patois*. 2nd ed. Oxford [England]: Pergamon.

Savage, John F. 2000. *For the Love of Literature: Children & Books in the Elementary Years*. Boston: McGraw Hill.

Shulevitz, Uri. 1997. *Writing with Pictures: How to Write and Illustrate Children's Books*. New York: Watson-Guptill.

Silvey, Anita, ed. 1995. *Children's Books and Their Creators*. Boston: Houghton Mifflin.

Sloan, Glenna. 1991. *The Child as Critic: Teaching Literature in Elementary and Middle Schools.* 3rd ed. New York: Teachers College Press.

Smith, Ray. 2000. *The Artist's Handbook.* New York: Knopf.

Something About the Author. 1971-. Detroit: Gale Research.

Something About the Author: Autobiography Series. 1986-. Detroit: Gale Research.

"Special Issue: Picture Books." *The Horn Book Magazine 74* (March/April): 141–206.

Staerkel, Kathleen, Nancy Hackett, and Linda Ward Callaghan. 1994. *The Newbery & Caldecott Mock Election Kit: Choosing Champions in Children's Books.* Chicago: Association for Library Service to Children, American Library Association.

Stewig, John W. 1995. *Looking at Picture Books.* Fort Atkinson, Wis.: Highsmith Press.

Sutherland, Zena. 1997. *Children and Books.* 9th ed. New York: Longman.

Thomas, Rebecca L. 1989. *Primary Plots: A Book Talk Guide for Use with Readers Ages 4-8.* New York: Bowker.

Thomas, Rebecca L.1993. *Primary Plots 2: A Book Talk Guide for Use with Readers Ages 4-8.* New York: Bowker.

Thompson, Stith. 1977. *The Folktale.* Berkeley: University of California Press.

Thompson, Stith. 1955. *Motif-Index for Folk-Literature.* 6 Vols. Bloomington, Ind.: Indiana University Press.

Tixier, Diana Herald. 2000. *Genreflecting.* Englewood, Colo.: Libraries Unlimited.

Tomlinson, Carl M., ed. 1998. *Children's Books from Other Countries.* Lanham, Md.: Scarecrow Press.

Trelease, Jim. 1992. *Hey, Listen to This! Stories to Read Aloud.* New York: Penguin.

Trelease, Jim. 1993. *Read All about It: Great Read-Aloud Stories, Poems and News-paper Articles for Preteens and Teens.* New York: Penguin.

Trelease, Jim. 1995. *The Read-Aloud Handbook.* 4th ed. New York: Penguin.

Trelease, Jim. 2001. *The Read-Aloud Handbook.* 5th ed. New York: Penguin.

Vandergrift, Kay. 1986. *Child and Story.* New York: Neal-Schuman.

Vandergrift, Kay. 1990. *Children's Literature: Theory, Research, and Teaching.* Englewood, Colo.: Libraries Unlimited.

Volz, Bridget Dealy. 2000. *Junior Genreflecting: A Guide to Good Reads and Series Fiction for Children.* Englewood, Colo.: Libraries Unlimited.

von Franz, Marie-Luise. 1997. *Archetypal Patterns in Fairy Tales.* Toronto: Inner City Books.

Vygotsky, Lev. 1986. *Thought and Language.* Translated by Alex Kozulin. Cambridge, Mass.: MIT Press.

Wachowiak, Frank. 1997. *Emphasis ART: A Qualitative Art Program for Elementary and Middle Schools.* 6th ed. New York: Longman.

What Do I Read Next? 1993. Detroit: Gale.

White, Mary Lou. 1976. *Children's Literature: Criticism and Response.* Columbus, Ohio: Merrill.

Wilson, Elizabeth B. 1994. *Bibles and Bestiaries: A Guide to Illuminated Manuscripts.* New York: Farrar, Straus and Giroux.

Yenawine, Philip. 1995. *Key Art Terms for Beginners.* New York: Abrams.

Yolen, Jane. 2000. *Touch Magic: Fantasy, Faerie and Folklore in the Literature of Childhood.* Little Rock, Ark.: August House.

Young, Sue. 1994. *The Scholastic Rhyming Dictionary.* New York: Scholastic.

Entries Arranged by Subject

Pura Belpré Award
Randolph Caldecott Medal
Robert F. Sibert Informational Book
  Award
Scott O'Dell Award for Historical
  Fiction

CRITICISM

Archetypal Criticism
Biographical Criticism
Classic
Convention
Criticism
Formalism
Genre
Mode
Psychological Criticism
Radical Change
Reader Response Theory
Sociological Criticism
Structural Criticism
Touchstone

FORMAT

Battledore
Big Book
Board Book
Book
Book on Tape
Book Size
CD-ROM
Chapbook
Chapter Book
Comic Strip
Easy Reader/Beginning Reader
Format
Graphic Novel
Hornbook

Illustrated Book
Picture Book
Toy Book or Pop-Up Book or Movable
  Book
Video/Videotape

ILLUSTRATION

Acetate
Aesthetic Scanning
Airbrush
Balance
Batik
Block Printing
Calligraphy
Cartoon
Collage
Color
Color Separation
Computer Generated Graphics
Decorative Frame
Die-Cutting
Double Spread or Double-page Spread
Drawing
Dummy
Embroidered Pictures
Endpapers
Etching
Fabric Relief
Graphic Art
Graphic Design
Gutter
Hand-Lettering
Hatching
Illustrator
Linoleum Block (Printing)
Lettrism
Lithograph
Mixed Media
Origami

Paper Cuts or Paper Cutting
Perspective
Photography
Potato Printing
Pulp Painting
Rebus
Scratchboard
Storyboard
Wash
Woodcut

LITERARY AND ARTISTIC MOVEMENTS

Abstract Art
Expressionism
Folk Art
Impressionism
Photo Realistic Art
Pointillism
Realistic Art
Realistic Fiction
Surrealism

NARRATIVE ELEMENTS

Analogy
Antagonist
Anthropomorphism
Archetype
Atmosphere
Character
Characterization
Cliff-Hanger
Climax
Closed Ending
Coincidence
Colloquialism
Comic Relief
Complication

Conflict
Denouement
Dialect
Dialogue
Didacticism
Episodic Plot
Exposition
Falling Action
Figurative Language
Flashback
Flat Character
Foil
Foreshadowing
Imagery
Irony
Metaphor
Mood
Motif
Nostalgia
Omniscient Point of View
Onomatopoeia
Open Ending
Plot
Poetic Justice
Point of View
Progressive Plot
Protagonist
Refrain
Resolution
Rising Action
Round Character
Setting
Simile
Static Character
Stereotype
Stock Character
Style
Subplot
Suspension of Disbelief
Symbol

Theme
Tone
Understatement
Wit and Humor

NARRATIVE TYPES

Adventure Story
Allegory
Alphabet Book
Arthurian Legends
Autobiography
Beast Fable
Bestiary
Bildungsroman
Biography
Cautionary Tale
Collected Biography
Comedy
Concept Book
Contemporary Realistic Fiction
Counting Book
Cumulative Tale
Detective Story
Diary
Dime Novel
Documentary Novel
Fable
Fairy Tale
Fantasy
Fiction
Fictional Biography
Folklore
Folktale
Formula
Fractured Tale
Framework Story
Gothic Novel
Historical Fiction
Information Book

Irony/Satire
Legend
Letter
Literary Tale
Magical Realism
Mystery
Myth
Nonlinear Text
Noodlehead Story
Novella
Pageant
Parody
Pattern Book
Photo Essay
Picture Book
Pourquoi Tale
Predictable Book
Problem Novel
Prose
Proverb
Regional Literature
Retelling
Romance
Satire
Science Fiction
Short Story
Survival Story
Tall Tale
Tragedy
Trickster Tale
Wordless Book

POETRY – ELEMENTS

Alliteration
Allusion
Assonance
End Rhyme
Imagery
Internal Rhyme

Meter
Refrain
Rhyme
Stanza

POETRY – FORMS

Anthem
Ballad
Chant
Cinquain
Clerihew
Concrete Poetry
Couplet
Epic
Folk Song
Free Verse
Haiku
Limerick
Lullaby
Lyric
Narrative Poetry
Nonsense Verse
Nursery Rhymes
Poetry
Spiritual
Tercet
Terse Verse

PUBLISHING

Abridgement
Adaptation
Afterward
Annotation
Anthology
Author
Bibliography
Binding
Blurb

Book Review
Censorship
Copyright
Dedication
Edition
Editor
Epigraph
Epilogue
Glossary
International Standard Book Number
    (ISBN)
Page Layout
Prequel
Pseudonym
Series
Subtitle
Translation
Trilogy
Typeface
Typography

WORDS AND WORDPLAY

Acrostic
Anagram
Briticism
Connotation (see Denotation)
Denotation
Dictionary
Eponym
Homonym
Hyperbole
Idiom
Lexicon
Palindromes
Personification
Pun
Riddle
Synonym
Tongue Twister

Title Index

Title	Author	Publisher/Producer	Term(s)
1 2 3 Pop!	Isadora, Rachel	Viking, 1999	computer-generated graphics
21st Century Synonym and Antonym Finder	Kipfer, Barbara Ann	Dell, 1993	synonym
26 Fairmont Avenue	DePaola, Tomie	Putnam, 1999	reading aloud
26 Letters and 99 Cents	Hoban, Tana	Greenwillow, 1987	counting book
500 Hats of Bartholomew Cubbins	Dr. Seuss	Random House, 1938	comedy
A. Nonny Mouse Writes Again!	Prelutsky, Jack	Knopf, 1993	pseudonym
A-Apple Pie	Pearson, Tracey Campbell	Putman Penguin, 1986	dictionary
Aardvarks, Disembark!	Jonas, Ann	Greenwillow, 1990	double spread
ABC Books and Activities: From Preschool to High School	Cooper, Cathie Hilterbran	Scarecrow, 1996	alphabet book
ABC Pop	Isadora, Rachel	Viking, 1999	computer-generated graphics
Abel's Island	Steig, William	Farrar, Straus & Giroux, 1976	adventure story, romance
Abraham Lincoln	D'Aulaire, Ingri and Edgar Parin	Doubleday, 1939	lithograph
Absentminded Fellow	Marshak, Samuel	Farrar, Straus & Giroux, 1999	cartoon
Ackamarackus	Lester, Julius	Scholastic, 2001	figurative language
Adventures of Robin Hood	Williams, Marcia	Candlewick, 1997	Arthurian legends
Aesop's Fables	Hague, Michael	Holt, Rinehart, Winston, 1985	fable
Aesop's Fables	Paxton, Tom	Morrow, 1988	beast fable

Title	Author	Publisher/Producer	Term(s)
After the Flood	Geisert, Arthur	Houghton Mifflin, 1994	woodcut
Alan Mendelsohn, the Boy from Mars	Pinkwater, Daniel	Dutton, 1978	science fiction
Alexander and the Wind-Up Mouse	Lionni, Leo	Knopf, 1969	character
Alice in Wonderland	Carroll, Lewis	Macmillan, 1950, 1866	classic
Alice Series	Naylor, Phyllis Reynolds	Atheneum	contemporary realistic fiction, series
Alice's Adventures Under Ground	Carroll, Lewis	Holt, Rinehart and Winston, 1985	edition
Aliens Ate My Homework	Coville, Bruce	Simon & Schuster, 1993	science fiction
Aliens in the Family	Mahy, Margaret	Scholastic, 1986	science fiction
Alison's Zinnia	Lobel, Anita	Greenwillow, 1990	alliteration
All Fall Down	Oxenbury, Helen	Dutton, 1994	wash
All Night, All Day—A Child's First Book of African-American Spirituals	Bryan, Ashley	Atheneum, 1991	spiritual
All the Places to Love	MacLachlan, Patricia	HarperCollins, 1994	realistic art
All the Small Poems and Fourteen More	Worth, Valerie	Farrar, Straus & Giroux, 1994	analogy
Alphabatics	MacDonald, Suse	Simon & Schuster, 1986	alphabet book
Alphabet City	Johnson, Stephen T.	Viking, 1995	alphabet book, double spread, hand-lettering, photo realistic art, picture book

Title	Author	Publisher/Producer	Term(s)
Always My Dad	Wyeth, Sharon Dennis	Knopf, 1995	impressionism
Always Room for One More	Leodhas, Sorche Nic	Henry Holt, 1965	hatching
Amazing Christmas Extravaganza	Shannon, David	Blue Sky, 1995	decorative frame
Amazing Grace	Hoffman, Mary	Dial, 1991	realistic art
Amazing Life of Benjamin Franklin	Giblin, James Cross	Scholastic, 2000	oil paint
Amber Spyglass	Pullman, Phillip	Knopf, 2000	trilogy
Amelia Bedelia	Parrish, Peggy	Harper, 1963	fantasy
American Girls Premier	The Learning Co.	The Learning Co., 1988	CD-ROM
Anagram Dictionary	Curl, Michael	Robert Hale, Ltd., 1996	anagram
Anansi and the Moss-Covered Rock	Kimmel, Eric A.	Holiday, 1988	trickster tale
Anansi and the Talking Melon	Kimmel, Eric A.	Holiday, 1993	trickster tale
Anastasia Series	Lowry, Lois	Houghton Mifflin	contemporary realistic fiction, series
Anatole and the Cat	Titus, Eve	McGraw, 1958	India ink
And the Green Grass Grew All Around: Folk Poetry from Everyone	Schwartz, Alvin	HarperCollins, 1999	stanza
Animal Farm	Orwell, George	Turtleback Books, 1954	allegory
Animalia	Base, Graeme	Henry Abrams, 1986	alphabet book
Animals of the Bible	Fish, Helen Dean	Lippincott, 1937	lithograph

Title	Author	Publisher/Producer	Term(s)
Anna Banana: 101 Jump-Rope Rhymes	Cole, Joanna	Beechtree, 1991	chant
Anne of Green Gables Series	Montgomery, Lucy Maud	Bantam, 1991	series
Anno's Aesop	Anno, Mitsumasa	Orchard, 1989	fable
Anno's Journey	Anno, Mitsumasa	Collins-World, 1978	wordless book
Annotated Mother Goose	Baring-Gould, William	Crown, 1988	nursery rhymes
Antarctic Antics	Sierra, Judy	Harcourt Brace, 1998	video/videotape
Antics!	Hepworth, Cathi	Putnam, 1992	dictionary, pastels
Appalachia: Voices of Sleeping Birds	Rylant, Cynthia	Harcourt Brace Jovanovich, 1991	biographical criticism, regional literature
Apples	Gibbons, Gail	Holiday, 2000	book size, graphic design
Apples, Alligators and also Alphabets	Johnson, Bruce	Oxford University, 1990	alliteration
April Wilson's Magpie Magic	Wilson, April	Dial, 1999	perspective
Archetypal Patterns in Fairy Tales	Von Franz, Marie-Luise	Inner City, 1997	archetype
Arctic Antics	Weston Woods	Weston Woods, 2000	video/videotape
Ark	Geisert, Arthur	Houghton Mifflin, 1988	etching, modeling clay
Arnold Lobel Book of Mother Goose: A Treasury of More Than 300 Classic Nursery Rhymes	Lobel, Arnold	Random House, 1997, 1986	nursery rhymes
Arrow to the Sun	McDermott, Gerald	Viking, 1974	collage

Title	Author	Publisher/Producer	Term(s)
Arthur and the Sword	Sabuda, Robert	Atheneum, 1995	Arthurian legends
Ashanti to Zulu: African Traditions	Musgrove, Margaret	Dial, 1976	alphabet book
Asleep, Asleep	Ginsburg, Mira	Greenwillow, 1992	pastels
Athletic Shorts	Crutcher, Chris	Greenwillow, 1991	short story
Autumn: An Alphabet Acrostic	Schnur, Steven	Clarion, 1997	acrostic
Baboushka and the Three Kings	Sidajakov, Nicolas	Parnassus, 1960	tempera
Babysitting Is a Dangerous Job	Roberts, Willo	Atheneum, 1987	mystery
Bad Day at Riverbend	Van Allsburg, Chris	Houghton Mifflin, 1995	crayon
Bad-Tempered Ladybird	Carle, Eric	Hamish Hamilton, 1978	Briticism
Bag I'm Taking to Grandma	Neitzel, Shirley	Greenwillow, 1995	rebus
Baker Street Irregulars Series	Dicks, Terrance	Elsevier/Nelson	detective story
Ballad of the Pirate Queens	Yolen, Jane	Harcourt Brace, 1995	refrain
Barn Cat	Saul, Carol P.	Little, Brown, 2000	woodcut
Barrio: José's Neighborhood	Ancona, George	Harcourt Brace, 1998	translation
Baseball in April	Soto, Gary	Harcourt Brace Jovanovich, 1991	short story
Bat 6	Wolff, Virginia Euwer	Scholastic, 1998	atmosphere, nonlinear text, radical change
Because of Winn-Dixie	Di Camillio, Kate	Candlewick, 2000	contemporary realistic fiction
Beezus and Ramona	Cleary, Beverly	Morrow, 1955	episodic plot

Title	Author	Publisher/Producer	Term(s)
Belle Prater's Boy	White, Ruth	Farrar, Straus & Giroux, 1996	cliff-hanger, closed ending, flashback, hyperbole, plot, psychological criticism, onomatopoeia
Belling the Cat: And Other Aesop's Fables	Paxton, Tom	Macmillan, 1987	beast fable
Bells of London	Wolff, Ashley	Dodd, Mead, 1985	linoleum block
Bembo's Zoo: An Animal ABC	De Cumptich, Roberto de Vicq	Henry Holt, 2000	alphabet book, letterism, typeface
Ben and Me	Lawson, Robert	Little, Brown, 1939	fictional biography, proverb
Ben's Trumpet	Isadora, Rachel	Greenwillow, 1979	India ink
Berlioz the Bear	Brett, Jan	Putnam, 1991	decorative frame
Best of Aesop	Clark, Margaret	Little Brown, 1990	beast fable
Best Town in the World	Baylor, Byrd	Macmillan, 1983	theme
Best Wishes	Rylant, Cynthia	Owen, 1992	autobiography, biographical criticism
Bestiary: An Illuminated Alphabet of Medieval Beasts	Hunt, John	Simon & Schuster, 1998	bestiary
Bibles and Bestiaries: A Guide to Illuminated Manuscripts	Wilson, Elizabeth	Pierpont Morgan Library and Farrar, Straus and Giroux, 1994	bestiary
Big Books for Little People	Davis, Robin	Scarecrow, 1999	big book
Big Fat Hen	Baker, Keith	Harcourt Brace, 1994	counting book

Title	Author	Publisher/Producer	Term(s)
Big Fat Worm	Van Laan, Nancy	Knopf, 1987	cumulative tale
Big Talk: Poems for Four Voices	Fleischman, Paul	Candlewick, 2000	choral speaking
Biggest Bear	Ward, Lynd	Houghton Mifflin, 1952	foreshadowing
Bigmama's	Crews, Donald	Greenwillow, 1991	typography
Bill Peet: An Autobiography	Peet, Bill	Houghton Mifflin, 1989	autobiography
Birthday Surprises: Ten Great Stories to Unwrap	Hurwitz, Johanna	Morrow, 1995	short story
Black and White	Macaulay, David	Houghton Mifflin, 1990	gouache, nonlinear text, parallel story
Black Cowboy, Wild Horses	Lester, Julius	Dial, 1998	drawing
Black Swan White Crow	Lewis, J. Patrick	Atheneum, 1995	woodcut
Blizzard! The Storm That Changed America	Murphy, Jim	Scholastic, 2000	sepia
Blue Willow	Gates, Doris	Viking, 1940	regional literature
Bodies from the Bog	Deem, James M.	Houghton Mifflin, 1998	page layout
Bone Detectives: How Forensic Anthropologists Solve Crimes and Uncover Mysteries of the Dead	Jackson, Donna M.	Little, Brown, 1996	detective story, photo essay
Book	Brookfield, Karen	Dorling Kindersley, 2000	book
Book of Nonsense	Lear, Edward	Everyman's Library, 1992	limerick, narrative poetry
Books and the Teenage Reader	Carlsen, G. Robert	Harper & Row, 198	classic, science fiction

Title	Author	Publisher/Producer	Term(s)
Bootmaker and the Elves	Lowell, Susan	Orchard, 1997	fractured tale
Bourgeois Gentleman	Moliere	Ivan R. Dee, 2000	prose
Boy, a Dog and a Frog	Mercer, Mayor	Dial, 1967	wordless book
Bread Bread Bread	Morris, Ann	Mulberry Big Books/ William Morrow, 1993	big book
Brian's Return	Paulsen, Gary	Delacorte, 1999	sequel
Brian's Winter	Paulsen, Gary	Delacorte, 1996	sequel
Bridge to Terabithia	Paterson, Katherine	Harper, 1977	censorship, conflict, poetic justice, round character, tragedy
Bright and Early Thursday Evening: A Tangled Tale	Wood, Audrey	Harcourt Brace, 1996	computer-generated graphics
Brown Angels: An Album of Pictures and Verse	Myers, Walter Dean	HarperCollins, 1993	sepia
Brown Bear, Brown Bear	Martin, Bill	Henry Holt, 1983	pattern book, predictable book
Brown Bear, Brown Bear (Board book)	Martin, Bill	Holt, 1996	board book
Brown Noney and Broomwheat Tea	Thomas, Joyce Carol	HarperCollins, 1993	oil paint
Bud, Not Buddy	Curtis, Christopher Paul	Delacorte, 1999	character, historical fiction, progressive plot, reading aloud, romance

Title	Author	Publisher/Producer	Term(s)
Bud, Not Buddy (book on tape)	Curtis, Christopher Paul	Listening Library, 2000	book on tape
Buffalo Days	Hoyt-Goldsmith, Diane	Holiday, 1997	photo essay
Building Big	Macaulay, David	Houghton Mifflin, 2000	drawing
Bull Run	Fleischman, Paul	HarperCollins, 1993	nonlinear text, radical change
Busy Year	Lionni, Leo	Scholastic, 1994	big book
But I'll Be Back Again	Rylant, Cynthia	Orchard, 1989	biographical criticism
But That's Another Story: Favorite Authors Introduce Popular Genres	Asher, Sandy	Walker, 1996	genre
Butterfly Alphabet	Sandved, Kjell	Scholastic, 1996	alphabet book
By the Dawn's Early Light: The Story of the Star-Spangled Banner	Kroll, Stephen	Scholastic, 1994	anthem
Cajun Night Before Christmas	Trosclair, Howard (editor)	Pelican, 1992	dialect, parody
Caldecott Celebration: Six Artists Share Their Paths to the Caldecott Medal	Marcus, Leonard	Walker & Company, 1998	illustrator
Calligraphy	Campbell, Fiona	Children's Press, 1998	calligraphy
Can't Sit Still	Lotz, Karen E.	Econoclad, 1999	pointillism
Canterbury Tales	Cohen, Barbara	Lothrop, Lee & Shepard, 1988	bowdlerize
Canterbury Tales	McCaughrean, Geraldine	Oxford University, 1999	bowdlerize
Carmen Sandiego Math Detective	Broderbund	Broderbund, 1999	CD-ROM
Carnaval	Ancona, George	Harcourt Brace, 1999	photography

Title	Author	Publisher/Producer	Term(s)
Carousel	Crews, Donald	Morrow, 1982	photography
Carrot Seed	Krauss, Ruth	Harper & Row, 1945	predictable book
Casey at the Bat: A Ballad of the Republic Sung in the Year 1888	Thayer, Ernest	Handprint, 2000	ballad, computer-generated graphics, framework story
Casey at the Bat: A Ballad of the Republic, Sung in 1888	Polacco, Patricia	Putnam, 1992; Star, 1997	narrative poetry
Castle	Macaulay, David	Houghton Mifflin, 1978	drawing, hatching, India ink
Castle of Otranto: A Gothic Story	Walpole, Horace	1764	gothic novel
Cat in the Hat	Dr. Seuss	Random House, 1957	easy reader
Cat in the Hat	Dr. Seuss	Broderbund, 1997	CD-ROM
Cathedral: The Story of Its Construction	Macaulay, David	Houghton Mifflin, 1973	drawing, hatching, India ink
Catherine Called Birdy	Cushman, Karen	Clarion, 1994	diary
Cats are Cats	Larrick, Nancy	Philomel, 1988	charcoal
Cay	Taylor, Theodore	Doubleday, 1969	prequel
CDB!	Steig, William	Simon & Schuster, 2000	visual literacy
Celebrations	Livingston, Myra Cohn	Holiday, 1985	tone
Cendrillon: A Caribbean Cinderella	San Souci, Daniel	Simon & Schuster, 1998	folktale
Chair for My Mother	Williams, Vera B.	Greenwillow, 1982	expressionism
Changes, Changes	Hutchins, Pat	Macmillan, 1971	wordless book

Title	Author	Publisher/Producer	Term(s)
Chanticleer and the Fox	Cooney, Barbara	Crowell, 1958	bowdlerize
Chanticleer and the Fox: A Chaucerian Tale	Roberts, Fulton	Disney, 1991	bowdlerize
Charlie Parker Played Be Bop	Raschka, Chris	Orchard, 1992	charcoal
Charlotte's Web	White, E. B.	Harper & Row, 1952	classic, climax, comedy, fantasy, flat character, foil, irony, omniscient point of view, reading aloud, static character, suspension of disbelief, theme, touchstone, wit and humor
Chato and the Party Animals	Soto, Gary	Putnam, 2000	glossary
Chato's Kitchen	Soto, Gary	Putnam, 1995	expressionism
Chicago Manual of Style	Grossman, John	University of Chicago, 1993	bibliography
Chicka Chicka Boom Boom	Archambault, John and Bill Martin	Simon & Schuster, 1989	alphabet book
Chicka Chicka Boom Boom	Martin, Bill and John Archambault	Simon & Schuster, 1989	choral speaking
Chicken Soup with Rice	Maurice Sendak	Scholastic, 1986	big book
Child's Bestiary	Gardner, John	Knopf, 1977	bestiary
Child's Book of Lullabies	McKellar, Shona	Dorling Kindersley, 1997	lullaby
Child's Celebration of Folk Music	Sendak, Maurice	Warner Bros.	folk song

Title	Author	Publisher/Producer	Term(s)
Child's Collection of Lullabies	Shona McKellar	Dorling Kindersley, 1997	lullaby
Child's Garden of Verses	Stevenson, Robert Louis	Vermilion, 1996	didacticism, stereotype
Child's Good Night Book	Brown, Margaret Wise	Schott, 1943	crayon
Chocolate War	Cormier, Robert	Pantheon, 1974	antagonist
Choose Your Own Adventure Series	Various	Bantam	adventure story
Christmas Alphabet	Sabuda, Robert	Little, Simon, 1994	toy book
Chronicles of Narnia	Lewis, C.S.	Macmillan	allegory, fantasy
Chuck Close, Up Close	Greenberg, Jan and Sandra Jordan	Dorling Kindersley, 1998	photo realistic art
Cinder Edna	Jackson, Ellen	Lothrop, Lee & Shepard, 1994	fractured tale
Cinderella	Perrault, Charles	Scribner, 1954	archetype, folktale
Cinderella: Or, the Little Glass Slipper	Brown, Marcia	Scribner, 1954	illustrator
Cinderella's Rat	Meddaugh, Susan	Houghton Mifflin, 1997	fractured tale
Cinder-Elly	Minters, Frances	Viking, 1994	fractured tale
Cindy Ellen: A Wild Western Cinderella	Lowell, Susan	HarperCollins, 2000	fractured tale
Circlemaker	Schur, Maxine	Dial, 1994	survival story
Circles, Triangles, and Squares	Hoban, Tana	Macmillan, 1974	concept
Clap Hands	Oxenbury, Helen	Dutton, 1994	wash

Title	Author	Publisher/Producer	Term(s)
Clap Your Hands	Cauley, Lorinda Bryan	Putnam, 1992	participation book
Cleopatra	Stanley, Diane	Morrow, 1994	biography
Click Clack Moo: Cows that Type	Cronin, Doreen	Simon & Schuster, 2000	cartoon, wash
Coffin in the Case	Bunting, Eve	HarperCollins, 1992	mystery
Color Dance	Jonas, Ann	Greenwillow, 1989	color
Color Farm	Ehlert, Lois	Lippincott, 1990	color, die-cutting
Color Zoo	Ehlert, Lois	Lippincott, 1989	color, concept, die-cutting, picture book
Color, Color, Color	Heller, Ruth	Putnam, 1995	color separation
Colors Everywhere	Hoban, Tana	Greenwillow, 1995	color, wordless book
Come to My Party	Richardson, Judith Benet	Macmillan, 1993	fabric relief
Coming Home: From the Life of Langston Hughes	Cooper, Floyd	Philomel, 1994	wash
Complete Book of Nonsense	Lear, Edward	Everyman's Library, 1992	nonsense verse
Contract with God: And Other Tenement Stories	Eisner, Will	DC Comics, 1978	graphic novel
Cook-a-Doodle-Doo!	Stevens, Janet and Susan	Harcourt Brace, 1999	computer-generated graphics
Cookie Count	Sabuda, Robert	Little, Simon, 1997	toy book
Cookie's Week	Ward, Cindy	Putnam, 1988	predictable book
Cool Melons—Turn to Frogs! The Life and Poems of Issa	Gollub, Matthew	Lee & Low, 1998	haiku

Title	Author	Publisher/Producer	Term(s)
Cotton in My Sack	Lensky, Lois	Lippincott, 1949	regional literature
Count	Fleming, Denise	Henry Holt, 1992	counting book
Counting Our Way to Maine	Smith, Maggie	Orchard 1995	counting book
Counting Wildflowers	McMillan, Bruce	Lothrop, Lee & Shepard, 1986	counting book
Counting Your Way through 1-2-3: Books and Activities	Cooper, Cathie Hilterbran	Scarecrow, 1997	counting book
Cowboys: Roundup on an American Ranch	Anderson, Joan	Scholastic, 1996	photo essay
Coyote: A Trickster Tale from the American Southwest	McDermott, Gerald	Harcourt Brace, 1994	trickster tale
Creatures of Earth, Sea, and Sky	Heard, Georgia	Boyds Mills, 1999, 1982	choral speaking
D'Aulaire's Book of Greek Myths	D'Aulaire, Ingri and Edgar Parin	Doubleday, 1962	anthology
Daddies Say Goodnight	Sugar Hill	Sugar Hill, 1994	lullaby
Dance Away	Shannon, George	Greenwillow, 1982	visual literacy
Dancing Kettle	Uchida, Yoshiko	Creative Arts, 1986	kamishibai
Dandelions	Bunting, Eve	Harcourt Brace, 1995	fictional biography, historical fiction
Dark is Rising	Cooper, Susan	Macmillan, 1973	suspension of disbelief
The Dark Is Rising Series	Cooper, Susan	Harcourt	Arthurian legends
Dark-thirty: Southern Tales of the Supernatural	McKissack, Patricia C.	Knopf, 1992	subtitle

Title	Author	Publisher/Producer	Term(s)
Daughter of the Earth: A Roman Myth	McDermott, Gerald	Delacorte, 1984	myth
David Copperfield	Dickens, Charles	1849–1850	bildungsroman
Dawn	Shulevitz, Uri	Farrar, Straus, & Giroux, 1974	color
Day at Damp Camp	Lyon, George Ella	Orchard, 1996	terse verse
Days Like This: A Collection of Small Poems	James, Simon	Candlewick, 1999	watercolor
Dear Mr. Henshaw	Cleary, Beverly	Morrow, 1983	complication, letters, point of view, problem novel, psychological criticism
Dear Peter Rabbit	Ada, Alma Flor	Atheneum, 1994	letters
Deep in the Forest	Turkle, Brinton	Dutton, 1976	fractured tale
Devil's Arithmetic	Yolen, Jane	Putnam, 1988	fantasy
Dia's Story Cloth	Cha, Dia	Lee & Low, 1996	embroidered pictures
Dick Whittington and His Cat	Brown, Marcia	Scribner, 1988, 1950	legend
Digital Field Trip to the Rain Forest	Digital Frog Int.	Digital Frog International, 1998	CD-ROM
Dinner at Margritte's	Garland, Michael	Dutton, 1995	surrealism
Doctor Coyote: A Native American Aesop's Fables	Bierhorst, John	Macmillan, 1987	beast fable
Doll People	Martin, Ann M. and Laura Godwin	Hyperion, 2000	illustrated book
Doodle Dandies	Lewis, J. Patrick	Atheneum, 1998	concrete poetry

Title	Author	Publisher/Producer	Term(s)
Dora's Book	Edwards, Michele	Carolrhoda, 1990	binding
Downriver	Hobbs, Will	Atheneum, 1991	adventure story
Dr. Seuss	McDonald, Ruth	Twayne, 1988	biographical criticism
Dr. Seuss' Kindergarten	Broderbund	Broderbund, 1999	CD-ROM
Dragon Shirt	Wells, Rosemary	Dial, 1991	wash
Draw 50 Famous Caricatures	Ames, Lee J.	Doubleday, 1990	drawing
Dreamsnow	Carle, Eric	Philomel, 2000	acetate
Drop of Water: A Book of Science and Wonder	Wick, Walter	Scholastic, 1997	photo essay, photography, radical change
Drummer Hoff	Emberley, Barbara	Prentice-Hall, 1967	pattern book, woodcut
Duke Ellington: The Piano Prince and the Orchestra	Pinkney, Andrea Davis	Hyperion, 1998	double spread, mixed media, scratch board, typeface
Each Peach Pear Plum	Ahlberg, Janet and Allan	Penguin, 1999	participation book
Ear, the Eye, & the Arm: A Novel	Farmer, Nancy	Orchard, 1994	genre, science fiction
Earth Verses and Water Rhymes	Lewis, J. Patrick	Atheneum, 1991	linoleum block
Eating the Alphabet: Fruits and Vegetables from A to Z	Ehlert, Lois	Harcourt Brace, 1989	alphabet book, big book
Edward's Portrait	Morrow, Barbara	Macmillan, 1991	photography
Egg Tree	Milhous, Katherine	Scribner, 1950	tempera
Egyptian Cinderella	Climo, Shirley	Crowell, 1979	folktale

Title	Author	Publisher/Producer	Term(s)
Eleanor Roosevelt: A Life of Discovery	Freedman, Russell	Clarion, 1993	subtitle
Elements of a Pop-up	Carter, David A. and James Diaz	Simon & Schuster, 1999	toy book
Elfwyn's Saga	Wisniewski, David	Lothrop, Lee & Shepard, 1990	paper cuts
Elijah's Angel: A Story of Chanukah and Christmas	Rosen, Michael J.	Harcourt Brace Jovanovich, 1992	folk art
Ella Enchanted	Levine, Gail Carson	HarperCollins, 1997	fractured tale
Elvis Lives	Agee, Jon	Farrar, Straus & Giroux, 2000	anagram
Emily	Bedard, Michael	Doubleday, 1992	imagery
Emily and The Crows	Greenstein, Elaine	Picture Book Studio, 1992	casein paint
Emperor and the Kite	Yolen, Jane	World, 1967	paper cuts
Emperor's New Clothes	Andersen, Hans Christian	Candlewick, 1997	literary tale, satire
Encarta Africana	Encarta	Microsoft, 2000	CD-ROM
Encarta Interactive World Atlas 2000	Encarta	Microsoft, 2000	CD-ROM
Encyclopedia Brown Series	Sobol, Donald	Dutton	detective story
Erewhon	Butler, Samuel	University of Delaware Press, 1981	anagram
Etcher's Studio	Gisert, Arthur	Houghton Mifflin, 1997	etching
Every Living Thing	Rylant, Cynthia	Bradbury, 1985	short story
Everything Book	Fleming, Denise	Henry Holt, 2000	pulp painting

Title	Author	Publisher/Producer	Term(s)
Evolution of a Graphic Concept: The Stonecutter	McDermott, Gerald	Weston Woods, 1976	visual literacy
"Excerpts from 'Write Me Another Verse'"	McCord, David	Horn Book 46 (August 1970)	clerihew
Extraordinary Women: Rulers, Rebels (And What the Neighbors Thought)	Krull, Kathleen	Harcourt Brace, 2000	collected biography
Eyewitness Series	Kindersley, Dorling	Dorling Kindersley	format
Fables	Lobel, Arnold	Harper & Row, 1980	beast fable, didacticism, fable, gouache
Fables from Aesop	Lynch, Tom	Viking, 2000	fabric
Faithful Friend	San Scuci, Robert D.	Simon & Schuster, 1995	scratch board
Fanny's Dream	Buehner, Caralyn	Dial, 1996	fractured tale
Fantastic Voyage	Asimov, Isaac	Bantam, 1988	science fiction
Far North	Hobbs, Will	Morrow, 1997	rising action
Farmer's Alphabet	Saul, Carol P.	Gocine, 1981	woodcut
Favorite Poems Old and New	Ferris, Helen	Doubleday, 1957	anthology
Feathers	Patent, Dorothy Hinshaw	Cobblehill, 1992	photo essay
Feathers and Tails: Animal Fables from Around the World	Kherdian, David	Philomel, 1992	beast fable
Feathers for Lunch	Ehlert, Lois	Harcourt Brace Jovanovich, 1989	book size

Title	Author	Publisher/Producer	Term(s)
Fingerprint Drawing Book	Emberley, Ed	Little Brown, 2001	drawing
First Thanksgiving	George, Jean Craighead	Philomel, 1993	oil paint
Fisherman and His Wife	Stewig, John Warren	Holiday, 1988	motif
Five Chinese Brothers	Bishop, Claire Huchet	Coward-McCann, 1938	stereotype
Flag for Grandma	Grindley, Sally	Dorling Kindersley, 1998	pointillism
Fledgling	Langton, Jane	Harper & Row, 1980	omniscient point of view, point of view, suspension of disbelief
Flicker Flash	Graham, Jan Bransfield	Houghton Mifflin, 1999	concrete poetry
Flossie and the Fox	McKissack, Patricia C.	Dial, 1986	abridgment, reading aloud
Fly With Poetry: An ABC of Poetry	Harley, Avis	Wordson/Boyds Mills, 2000	cinquain
Flying	Crews, Donald	Greenwillow, 1986	air brush
Fox's Dream	Tejima, Keizaburo	Philomel, 1986	woodcut
Freaky Friday	Rodgers, Mary	Harper & Row, 1972	satire
Frederick	Lionni, Leo	Pantheon, 1967	fable
Frederick (big book)	Lionni, Leo	Scholastic	big book
Free Lunch	Seibold, J. Otto	Viking, 1996	computer-generated graphics
Freedom River	Collier, Bryan	Hyperion, 2000	collage
Freight Train	Crews, Donald	HarperCollins, 1978	air brush, color, expressionism

Title	Author	Publisher/Producer	Term(s)
Freight Train (big book)	Crews, Donald	Mulberry Big Book/ William Morrow, 1993	big book
Frog and ToadAare Friends	Lobel, Arnold	HarperCollins, 1979	mood, wit and humor
Frog and Toad Series	Lobel, Arnold	Harper & Row	comic strip, episodic plot
Frog and Toad Together	Lobel, Arnold	Harper, 1972	easy reader
Frog Prince Continued	Scieszka, Jon	Viking, 1991	allustion, fractured tale
Frog Went A-Courtin'	Langstaff, John	Harcourt, 1955	folk song
Froggie Went A-Courtin'	Priceman, Marjorie	Little Brown, 2000	folk song
From Pictures to Words: A Book about Making a Book	Stevens, Janet	Holiday House, 1995	author, dummy, illustrator, storyboard
From Sea to Shining Sea: A Treasury of American Folklore and Folk Songs	Cohn, Amy L.	Scholastic, 1993	folk song
From the Bellybutton of the Moon and Other Summer Poems/Del Ombligo de la Luna y otros poemas de verano	Alardûn, Francisco X.	Children's Press, 1998	translation
From the Hills of Georgia: An Autobiography in Paintings	O'Kelly, Mattie Lou	Little, Brown, 1983	folk art
From the Mixed-Up Files of Mrs. Basil E. Frankweiler	Konigsburg, E. L.	Atheneum, 1967	coincidence, foil
Frozen Stiff	Shahan, Sherry	Delacorte, 1998	survival story
Fun with Modeling Clay	Reid, Barbara	Kids Can, 1998	modeling clay

Title	Author	Publisher/Producer	Term(s)
G Is for Googol: A Math Alphabet Book	Schwartz, David M.	Tricycle, 1998	alphabet book
Gardener	Small, David	Dutton, 1997	crayon
Gardener	Stewart, Sarah	Farrar, Straus & Giroux, 1997	India ink, letters
Gathering of Days: A New England Girl's Journal, 1830-32	Blos, Joan W.	Scribner, 1979	diary
Gathering the Sun: An Alphabet in Spanish and English	Simún, Silva	Lothrop, Lee & Shepard, 1997	translation
Getting Near to Baby	Couloumbis, Audrey	Putnam, 1999	contemporary realistic fiction
Getting to Know Gerald McDermott	Soundworks	Soundworks, 1996	biographical criticism
Gift of the Magi	Henry, O.	Neugebauer, 1982	calligraphy
Gift of the Sacred Dog	Goble, Paul	Bradbury, 1980	pourquoi
Girl from Yamhill: A Memoir	Cleary, Beverly	Morrow, 1988	autobiography, biographical criticism
Girl Who Loved Wild Horses	Goble, Paul	Bradbury, 1978	imagery
Give a Boy a Gun	Strasser, Todd	Simon & Schuster, 2000	documentary novel
Giver	Lowry, Lois	Houghton Mifflin, 1993	open ending, science fiction
Glorious Fight: Across the Channel with Louis Bleriot, July 25, 1909	Provensen, Alice and Martin	Viking, 1987	perspective
Go Hang a Salami! I'm a Lasagna Hog!	Agee, Jon	Farrar, Straus & Giroux, 1991	palindromes

Title	Author	Publisher/Producer	Term(s)
Golden Compass	Pullman, Phillip	Knopf, 1995	trilogy
Golden Compass (book on tape)	Pullman, Phillip	Listening Library, 1999	book on tape
Goldilocks and the Three Bears	Marshall, James	Dial, 1988	India ink
Golem	Wisniewski, David	Clarion, 1996	paper cuts, perspective
Gonna Sing My Head Off! American Folk Songs for Children	Krull, Kathleen	Knopf, 1992	folk song
Good Night Moon (board book)	Brown, Margaret Wise	Harper Festival, 1991	board book
Good Night, Gorilla (big book)	Rathmann, Peggy	Scholastic, 1996, 1994	big book
Good Night, Gorilla (board book)	Rathmann, Peggy	Puffin, 2000	board book
Goodnight Moon	Brown, Margaret Wise	Harper & Row, 1947	classic, pattern book
Goodnight Moon: A Pop-up Book	Brown, Margaret Wise	HarperCollins, 1985	toy book
Goody Hall	Babbitt, Natalie	Farrar, Straus & Giroux, 1971	mystery
Gorilla Walk	Lewin, Ted and Betsy	Lothrop, Lee & Shepard, 1999	diary
Grandfather Tang's Story	Tompert, Ann	Crown, 1990	tangram
Grandfather's Journey	Say, Allen	Houghton, 1993	picture book, realistic art, watercolor
Graphic Alphabet	Pelletier, David	Orchard, 1996	alphabet book, computer-generated graphics
Grass Sandals: The Travels of Basho	Spivak, Dawnine	Atheneum, 1997	haiku
Great Expectations	Dickens, Charles	1861	bildungsroman

Title	Author	Publisher/Producer	Term(s)
Great Frog Race and Other Poems	George, Kristen O'Connell	Clarion, 1997	free verse
Great Gilly Hopkins	Paterson, Katherine	Crowell, 1978	antagonist
Grey Lady and the Strawberry Snatcher	Bang, Molly	Four Winds, 1980	surrealism
Grouchy Ladybug	Carle, Eric	HarperCollins, 1996	Briticism, page shape
Grow Big Songs	Guthrie, Woody	Warner Brothers, 1992	fold song
Growing Colors	McMillan, Bruce	Lothrop, Lee & Shepard, 1988	photography, picture book
Guess How Much I Love You	McBratney, Sam	Candlewick, 1996	board book, wash
Gulliver in Lilliput	Hodges, Margaret, reteller	Holiday, 1995	abridgment
Gulls...Gulls...Gulls...	Gibbons, Gail	Holiday, 2001	graphic design
Guppies in Tuxedos	Terban, Marvin	Clarion, 1988	eponym
Gypsy Rizka	Alexander, Lloyd	Harcourt Brace, 1999	cliff-hanger
Hailstones and Halibut Bones	O'Neill, Mary	Doubleday, 1989	color
Hair in Funny Places: A Book about Puberty	Cole, Babette	Hyperion, 2000	anthropomorphism
Handmade Alphabet	Rankin, Laura	Penguin, 1991	alphabet book
Hands	Ehlert, Lois	Harcourt Brace, 1997	die-cutting, page shape
Hans Christian Andersen: The Complete Fairy Tales & Stories	Haugaard, Erik	Doubleday, 1983	folktale
Hansel and Gretel	Grimm, Jacob and Wilhelm	McGraw-Hill, 1982	poetic justice

Title	Author	Publisher/Producer	Term(s)
Hansel and Gretel	Grimm, Jacob and Wilhelm	Morrow, 1979	motif
Hansel and Gretel	Lesser, Rika	Dodd, 1984	archetype, oil paint
Harlem: A Poem	Myers, Walter Dean	Orchard, 1997	gouache
Harriet the Spy	Fitzhugh, Louise	Harper, 1996	adaptation, diary
Harry Potter and the Chamber of Secrets	Rowling, J. K.	Listening Library, 1999	book on tape
Harry Potter and the Goblet of Fire	Rowling, J. K.	Scholastic, 2000	alliteration
Harry Potter and the Philosopher's Stone	Rowling, J. K.	Bloomsbury, 2001	Briticism
Harry Potter and the Sorcerer's Stone	Rowling, J. K.	Scholastic, 1998	antagonist, Briticism, censorship, cliff-hanger
Harry Potter and the Sorcerer's Stone (book on tape)	Rowling, J. K.	Listening Library, 1999	book on tape
Harry Potter Series	Rowling, J. K.	Scholastic	archetypal criticism, series
Hatchet	Paulsen, Gary	Bradbury, 1987	adventure story, antagonist, sequel
Hatseller and the Monkeys: A West African Folktale	Diakite, Baba Wague	Scholastic, 1999	folk art
Haunted House	Pienkowski, Jan	Dutton, 1979	toy book
Have You Seen Birds?	Oppenheim, Joanne	Scholastic, 1986	modeling clay
Heavens to Betsy and Other Curious Sayings	Funk, Charles Earle	Harper & Row, 1955	idiom

Title	Author	Publisher/Producer	Term(s)
Helen Oxenbury Nursery Rhyme Book	Alderson, Brian	William Morrow, 1986, 1974	nursery rhymes
Henry and Mudge Series	Rylant, Cynthia	Simon & Schuster	comic strip, episodic plot
Her Seven Brothers	Goble, Paul	Bradbury, 1988	pourquoi
Here Come Poppy and Max	Gardnier, Lindsay	Little, Brown, 2000	fabric
Here Comes Mother Goose	Opie, Iona	Candlewick, 1999	pattern book
Here Comes Mother Goose	Wells, Rosemary	Candlewick, 1999	nursery rhymes
Hershel and the Hanukkah Goblins	Hyman, Trina Schart	Holiday, 1989	India ink
Hey, Al	Yorinks, Arthur	Farrar, Straus, & Giroux, 1986	endpapers
Hey, Hay! A Wagonful of Funny Homonym Riddles	Terban, Marvin	Clarion, 1991	homonym
Hieroglyphs from A to Z: A Rhyming Book with Ancient Egyptian Stencils for Kids	Der Manuelian, Peter	Scholastic, 1991	hand-lettering
High King	Alexander, Lloyd	Holt, 1968	character, romance
History of Making Books	Brookfield, Karen	Scholastic, Voyages of Discovery, 1995	book
Hog on Ice and Other Curious Expressions	Funk, Charles Earle	Harper & Row, 1948	idiom
Holes	Sachar, Louis	Farrar, Straus & Giroux, 1998	contemporary realistic fiction, flashback, palindromes
Holes (book on tape)	Sachar, Louis	Listening Library, 1999	book on tape

Title	Author	Publisher/Producer	Term(s)
Hush Little Baby: A Folk Song with Pictures	Frazee, Marla	Browndeer, 1999	lullaby
Hush!: A Thai Lullaby	Ho, Minfong	Orchard Books, 1996	lullaby
I Am Phoenix: Poems for Two Voices	Fleischman, Paul	HarperCollins, 1985	choral speaking
I Had Seen Castles	Rylant, Cynthia	Harcourt Brace, 1993	novella
I Hear America Singing	Whitman, Walt	Philomel, 1991	linoleum block
I Love You: A Rebus Poem	Marzollo, Jean	Cartwheel, 2000	rebus
I Saw Esau: The School Child's Pocket Book	Opie, Iona and Peter	Candlewick, 1992	rhyme
I Was a Rat!	Pullman, Phillip	Random, 2000	fractured tale
I've Got Chicken Pox	Kelley, True	Dutton, 1994	wash
If You Find a Rock	Christian, Peggy	Harcourt, 2000	photography
If You Give a Mouse a Cookie	Numeroff, Laura Joffe	HarperCollins, 1985	cumulative tale, reading aloud
Iguana Brothers: A Tale of Two Lizards	Johnston, Tony	Cartwheel, 1995	mood, wit and humor
In a Pickle and Other Funny Idioms	Terban, Marvin	Houghton, 1983	idiom
In Coal Country	Hendershot, Judith	Knopf, 1987	charcoal
In the Beginning: Creation Stories From Around the World	Hamilton, Virginia	Harcourt Brace Jovanovich, 1988	pourquoi
In the Forest	Ets, Marie Hall	Viking, 1945	batik

Title	Author	Publisher/Producer	Term(s)
Jack Tales	Chase, Richard	Houghton Mifflin, 1971	motif, structural criticism
Jackal's Flying Lesson: A Koikhoi Tale	Aardema, Verna	Apple Soup/Knopf, 1995	onomatopoeia
Jacket I Wear in the Snow	Neitzel, Shirley	Greenwillow, 1989	rebus
Jacket I Wear to the Party	Neitzel, Shirley	Greenwillow, 1992	rebus
Jacob Have I Loved	Paterson, Katherine	Crowell, 1980	antagonist, bildungsroman, formalism, point of view, symbol
Jade Green: A Ghost Story	Naylor, Phyllis Reynolds	Simon & Schuster, 2000	gothic novel
Jambo Means Hello: Swahili Alphabet Book	Feelings, Muriel	Puffin, 1981	alphabet book, graphite
James and the Giant Peach	Dahl, Roald	Knopf, 1961	dialogue, reading aloud
Jason's Gold	Hobbs, Will	Morrow, 1999	conflict, survival story
Jelly Beans for Sale	McMillan, Bruce	Scholastic, 1996	counting book, photography
Jeremy Thatcher, Dragon Hatcher	Coville, Bruce	Simon & Schuster, 1991	theme
Jesse	Soto, Gary	Listening Library, 1998	book on tape
Joey Pigza Swallowed the Key	Gantos, Jack	Farrar, Straus & Giroux, 2000	contemporary realistic fiction, sociological criticism
Joey Pigza Swallowed the Key	Gantos, Jack	Listening Library, 1999	book on tape
John Henry	Lester, Julius	Dial, 1994	drawing, retelling
Johnny Appleseed	Kellog, Steven	Morrow, 1988	tall tale, wit and humor

Title	Author	Publisher/Producer	Term(s)
Johnny Appleseed: A Poem	Lindbergh, Reeve	Little Brown, 1993	folk art
Jolly Pocket Postman	Ahlberg, Janet and Allan	Little, Brown, 1995	letters
Jolly Postman: Or, Other People's Letters	Ahlberg, Janet and Allan	Little, Brown, 1986	Briticism, letters, participation book
Jolly Roger	Pinkwater, Daniel	Lothrop, Lee & Shepard, 1985	endpapers
Joseph Had a Little Overcoat	Taback, Simms	Viking, 1999	die-cutting, expressionism, gouache, mixed media
Joyful Noise: Poems for Two Voices	Fleischman, Paul	HarperCollins, 1988	choral speaking
Jubal's Wish	Wood, Audrey	Blue Sky, 2000	computer-generated graphics
Julian's Glorious Summer	Cameron, Ann	Random, 1987	chapter book
Julie of the Wolves	George, Jean Craighead	Harper & Row, 1972	adventure story
Julius	Johnson, Angela	Orchard, 1993	fabric
Jumanji	Van Allsburg, Chris	Houghton Mifflin, 1981	illustrator, surrealism
Jump	Parks, Van Dyke	Harcourt Brace, 1986	dialect
Jump Again	Parks, Van Dyke	Harcourt Brace, 1987	dialect
Jump Again! More Adventures of Brer Rabbit	Harris, Joel Chandler	Harcourt, Brace, Jovancvich, 1987	trickster tale
Jump on Over! The Adventures of Brer Rabbit and His Family	Harris, Joel Chandler	Harcourt, Brace, Jovanovich, 1989	trickster tale
Jump! The Adventures of Brer Rabbit	Harris, Joel Chandler	Harcourt, Brace, Jovanovich 1986	trickster tale

Title	Author	Publisher/Producer	Term(s)
Just Me	Ets, Marie Hall	Viking, 1966	batik
Kate and the Beanstalk	Osborne, Mary Pope	Atheneum/Ann Schwartz, 2000	fractured tale, setting
Keep On Singing: A Ballad of Marian Anderson	Livingston, Myra Cohn	Holiday, 1994	ballad
Keeping Quilt	Polacco, Patricia	Simon & Schuster, 1988	nostalgia
Kids at Work	Freedman, Russell	Clarion, 1993	radical change
King Arthur & the Legends of Camelot	Perham, Molly	Viking, 1993	anthology
Knock at a Star: A Child's Introduction to Poetry	Kennedy, X. J. and Dorothy	Little, Brown, 1982, 1999	choral speaking
Knots in My Yo-Yo String	Spinelli, Jerry	Knopf, 1998	autobiography
Larousse World Mythology	Grimal, Pierre	Hamlyn, 1973, 1965	mystery
Laughing Out Loud, I Fly: Poems in English and Spanish	Belpré, Pura	HarperCollins, 1998	translation
Legend of the Bluebonnet	DePaola, Tomie	Putnam, 1983	pourquoi
Legend of the Veery Bird	Hague, Kathleen	Harcourt Brace Jovanovich, 1985	fairy tale
Let It Shine: Stories of Black Women Freedom Fighters	Pinkney, Andrea Davis	Gulliver Books, 2000	collected biography, oil paint
Letters from Rifka	Hesse, Karen	Henry Holt, 1992	letters
Library	Stewart, Sarah	Farrar, Straus & Giroux, 1995	dedication
Library Lil	Williams, Suzanne	Dial, 1997	hyperbole
LIFE: Our Century in Pictures for Young People	Stolley, Richard B.	Little, Brown, 2000	photography

Title	Author	Publisher/Producer	Term(s)
Little Snake	Reinl, Edda	Simon & Schuster, 1991	batik
Living with Books	Haines, Helen	Columbia University, 1950	annotation
Lon Po Po	Young, Ed	Philomel, 1989	cautionary tale, impressionism, retelling
Long Way from Chicago: A Novel in Stories	Peck, Richard	Dial, 1998	colloquialism, episodic plot, plot, poetic justice, sequel, understatement
Long Way from Chicago: A Novel in Stories (book on tape)	Peck, Richard	Listening Library, 1999	book on tape
Look! Look! Look!	Hoban, Tana	Greenwillow, 1988	die-cutting, photography
Looking Back: A Book of Memories	Lowry, Lois	Houghton Mifflin, 1989	autobiography
Lord of the Rings	Tolkien, J.R.R.	Ballantine, 1991	science fiction
Lots of Limericks	Livingston, Myra Cohn	M. K. McElderry, 1991	limerick
Lou Gehrig: The Luckiest Man	Adler, David	Gulliver, 1997	biography
Love Letters	Adoff, Arnold	Scholastic/Blue Sky, 1997	dedication
Lucy Cousins Book of Nursery Rhymes	Cousins, Lucy	Dutton, 1989	nursery rhymes
Lullabies: An Illustrated Songbook	Meade, Holly	Harcourt, 1997	lullaby
Lullaby: A Collection		Music for Little People, 1994	lullaby
Lunch	Fleming, Denise	Henry Holt, 1992	pulp painting
Lyddie	Paterson, Katherine	Dutton, 1991	antagonist

Title	Author	Publisher/Producer	Term(s)
Madeline	Bemelman, Ludwig	Viking, 1939	expressionism
Magic School Bus Explores the World of Animals	Microsoft	Microsoft, 1999	CD-ROM
Magic Windows/Ventanas M·gicas	Garza, Carmen Lomas	Children's Book, 1999	paper cuts
Mailing May	Tunnell, Michael O.	Greenwillow, 1997	book size
Maisy's Pop-up Playhouse	Cousins, Lucy	Candlewick, 1995	toy book
Make Way for Ducklings	McCloskey, Robert	Viking, 1941	balance, gutter, illustrator, lithograph, sepia
Make Way for Ducklings (Big book)	McCloskey, Robert	Puffin, 1941	big book
Making Magic Windows	Garza, Carmen Lomas	Children s Book, 1999	paper cuts
Making Up Megaboy	Walter, Virginia	Delacorte, 1998	nonlinear text, radical change
Maniac Magee	Spinelli, Jerry	Little, Brown, 1991	realistic fiction
Many Moons	Thurber, James	Harcourt Brace Jovanovich, 1943	India ink
Mary Had a Little Lamb	Hale, Josepha	Orchard, 1995	fabric relief, nursery rhymes
Mary Poppins	Travers, Pamela	Harcourt Trade, 1934	stereotype
Maus: A Survivor's Tale	Spiegelman, Art	Random House, 1986	graphic novel
Max's Breakfast	Wells, Rosemary	Dial, 1985	board book
Meteor!	Polacco, Patricia	Spoken Arts, 1999	book on tape
Michael Hague's Favorite Hans Christian Andersen Fairy Tales	Hague, Michael	Henry Holt, 1981	fairy tale

Title	Author	Publisher/Producer	Term(s)
Middle Ages	Howarth, Sarah	Viking, 1993	acetate
Middle Passage: White Ships, Black Cargo	Feelings, Tom	Dial, 1995	wordless book
Midnight Fox	Byars, Betsy	Viking, 1968	foreshadowing
Midnight Magic	Avi	Scholastic, 1999	gothic novel
Midwife's Apprentice	Cushman, Karen	Houghton Mifflin, 1995	historical fiction
Mike Mulligan and His Steam Shovel	Burton, Virginia Lee	Houghton Mifflin, 1939	climax
Miller, the Boy and the Donkey	Wildsmith, Brian	Oxford University, 1969	fable
Million Fish...More or Less	McKissack, Patricia C.	Random, 1992	hyperbole
Millions of Cats	Gag, Wanda	Coward-McCann, Putnam, 1928	hand-lettering
Minty: A Story of Young Harriet Tubman	Schroeder, Alan	Dial, 1996	biography
Mirandy and Brother Wind	McKissack, Patricia C.	Random, 1988	drawing
Mirette on the High Wire	McCully, Emily Arnold	Putnam, 1992	picture book, impressionism
Miss Rumphius	Cooney, Barbara	Viking, 1982	setting
Missing May	Rylant, Cynthia	Orchard, 1992	regional literature
Mist Over the Mountains: Appalachia and Its People	Bial, Raymond	Houghton Mifflin, 1997	regional literature
Mitten: A Ukranian Folktale	Brett, Jan	Putnam, 1990	cumulative tale, decorative frame

Title	Author	Publisher/Producer	Term(s)
Mr. Rabbit and the Lovely Present	Zolotow, Charlotte	Harper & Row, 1962	impressionism
Mr. T.W. Anthony Woo	Ets, Marie Hall	Viking, 1952	batik
Mrs. Rose's Garden	Greenstein, Elaine	Schuster, 1996	casein paint
Mufaro's Beautiful Daughters: An African Tale	Steptoe, John	Lothrop, 1987	hatching, static character
Mummy, the Will and the Crypt	Bellairs, John	Dial, 1983	mystery
My Amazing Human Body	DK Multimedia	DK Multimedia, 1998	CD-ROM
My America: A Poetry Atlas of the United States	Hopkins, Lee Bennet	Simon & Schuster, 2000	casein paint
My Dog Rosie	Harper, Isabelle	Blue Sky, 1994	realistic art
My First Photography Book	King, Dave	Dorling Kindersley, 1994	photography
My Head Is Red and Other Riddle Rhymes	Livingston, Myra Cohn	Holiday, 1990	riddle
My Little Red Toolbox	Johnson, Stephen T.	Silver Whistle, 2000	page shape, toy book
My Louisiana Sky	Holt, Kimberly Willis	Holt, 1998	problem novel
My Louisiana Sky (book on tape)	Holt, Kimberly Willis	Listening Library, 1998	book on tape
My Mama Had a Dancing Heart	Gray, Libba Moore	Orchard, 1995	impressionism
My Mom Is Magic!	Roche, Hanna	De Agostini, 1996	hatching
My Name is Georgia: A Portrait	Winter, Jeanette	Silver Whistle, 1998	biography
My New York	Jakobsen, Kathy	Little Brown, 1993	folk art

Title	Author	Publisher/Producer	Term(s)
My Own Two Feet: A Memoir	Cleary, Beverly	Morrow, 1995	autobiography, biographical criticism
You Are My Perfect Baby	Thomas, Joyce Carol	HarperCollins, 1999	board book
My Season with Penguins: An Antarctic Journal	Webb, Sophie	Houghton Mifflin, 2000	diary
My Side of the Mountain	George, Jean Craighead	Dutton, 1959	conflict, flashback
My Trip to Alpha I	Slote, Alfred	Harper, 1978	science fiction
My Very First Mother Goose	Wells, Rosemary	Candlewick, 1996	nursery rhymes
Mysteries of Harris Burdick	Van Allsburg, Chris	Houghton Mifflin, 1984	surrealism
Name of the Game Was Murder	Nixon, Joan Lowery	Delacorte, 1993	detective story
Napping House	Wood, Audrey	Harcourt Brace Jovanovich, 1984	color, cumulative tale
Nate the Great Series	Sharmat, Marjorie	Coward, McCann & Georghegan	detective story
New Baby Calf	Chase, Edith Newlin	Scholastic, 1986	modeling clay
New Kid on the Block	Prelutsky, Jack	Greenwillow, 1984	alliteration, assonance
New Way Things Work	Macaulay, David	Houghton Mifflin, 1998	drawing
Night Before Christmas	Brett, Jan	Putnam, 1998	narrative poetry
Night Before Christmas or a Visit from St. Nicholas	Moore, Clement Clark	Philomel Books, 1989	parody
Night of the Pufflings	McMillan, Bruce	Houghton, 1995	photo essay
No Kidding	Brooks, Bruce	Harper, 1989	science fiction

Title	Author	Publisher/Producer	Term(s)
No, David!	Shannon, David	Blue Sky/Scholastic, 1998	acrylic, typeface
Noah and the Great Flood	Gerstein, Mordicai	Simon & Schuster, 1999	modeling clay
Noah's Ark	Spier, Peter	Doubleday, 1977	modeling clay
Noisy Book	Brown, Margaret Wise	HarperCollins, 1983	abstract art
Nonsense Songs	Lear, Edward	McElderry, 1997	nonsense verse
Nothing But the Truth: A Documentary Novel	Avi	Orchard, 1991	point of view, subtitle
Nothing Ever Happens on my Block	Raskin, Ellen	Atheneum, 1996	irony
Not-Just-Anybody Family	Byars, Betsy	Delacorte, 1986	dialogue
Number Devil: A Mathematical Adventure	Enzensberger, Hans Magnus	Henry Holt/Metropolitan, 1998	illustrated book
Number the Stars	Lowry, Lois	Houghton Mifflin, 1989	afterward, climax, conflict, historical fiction
Nutshell Library	Sendak, Maurice	Harper & Row, 1964	book size
October 45	Besson, Jean-Louis	Creative Editions, 1995	typeface
Of Pelicans and Pussycats	Lear, Edward	Dial, 1990	limerick
Officer Buckle and Gloria	Rathmann, Peggy	Putnam, 1995	cartoon, climax, picture book, watercolor
Oink	Geisert, Arthur	Houghton Mifflin, 1991	etching
Old Elm Speaks: Tree Poems	George, Kristen O'Connell	Clarion, 1998	free verse
Old MacDonald Has a Farm	Jones, Carol	Houghton Mifflin, 1998	participation book

Title	Author	Publisher/Producer	Term(s)
Olive, the Other Reindeer	Walsh, Vivian	Chronicle, 1997	computer-generated graphics
Olivia	Falconer, Ian	Atheneum, 2000	charcoal
On Market Street	Lobel, Arnold	Greenwillow, 1981	alphabet book, dictionary
On My Honor	Bauer, Marion Dane	Clarion, 1986	conflict
On the Edge: Stories on the Brink	Duncan, Lois	Simon & Schuster, 2000	short story
Once a Mouse	Brown, Marcia	Scribner, 1961	fable, woodcut
Once a Mouse	Ormerod, Jan	Scribner, 1981	wordless book
One at a Time: His Collected Poems for the Young	McCord, David	Little, 1977	meter
One Good Horse: A Cowpuncher's Counting Book	Herbert Scott, Ann	Greenwillow, 1990	counting book
One Potato: A Counting Book of Potato Prints	Pomeroy, Diana	Harcourt Brace, 1996	potato printing
One Sun: A Book of Terse Verse	McMillan, Bruce	Holiday, 1991	terse verse
One Thousand and One Arabian Nights	McCaughrean, Geraldine	Oxford University, 2000	framework story, folktale
Onions and Garlic: An Old Tale	Kimmel, Eric	Holiday, 1996	noodlehead story
Orchard Book of Nursery Rhymes	Sutherland, Zena	Orchard, 1990	nursery rhymes
Origami Magic	Temko, Florence	Scholastic, 1993	origami
Origami Safari	Biddle, Steve and Megumi	Morrow, 1994	origami

Title	Author	Publisher/Producer	Term(s)
Orvis	Hoover, H. M.	Viking, Penguin, 1987	science fiction
Other Side of Dark	Nixon, Joan Lowery	Delacorte, 1986	mystery
Our Cancer Year	Pekar, Harvey and Joyce Brabner	Four Walls Eight Windows, 1994	graphic novel
Our Only May Amelia	Holm, Jennifer L.	HarperCollins, 1999	static character
Out of the Dust	Hesse, Karen	Scholastic, 1997	free verse, historical fiction, reading aloud, setting, sociological criticism
Outside Over There	Sendak, Maurice	Harper & Row, 1981	fairy tale
Outsiders	Hinton, S. E.	Viking, 1967	problem novel
Over Sea Under Stone	Cooper, Susan	Harcourt, 1966	Arthurian legends
Owen	Henkes, Kevin	Greenwillow, 1993	India ink
Owl Moon	Yolen, Jane	Philomel, 1987	imagery, India ink, setting, watercolor
Ox-Cart Man	Hall, Donald	Viking, 1979	folk art
Oxford Book of Children's Verses in America	Hall, Donald	Oxford University, 1985	stanza
Oxford Dictionary of Nursery Rhymes	Opie, Iona and Peter	Oxford University, 1951, 1998	nursery rhymes
Oxford Nursery Rhyme Book	Opie, Iona and Peter	Oxford University, 1955	nursery rhymes
Painting with Paper: Easy Paper-making Fun for the Entire Family	Fleming, Denise	Holt, 1994	pulp painting

Title	Author	Publisher/Producer	Term(s)
Pajamas	Taylor, Maggie	Harcourt Brace Jovanovich, 1988	perspective
Pancakes for Breakfast	DePaola, Tomie	Harcourt, 1978	reader response theory, wordless book
Paper Crane	Bang, Molly	Greenwillow, 1985	origami
Paper Dragon	Davol, Marguerite W.	Atheneum, 1997	kamishibai, paper cuts
Paper Trail	Gilbert, Barbara Snow	Front Street, 2000	documentary novel, fiction
Paperboy	Pilkey, Dav	Orchard, 1996	acrylic, India ink
Passage to Freedom: The Sugihara Story	Mochizuki, Ken	Lee & Low Books, 1997	sepia
Pat the Bunny	Kunhardt, Dorothy	Golden, 1962, 1940	participation book
Paul Bunyan	Kellog, Steven	Morrow, 1936	wit and humor
Paul Revere's Ride	Longfellow, Henry Wadsworth	Mulberry, 1993	ballad, narrative poetry
Peaceable Kingdom: The Shaker Abecedarius	Provensen, Alice and Martin	Viking, 1978	acrostic
Pecos Bill	Kellog, Steven	Morrow, 1986	wit and humor
Pedro and Me: Friendship, Loss and What I Learned	Winick, Judd	Holt, 2000	graphic novel
Penguin Dreams	Seibold, J. Otto	Chronicle, 1999	computer-generated graphics
People Could Fly: American Black Folktales	Hamilton, Virginia	Knopf, 1985	anthology

Title	Author	Publisher/Producer	Term(s)
Perrault's Fairy Tales	Perrault, Charles	Didier, 1946; Dover, 1969	cautionary tale
Persephone	Hutton, Warrick	Macmillan, 1994	myth
Pete's Pizza	Steig, William	HarperCollins, 1999	endpapers
Phantom Tollbooth	Juster, Norman	Random, 1961	fantasy
Piano Discovery for Kids	Jump! Music	Jump! Music, 1998	CD-ROM
Picnic	McCully, Emily Arnold	Harper & Row, 1984	wordless book
Pied Piper of Hamelin	Holden, Robert	Houghton Mifflin, 1998	legend
Pigericks	Lobel, Arnold	Harper, 1989	limerick
Pigman	Zindel, Paul	Harper & Row, 1968	problem novel
Pigs from 1 to 1	Geisert, Arthur	Houghton Mifflin, 1992	counting book
Pigs from A to Z	Geisert, Arthur	Houghton Mifflin, 1996	etching
Pilgrim's Progress	Bunyan, John	1678	allegory
Pish Posh, Said Hieronymous Bosch	Willard, Nancy	Harcourt Brace Jovanovich, 1991	decorative frame
Pizza the Size of the Sun	Prelutsky, Jack	Listening Library, 1999	book on tape
Planting a Rainbow	Ehlert, Lois	Harcourt Brace Jovanovich, 1988	page shape
Play Day: A Book of Terse Verse	McMillan, Bruce	Holiday, 1991	terse verse
Play with Me	Ets, Marie Hall	Viking, 1955	visual literacy
Playing	Oxenbury, Helen	Dutton, 1994	wash

Title	Author	Publisher/Producer	Term(s)
Quilt	Jonas, Ann	Greenwillow, 1984	endpapers
Rabbit Hill	Lawson, Robert	Viking, 1944	wit and humor
Rabbits, Rabbits & More Rabbits!	Gibbons, Gail	Holiday, 2000	graphic design
Rain Player	Wisniewski, David	Clarion, 1991	paper cuts
Ramona the Pest	Cleary, Beverly	Morrow, 1968	plot
Ramona's World	Cleary, Beverly	Listening Library, 1999	book on tape
Random House Book of Poetry for Children: A Treasury of 572 Poems for Today's Child	Prelutsky, Jack	Random House, 1983	anthology, couplet, dialogue, tercet (12)
Rapunzel	Zelinsky, Paul O.	Dutton, 1997	motif, oil paint
Raven: A Trickster Tale from the Pacific Northwest	McDermott, Gerald	Harcourt Brace Jovanovich, 1993	motif , trickster tale
Red Leaf, Yellow Leaf	Ehlert, Lois	Harcourt Brace Jovanovich, 1991	collage
Red-Eyed Tree Frog	Cowley, Joy	Scholastic, 1999	photography
Relatives Came	Rylant, Cynthia	Bradbury, 1985	graphite, reading aloud, regional literature
Riddle-icious	Lewis, J. Patrick	Knopf, 1996	riddle
Rifle	Paulsen, Gary	Harcourt Brace, 1995	novella
Rifles for Watie	Keith, Harold	Crowell, 1957	stereotype
River	Paulsen, Gary	Delacorte, 1991	sequel

Title	Author	Publisher/Producer	Term(s)
River of No Return	Lahey, Vince	Bantam, 1997	adventure story
Rocket in My Pocket: The Rhymes and Chants of Young Americans	Withers, Carl	Holt, 1988, 1948	chant, pun, riddle
Roll of Thunder, Hear my Cry	Taylor, Mildred	Dial 1976	dialect
Rooster Crows	Petersham, Maud and Miska	Macmillan, 1945	lithograph
Rose Blanche	Innocenti, Roberto	Creative Education, 1985	antagonist, point of view
Rosie's Walk	Hutchins, Pat	Macmillan, 1968	predictable book
Round Trip	Jonas, Ann	Morrow, 1990	double spread, graphic design
Ruby	Emberley, Michael	Little, Brown, 1990	fractured tale
Rumpelstiltskin	Zelinsky, Paul O.	Dutton, 1936	conflict, oil paint
Runaway Tortilla	Kimmel, Eric	Winslow, 2000	fractured tale
Sail Away	Crews, Donald	Greenwillow, 1996	air brush, expressionism
Sailor's Alphabet	McCurdy, Michael	Houghton Mifflin, 1998	alphabet book
Saint George and the Dragon	Hodges, Margaret	Little, Brown, 1984	Arthurian legends, calligraphy, epic, India ink
Saint George and the Dragon	Hyman, Trina Schart	Holiday, 1934	decorative frame
Sally Ann Thunder Ann Whirlwind Crockett	Kellog, Steven	Morrow, 1995	wit and humor
Sally Goes to the Beach	Huneck, Stephen	Abrams, 2000	perspective
Salting the Ocean: 100 Poems by Young Children	Nye, Naomi Shihab	Greenwillow, 2000	anthology

Title	Author	Publisher/Producer	Term(s)
Santa Calls	Joyce, William	HarperCollins, 1993	letters
Sarah Plain and Tall	MacLachlan, Patricia	HarperCollins, 1985	sequel
Say Goodnight	Oxenbury, Helen	Dutton, 1994	wash
Say It!	Zolotow, Charlotte	Greenwillow, 1980	impressionism
Scary Stories to Tell in the Dark	Schwartz, Alvin	J. B. Lippincott, 1981	tone
Scholastic Dictionary of Idioms	Terban, Marvin	Scholastic, 1998	idiom
Scholastic Rhyming Dictionary	Young, Sue	Scholastic, 1997	end rhyme, rhyme, tercet
School	McCully, Emily Arnold	Harper & Row, 1987	wordless book
Seasons Sewn: A Year in Patchwork	Paul, Ann Whitford	Harcourt Brace, 1996	scratch board
Secret Stars	Slate, Joseph	Marshall Cavendish, 1985	decorative frame
Sector 7	Wiesner, David	Clarion, 1999	watercolor
Seeing Things	Froman, Robert	Crowell, 1974	concrete poetry
Seven Blind Mice	Young, Ed	Philomel, 1992	retelling
Seven Chinese Brothers	Mahy, Margaret	Scholastic, 1990	stereotype
Seven Spools of Thread: A Kwanzaa Story	Medearis, Angela Shelf	Albert Whitman, 2000	linoleum block
Shades of Black: A Celebration of Our Children	Pinkney, Sandra L.	Scholastic, 2000	photography
Shake It to the One That You Love the Best: Play Songs and Lullabies from Black Musical Traditions	Mattox, Cheryl	Warren-Mattox Productions, 1989	lullaby

Title	Author	Publisher/Producer	Term(s)
Sir Gawain and the Loathly Lady	Wijngaard, Juan	Morrow, 1985	decorative frame
Sir Walter Ralegh and the Quest for El Dorado	Aronson, Marc	Houghton Mifflin, 2000	editor, information book, Robert F. Sibert Informational Book Award
Six Brave Explorers	Moerbeek, Kees	Price Stern Sloan, 1988	page shape
Six Sick Sheep: 101 Tongue Twisters	Cole, Joanna	Morrow, 1993	tongue twister
Sky Full of Poems	Merriam, Eve	Dell, 1986	concrete poetry
Skylark	MacLachlan, Patricia	HarperCollins, 1994	sequel
Slake's Limbo	Holman, Felice	Aladdin, 1986	survival story
Sleeping Beauty	Hyman, Trina Schart	Little Brown, 1974	motif
Sleeping Ugly	Yolen, Jane	Coward, McCann & Geoghegan, 1981	fairy tale, fractured tale
Smoky Night	Bunting, Eve	Harcourt Brace, 1994	collage, expressionism
Smoky Night	Diaz, David	Harcourt Brace, 1994	hand-lettering
Snow	Shulevitz, Uri	Farrar, Straus & Giroux, 1998	India ink, typeface, watercolor
Snow Queen	Anderson, Hans Christian	HarperCollins, 1996	pageant
Snow White	Grimm, Jacob and Wilhelm	Farrar, Straus & Giroux, 1972	motif
Snowflake Bentley	Briggs, Jacqueline	Houghton Mifflin, 1999	woodcut
Snowman	Briggs, Raymond	Random, 1970	comic strip
Snowy Day	Keats, Ezra Jack	Viking, 1962	collage, imagery

Title	Author	Publisher/Producer	Term(s)
So Many Dynamos! And Other Palindromes	Agee, Jon	Farrar, Straus & Giroux, 1994	palindromes
So You Want to be President?	St. George, Judith	Philomel, 2000	cartoon, watercolor
Soldier's Heart	Paulsen, Gary	Delacorte, 1998	novella
Some Smug Slug	Edward, Pamela	HarperCollins, 1996	alliteration
Something about the Author		Gale Research, 1971-	author
Something about the Author: Autobiography Series		Gale Research, 1971-	author
Song and Dance Man	Ackerman, Karen	Knopf, 1988	analogy
Song of the Swallows	Politi, Leo	Scribner, 1949	tempera
Songs for Survival: Songs and Chants from Tribal People Around the World	Siegen-Smith, Nikki	Dutton, 1996	chant
Sounder	Armstrong, William	Harper & Row, 1969	poetic justice, sociological criticism, tragedy
Sparrowboy	Pinkney, Brian	Simon & Schuster	comic strip
Spindle's End	McKinley, Robin	Putnam, 2000	comedy
Splish, Splash	Graham, Jan Bransfield	Ticknor & Fields, 1994	concrete poetry
Spoon for Every Bite	Hayes, Joe	Orchard, 1996	pastels
Spring: An Alphabet Acrostic	Schnur, Steven	Clarion, 1999	acrostic
Squanto's Journey: The Story of the First Thanksgiving	Bruchac, Joseph	Harcourt, 2000	glossary

Title	Author	Publisher/Producer	Term(s)
Squids Will Be Squids: Fresh Morals: Beastly Fables	Scieszka, Jon	Viking, 1998	fable
St. Jerome and the Lion	Hodges, Margaret	Orchard, 1991	hand-lettering
Star Spangled Banner	Key, Francis Scott	Doubleday, 1973	anthem
Stay!: Keepers Story	Lowry, Lois	Houghton Mifflin, 1997	couplet
Steadfast Tin Soldier	Andersen, Hans Christian	Turtleback, 1997	literary tale
Stevie	Steptoe, John	Harper & Row, 1969	chalk
Stinker from Space	Service, Pamela	Scribner, 1988	science fiction
Stinky Cheeseman and Other Fairly Stupid Tales	Scieszka, Jon	Viking, 1992	fractured tale
Stone Bench in an Empty Park	Janezko, Paul B.	Orchard, 2000	haiku
Stone Bench in an Empty Park	Silberman, Henri	Orchard, 2000	visual literacy
Stone Fox	Gardiner, John	Crowell, 1980	conflict
Stonecutter	McDermott, Gerald	Penguin, 1975	motif, visual literacy
Stonewords	Conrad, Pam	HarperCollins, 1990	fantasy
Stopping by Woods on a Snowy Evening	Frost, Robert	Dutton, 1978	lyric
Stories that Julian Tells	Cameron, Ann	Random, 1981	chapter book, reader response theory
Storm in the Night	Stolz, Mary	HarperCollins, 1988	realistic art
Story of Jumping Mouse	Steptoe, John	Lothrop, 1984	graphite, pourquoi

Title	Author	Publisher/Producer	Term(s)
Story of the Milky Way	Bruchac, Joseph & Gayle Ross	Dial, 1995	pourquoi
Story Puzzles: Tales in Tangram Tradition	Marsh, Valerie	Highsmith, 1996	tangram
Stowaway	Hesse, Karen	Simon & Schuster, 2000	setting
Strawberry Girl	Lensky, Lois	Harper & Row, 1945	regional literature
Street Called Home	Robinson, Aminah Brenda Lynn	Harcourt Brace, 1997	folk art
Strega Nona	DePaola, Tomie	Prentice, 1975	graphite
Strega Nona (Book on tape)	DePaola, Tomie	Recorded Books, Inc., 1999	book on tape
Strega Nona: An Old Tale	DePaola, Tomie	Simon & Schuster, 1975	climax
Stuck Rubber Baby	Cruse, Howard	Paradox, 1995	graphic novel
Subtle Knife	Pullman, Phillip	Knopf, 1997	trilogy
Sugarbush Spring	Chall, Marsha Wilson	Lothrop, Lee & Shepard, 2000	realistic art
Sukey and the Mermaid	Pinkney, Brian	Four Winds, 1992	pastels
Summer of the Swans	Byars, Betsy	Viking, 1970	autobiography
Sun and Spoon	Henkes, Kevin	Greenwillow, 1997	contemporary realistic fiction
Sun Moon Star	Vonnegut, Kurt	Harper & Row, 1980	abstract art
Sundiate, Lion King of Mali	Wisniewski, David	Clarion, 1999	paper cuts
Surfeit of Similes	Juster, Norman	William Morrow, 1989	simile
Surprising Myself	Fritz, Jean	Owen, 1992	autobiography

Title	Author	Publisher/Producer	Term(s)
Swamp Angel	Isaacs, Anne	Dutton, 1994	oil paint
Sweetest Fig	Van Allsburg, Chris	Houghton Mifflin, 1993	irony
Sylvester and the Magic Pebble	Steig, William	Simon & Schuster, 1969	cartoon, illustrator
Synonym Finder	Rodale, J. I.	Warner, 1986	synonym
Tale of Peter Rabbit	Potter, Beatrix	Frederick Warne, 1902	antagonist, book size, character, imagery, poetic justice, romance
Tale of Rabbit and Coyote	Johnston, Tony	Putnam, 1994	motif
Tales of Mother Goose	Perrault, Charles	1697	nursery rhymes
Tales of Uncle Remus	Lester, Julius	Penguin Putnam, 1988, 1989	dialect, trickster tale
Talking with the Artists	Cummings, Pat	Bradbury, 1992	collected biography, illustrator
Talking with the Artists, Volume Three	Cummings, Pat	Clarion, 1999	collected biography, illustrator
Talking with the Artists, Volume Two	Cummings, Pat	Simon & Schuster, 1995	collected biography, illustrator
Tangram Discovery Box	Tompert, Ann	Scholastic, 1997	tangram
Tar Beach	Ringgold, Faith	Crown, 1991	acrylic, allusion, fabric
Tattercoats	Watts, Bernadette	Holt, 1989	folktale
Teammates	Golenbock, Peter	Harcourt Brace, 1990	biography
Telling of the Tales: Five Stories	Brooke, William J.	Harper & Row, 1990	fractured tale

Title	Author	Publisher/Producer	Term(s)
Ten Queens: Portraits of Women of Power	Meltzer, Milton	Dutton, 1998	collected biography
Ten, Nine, Eight	Bang, Molly	Putnam, 1998	counting book
Thank You, Mr. Falker!	Polacco, Patricia	Spoken Arts, 1999	book on tape
There Was a Hill	Carrier, Lark	Picture Book Studio, 1984	page shape
There Was an Old Lady Who Swallowed a Fly	Taback, Simms	Viking 1997	cumulative tale, die-cutting, retelling
This Is the Sunflower	Schaefer, Lola	Greenwillow, 2000	air brush
This Is the Way We Eat Our Lunch	Baer, Edith	Scholastic, 1995	parallel story
This Is the Way We Go to School	Baer, Edith	Scholastic, 1990	parallel story
This Land Is Your Land	Guthrie, Woody	Little, Brown, 1998	folk art, folk song
Three Bears	Galdone, Paul	Clarion, 1972	predictable book
Three Billy Goats Gruff	Stevens, Janet	Harcourt Brace, 1987	big book
Three Little Kittens	Galdone, Paul	Houghton Mifflin, 1986	nursery rhymes
Three Little Pigs	Galdone, Paul	Clarion, 1979	archetype
Three Little Pigs	Reinl, Edda	Simon & Schuster, 1991	batik
Through the Looking Glass	Carroll, Lewis	Random House, 1946	nonsense verse
Through the Looking-Glass and What Alice Found There	Carroll, Lewis	1872	onomatopoeia
Throwing Smoke	Brooks, Bruce	HarperCollins, 2000	magical realism

Title	Author	Publisher/Producer	Term(s)
Thump, Thump, Rat-A-Tat-Tat	Baer, Gene	Harper & Row, 1989	pattern book
Thunder Cake	Polacco, Patricia	Philomel, 1990	pastels
Tibet: Through the Red Box	Sis, Peter	Farrar, Straus & Giroux, 1998	mixed media, typeface
Tickle, Tickle	Oxenbury, Helen	Dutton, 1994	wash
'Til Their Eyes Shine: The Lullaby Album	Sony, Campbell	Sony/Campbell, 1992	Lullaby
Time of Wonder	McCloskey, Robert	Viking, 1957	casein paint, color
Timothy of the Cay	Taylor, Theodore	Harcourt Brace, 1993	prequel
Tin Heart	Ackerman, Karen	Atheneum, 1997	style
To Be a Drum	Coleman, Evelyn	Albert Whitman, 1998	folk art
To Market, To Market	Miranda, Anne	Harcourt Brace, 1997	nursery rhymes
A to Z Picture Book	Fujikawa, Gyo	Grosset & Dunlap, 1984	pointillism
Today is Monday	Carle, Eric	Philomel, 1993	predictable book
Tom Sawyer	Twain, Mark	1876	classic
Too Hot to Hoot: Funny Palindrome Riddles	Treban, Marvin	Houghton, 1985	palindromes
Tops and Bottoms	Stevens, Janet	Harcourt Brace, 1995	double spread, mixed media, page layout, retelling, trickster tale
Touch Magic: Fantasy, Faerie and Folklore in the Literature of Children	Yolen, Jane	August, 2000	literary tale

Title	Author	Publisher/Producer	Term(s)
Twentieth Century Children's Poetry Treasury	Prelutsky, Jack	Knopf, 1999	stanza
Two by Two	Reid, Barbara	Scholastic, 1993	modeling clay
Two of Everything	Hong, Lily Toy	Whitman, 1993	air brush
Tyger	Blake, William	Harcourt Brace Jovanovich, 1993	lyric
Ugly Duckling	Andersen, Hans Christian	Morrow, 1999	endpapers, literary tale, retelling, satire
Ultimate Alphabet	Wilks, Mike	Holt, 1986	dictionary
Uncle Jed's Barbershop	Mitchell, Margaree King	Simon & Schuster, 1993	realistic art
Up Goes the Skyscraper	Gibbons, Gail	Four Winds, 1986	book size
Up in the Air	Livingston, Myra Cohn	Holiday; 1989	metaphor
Velveteen Rabbit	Williams, Margery	Doubleday, 1922	fantasy
Very Hungry Caterpillar	Carle, Eric	Philomel, 1969	pattern book, reader response theory
View from Saturday	Konigsburg, E. L.	Atheneum, 1996	contemporary realistic fiction, exposition, psychological criticism, stanza, style, symbol
Village of Round and Square Houses	Grifilconi, Ann	Little, Brown, 1986	chalk
Virgie Goes to School with Us Boys	Howard, Elizabeth	Simon & Schuster, 2000	watercolor
Voices in the Park	Brown, Anthony	DK, 1998	radical change

Title	Author	Publisher/Producer	Term(s)
Voices in the Park	Browne, Anthony	Dorling Kindersley, 1998	surrealism
Waiting for Wings	Ehlert, Lois	Harcourt, 2001	page shape
Walk Two Moons	Creech, Sharon	HarperCollins, 1994	contemporary realistic fiction, setting, subplot
Wanderer	Creech, Sharon	HarperCollins, 2000	adventure story
Wash Day on Noah's Ark	Rounds, Glen	Holiday, 1985	chalk
Watch William Walk	Jonas, Ann	Greenwillow, 1997	alliteration
Watership Down	Adams, Richard	Macmillan, 1972	bestiary
Wave of the Sea-World	Wisniewski, David	Clarion, 1994	paper cuts
We're Going on a Bear Hunt	Rosen, Michael	Macmillan, 1989	reader response theory
We're Making Breakfast for Mother	Neitzel, Shirley	Greenwillow, 1997	rebus
Welcome to the Green House	Yolen, Jane	Putnam, 1993	internal rhyme
Welcome to the Ice House	Yolen, Jane	Putnam, 1998	imagery
Wemberly Worried	Henkes, Kevin	Greenwillow, 2000	watercolor
Westing Game	Raskin, Ellen	Dutton, 1978	irony, mystery
What Do Illustrators Do?	Christelow, Eileen	Clarion, 1999	illustrator, storyboard
When Birds Could Talk and Bats Could Sing: The Adventures of Bruh Sparrow, Sis Wren and Her Friends	Hamilton, Virginia	Scholastic, 1996	dialect, fable
When Cats Dream	Pilkey, Dav	Orchard, 1992	surrealism

Title	Author	Publisher/Producer	Term(s)
When I Was Young in the Mountains	Rylant, Cynthia	Dutton, 1982	biographical criticism, nostalgia, regional literature
When Sophie Gets Angry—Really, Really Angry	Bang, Molly	Scholastic, 1999	gouache
When This Box is Full	Lillie, Patricia	Greenwillow, 1993	photography
When Zachary Beaver Came to Town	Holt, Kimberly Willis	Holt, 1999	flat character, problem novel
Where the Forest Meets the Sea	Baker, Jeannie	Greenwillow, 1987	collage
Where the River Begins	Locker, Thomas	Dial, 1984	oil paint
Where the Sidewalk Ends	Silverstein, Shel	Harper & Row, 1974	assonance, reading aloud
Where the Wild Things Are	Sendak, Maurice	Harper & Row, 1963	adaptation, atmosphere, color, foreshadowing, illustrator, romance, tempera
Where's Spot	Hall, Eric	Putnam, 1980	participation book
Where's Spot?	Hill, Eric	Putnam, 1980	predictable book
Whose Mouse are You?	Kraus, Robert	Macmillan, 1970	pattern book
Why Mosquitoes Buzz in People's Ears	Aardema, Verna	Dial, 1975	air brush, pourquoi
Wild Children	Holman, Felice	Puffin, 1985	survival story
Wildflower ABC: An Alphabet of Potato Prints	Pomeroy, Diana	Harcourt Brace, 1997	potato printing
Will Rogers: Larger Than Life	Dadey, Debbie	Walker, 1999	hyperbole

Title	Author	Publisher/Producer	Term(s)
Winter Room	Paulsen, Gary	Orchard Books, 1989	imagery
Wish You Were Here and I Wasn't: A Book of Poems and Pictures for Globe-Trotters	McNaughton, Colin	Candlewick, 2000	anthology
Witch of Blackbird Pond	Speare, Elizabeth	Houghton Mifflin, 1958	complication, conflict
With a Whoop and a Holler: A Bushel of Lore from Way Down South	Van Laan, Nancy	Atheneum 1998	anthology, dialect
Wonderful Wizard of Oz: A Commemorative Pop-up	Sabuda, Robert	Little, Simon, 2000	toy book
Word to the Wise and other Proverbs	Johanna Hurwitz	Morrow, 1994	proverb
Words from the Myths	Asimov, Isaac	Houghton, 1961	myth
Working Cotton	Williams, Sherley Ann	Harcourt Brace Jovanovich, 1992	dialect, impressionism
World Sings Goodnight, Volumes 1 and 2		Silver Wave, 1993	lullaby
World's Toughest Tongue Twisters	Rosenbloom, Joseph	Sterling, 1987	tongue twister
Wrapping Paper Romp	Hubbell, Patricia	HarperCollins, 1998	board book
Wright Brothers: How They Invented the Airplane	Freedman, Russell	Holiday, 1991	bibliography, subtitle
Wringer	Spinelli, Jerry	HarperCollins, 1997	comic relief, psychological criticism

Title	Author	Publisher/Producer	Term(s)
Wrinkle in Time	L'Engle, Madeleine	Farrar, Straus & Giroux, 1962	science fiction
Year Down Yonder	Peck, Richard	Dial, 2000	historical fiction, sequel
Year of Beasts	Wolff, Ashley	Dutton, 1986	linoleum block
Year of Birds	Wolff, Ashley	Dodd, Mead, 1984	linoleum block
Year with Grandma Moses	Nikola-Lisa, W.	Henry Holt, 2000	folk art
Yeh Shen: A Cinderella Story from China	Louie, Ai-Ling	Putnam, 1982	folktale
Yo, Hungry Wolff A Nursery Rap	Vozar, David	Delacorte, 1993	internal rhyme
You Are Here	Crews, Nina	Greenwillow, 1998	aesthetic scanning, photography
Young Black Stallion	Farley, Walter and Steven	Random House, 1989	prequel
Yours Truly, Goldilocks	Ada, Alma Flor	Atheneum, 1998	letters
Zin! Zin! Zin! A Violin	Moss, Lloyd	Simon & Schuster, 1995	double spread, gouache
Zin! Zin! Zin! A Violin	Priceman, Marjorie	Weston Woods, 1999	book on tape
Zoom City	Hurd, Thatcher	Harper Festival, 1998	board book

Author Index

This index is provided to facilitate access to terms for readers looking for entries referring to a particular author. Full information for each title listed below is contained in the preceding index, pages 195–256.

Author	Title
Ames, Lee J.	*Draw 50 Famous Caricatures*
Ancona, George	*Barrio: José's Neighborhood*
Ancona, George	*Carnaval*
Andersen, Hans Christian	*The Emperor's New Clothes*
Andersen, Hans Christian	*The Snow Queen*
Andersen, Hans Christian	*The Steadfast Tin Soldier*
Andersen, Hans Christian	*The Ugly Duckling*
Anderson, Joan	*Cowboys: Roundup on an American Ranch*
Anno, Mitsumasa	*Anno's Aesop*
Anno, Mitsumasa	*Anno's Journey*
Archambault, John and Bill Martin	*Chicka Chicka Boom Boom*
Armstrong, William	*Sounder*
Aronson, Marc	*Sir Walter Ralegh and the Quest for El Dorado*
Asher, Sandy	*But That's Another Story: Favorite Authors Introduce Popular Genres*
Asimov, Isaac	*The Fantastic Voyage*
Asimov, Isaac	*Words from the Myths*
Avi	*Midnight Magic*
Avi	*Nothing But the Truth: A Documentary Novel*
Avi	*The True Confessions of Charlotte Doyle*
Babbitt, Natalie	*Goody Hall*
Babbitt, Natalie	*Tuck Everlasting*
Baer, Edith	*This Is the Way We Eat Our Lunch*
Baer, Edith	*This Is the Way We Go to School*
Baer, Gene	*Thump, Thump, Rat-A-Tat-Tat*
Baker, Jeannie	*Where the Forest Meets the Sea*
Baker, Keith	*Big Fat Hen*
Bang, Molly	*The Grey Lady and the Strawberry Snatcher*
Bang, Molly	*The Paper Crane*
Bang, Molly	*Ten, Nine, Eight*
Bang, Molly	*When Sophie Gets Angry—Really, Really Angry*
Baring-Gould, William	*Annotated Mother Goose*
Base, Graeme	*Animalia*
Bauer, Joan	*Hope Was Here*
Bauer, Marion Dane	*On My Honor*
Baylor, Byrd	*The Best Town in the World*
Bedard, Michael	*Emily*
Bellairs, John	*The Mummy, the Will and the Crypt*
Belpré, Pura	*Laughing Out Loud, I Fly: Poems in English and Spanish*
Bemelman, Ludwig	*Madeline*
Ben-Ezer, Ehud	*Hosni the Dreamer: An Arabian Tale*
Besson, Jean-Louis	*October 45*
Bial, Raymond	*Mist Over the Mountains: Appalachia and Its People*

Author	Title
Butler, Samuel	*Erewhon*
Byars, Betsy	*The Midnight Fox*
Byars, Betsy	*The Moon and I*
Byars, Betsy	*The Not-Just-Anybody Family*
Byars, Betsy	*The Summer of the Swans*
Cameron, Ann	*Julian's Glorious Summer*
Cameron, Ann	*More Stories Julian Tells*
Cameron, Ann	*The Stories that Julian Tells*
Campbell, Fiona	*Calligraphy*
Capucilli, Alyssa	*Inside a Barn in the Country: A Read Along Story*
Carle, Eric	*The Bad-Tempered Ladybird Hamilton*
Carle, Eric	*Dreamsnow.*
Carle, Eric	*The Grouchy Ladybug*
Carle, Eric	*Today is Monday*
Carle, Eric	*The Very Hungry Caterpillar*
Carlsen, G. Robert	*Books and the Teenage Reader*
Carrier, Lark	*There Was a Hill*
Carroll, Lewis	*Alice in Wonderland*
Carroll, Lewis	*Alice's Adventures Under Ground*
Carroll, Lewis	*Through the Looking-Glass and What Alice Found There*
Carter, David A. and James Diaz	*Elements of a Pop-up*
Cauley, Lorinda Bryan	*Clap Your Hands*
Cha, Dia	*Dia's Story Cloth*
Chalk, Gary	*Mr. Frog Went a Courting*
Chall, Marsha Wilson	*Sugarbush Spring*
Chase, Edith Newlin	*The New Baby Calf*
Chase, Richard	*The Jack Tales*
Christelow, Eileen	*What Do Illustrators Do?*
Christian, Peggy	*If You Find a Rock*
Ciardi, John	*The Hopeful Trout and Other Limericks*
Clark, Margaret	*The Best of Aesop*
Cleary, Beverly	*A Girl from Yamhill: A Memoir*
Cleary, Beverly	*Beezus and Ramona*
Cleary, Beverly	*Dear Mr. Henshaw*
Cleary, Beverly	*The Mouse and the Motorcycle*
Cleary, Beverly	*My Own Two Feet: A Memoir*
Cleary, Beverly	*Ramona the Pest*
Cleary, Beverly	*Ramona's World*
Climo, Shirley	*The Egyptian Cinderella*
Cohen, Barbara	*Canterbury Tales*
Cohn, Amy L.	*From Sea to Shining Sea: A Treasury of American Folklore and Folk Songs*
Cole, Babette	*Hair in Funny Places: A Book about Puberty*

Author	Title
Cole, Babette	*Prince Cinders*
Cole, Joanna	*Anna Banana: 101 Jump-Rope Rhymes*
Cole, Joanna	*Six Sick Sheep: 101 Tongue Twisters*
Coleman, Evelyn	*To Be a Drum*
Colller, Bryan	*Freedom River*
Conrad, Pam	*Stonewords*
Cooney, Barbara	*Chanticleer and the Fox*
Cooney, Barbara	*Miss Rumphius*
Cooper, Cathie Hilterbran	*ABC Books and Activities: From Preschool to High School*
Cooper, Cathie Hilterbran	*Counting Your Way through 1-2-3: Books and Activities*
Cooper, Floyd	*Coming Home: From the Life of Langston Hughes*
Cooper, Susan	*Dark Is Rising*
Cooper, Susan	*Dark is Rising Series*
Coopor, Susan	*Over Sea Under Stone*
Cormier, Robert	*The Chocolate War*
Couloumbis, Audrey	*Getting Near to Baby*
Cousins, Lucy	*The Lucy Cousins Book of Nursery Rhymes*
Cousins, Lucy	*Maisy's Pop-up Playhouse*
Coville, Bruce	*Aliens Ate My Homework*
Coville, Bruce	*Jeremy Thatcher, Dragon Hatcher*
Cowley, Joy	*Red-Eyed Tree Frog*
Creech, Sharon	*Walk Two Moons*
Creech, Sharon	*The Wanderer*
Crews, Donald	*Bigmama's*
Crews, Donald	*Carousel*
Crews, Donald	*Flying*
Crews, Donald (big book)	*Freight Train*
Crews, Donald	*Sail Away*
Crews, Nina	*You Are Here*
Cronin, Doreen	*Click Clack Moo: Cows that Type*
Cruse, Howard	*Stuck Rubber Baby*
Crutcher, Chris	*Athletic Shorts*
Cummings, Pat	*Talking with the Artists*
Cummings, Pat	*Talking with the Artists*, Volume Two
Cummings, Pat	*Talking with the Artists*, Volume Three
Curl, Michael	*The Anagram Dictionary*
Curtis, Christopher Paul	*Bud, Not Buddy*
Curtis, Christopher Paul (book on tape)	*Bud, Not Buddy*
Cushman, Karen	*Catherine Called Birdy*
Cushman, Karen	*The Midwife's Apprentice*
D'Aulaire, Ingri and Edgar Parin	*Abraham Lincoln*
D'Aulaire, Ingri and Edgar Parin	*D'Aulaire's Book of Greek Myths*

Author	Title
Dadey, Debbie	*Will Rogers: Larger Than Life*
Dahl, Roald	*James and the Giant Peach*
Davis, Robin	*Big Books for Little People*
Davol, Marguerite W.	*The Paper Dragon*
De Cumptich, Roberto de Vicq	*Bembo's Zoo: An Animal ABC*
De Regnier, Beatrice Schenk	*Sing a Song of Popcorn: Every Child's Favorite Book of Poems*
Deem, James M.	*Bodies from the Bog*
DePaola, Tomie	*The Legend of the Bluebonnet*
DePaola, Tomie	*Pancakes for Breakfast*
DePaola, Tomie	*The Popcorn Book*
DePaola, Tomie	*Strega Nona: An Old Tale*
DePaola, Tomle	*26 Falrmont Avenue*
Der Manuelian, Peter	*Hieroglyphs from A to Z: A Rhyming Book with Ancient Egyptian Stencils for Kids*
Di Camillio, Kate	*Because of Winn-Dixie*
Diakite, Baba Wague	*The Hatseller and the Monkeys: A West African Folktale*
Diaz, David	*Smoky Night*
Dickens, Charles	*David Copperfield*
Dickens, Charles	*Great Expectations*
Dicks, Terrance	*The Baker Street Irregulars Series*
Dorling Kindersley	*Eyewitness Series*
Dr. Seuss	*The Cat in the Hat*
Dr. Seuss	*The 500 Hats of Bartholomew Cubbins*
Dr. Seuss	*How the Grinch Stole Christmas*
Dragonwagon, Crescent	*Home Place*
Duncan, Lois	*On the Edge: Stories on the Brink*
Edmiston, Jim	*Little Eagle and Lots of Owls*
Edward, Pamela	*Some Smug Slug*
Edwards, Michele	*Dora's Book*
Ehlert, Lois	*Color Farm*
Ehlert, Lois	*Color Zoo*
Ehlert, Lois	*Eating the Alphabet: Fruits and Vegetables from A to Z*
Ehlert, Lois	*Feathers for Lunch*
Ehlert, Lois	*Hands*
Ehlert, Lois	*Planting a Rainbow*
Ehlert, Lois	*Red Leaf, Yellow Leaf*
Ehlert, Lois	*Waiting for Wings*
Eisner, Will	*A Contract with God: And Other Tenement Stories*
Emberley, Barbara	*Drummer Hoff*
Emberley, Ed	*Fingerprint Drawing Book*
Emberley, Michael	*Ruby*

Author	Title
Enzensberger, Hans Magnus	The Number Devil: A Mathematical Adventure
Ernst, Lisa Campbell	Little Red Riding Hood: A Newfangled Prairie Tale
Ets, Marie Hall	In the Forest
Ets, Marie Hall	Just Me
Ets, Marie Hall	Mr. Penny's Race Horse
Ets, Marie Hall	Mr. T.W. Anthony Woo
Ets, Marie Hall	Play with Me
Falconer, Ian	Olivia
Farley, Walter and Steven	The Young Black Stallion
Farmer, Nancy	The Ear, the Eye, & the Arm: A Novel
Feelings, Muriel	Jambo Means Hello: Swahili Alphabet Book
Feelings, Muriel	Moja Means One: Swahili Counting Book
Feelings, Tom	The Middle Passage: White Ships, Black Cargo
Ferris, Helen	Favorite Poems Old and New
Field, Eugene	Poems of Childhood
Fish, Helen Dean	Animals of the Bible
Fitzhugh, Louise	Harriet the Spy
Fleischman, Paul	Big Talk: Poems for Four Voices
Fleischman, Paul	Bull Run
Fleischman, Paul	I Am Phoenix: Poems for Two Voices
Fleischman, Paul	Joyful Noise: Poems for Two Voices
Fleming, Denise	Count
Fleming, Denise	The Everything Book
Fleming, Denise	In the Small, Small Pond
Fleming, Denise	In the Tall, Tall Grass
Fleming, Denise	Lunch
Fleming, Denise	Painting with Paper: Easy Papermaking Fun for the Entire Family
Frazee, Marla	Hush Little Baby: A Folk Song with Pictures
Freedman, Russell	Eleanor Roosevelt: A Life of Discovery
Freedman, Russell	Kids at Work
Freedman, Russell	Lincoln: A Photobiography
Freedman, Russell	The Wright Brothers: How They Invented the Airplane
Freeman, Don	A Pocket for Corduroy
Freeman, Judy	More Books Kids Will Sit Still For: A Read Aloud Guide
Friedman, Robin	How I Survived My Summer Vacation and Lived to Write About It
Fritz, Jean	Homesick: My Own Story
Fritz, Jean	Surprising Myself
Froman, Robert	Seeing Things
Frost, Robert	Stopping by Woods on a Snowy Evening
Fujikawa, Gyo	A to Z Picture Book

Author	Title
Funk, Charles Earle	*A Hog on Ice and Other Curious Expressions*
Funk, Charles Earle	*Heavens to Betsy and Other Curious Sayings*
Gag, Wanda	*Millions of Cats*
Galdone, Paul	*The Three Bears*
Galdone, Paul	*The Three Little Kittens*
Galdone, Paul	*The Three Little Pigs*
Gallow, Donald	*Short Circuits: Thirteen Shocking Stories by Outstanding Writers for Young Adults*
Gantos, Jack	*Joey Pigza Swallowed the Key*
Gardiner, John	*Stone Fox*
Gardner, John	*A Child's Bestiary*
Gardnier, Lindsay	*Here Come Poppy and Max*
Garland, Michael	*Dinner at Margritte's*
Garza, Carmen Lomas	*Magic Windows/Ventanas M·gicas*
Garza, Carmen Lomas	*Making Magic Windows*
Gates, Doris	*Blue Willow*
Geisert, Arthur	*After the Flood*
Geisert, Arthur	*The Ark*
Geisert, Arthur	*Oink*
Geisert, Arthur	*Pigs from 1 to 1*
Geisert, Arthur	*Pigs from A to Z*
George, Jean Craighead	*The First Thanksgiving*
George, Jean Craighead	*Julie of the Wolves*
George, Jean Craighead	*My Side of the Mountain*
George, Kristen O'Connell	*The Great Frog Race and Other Poems*
George, Kristen O'Connell	*Little Dog Poems*
George, Kristen O'Connell	*Old Elm Speaks: Tree Poems*
Gerstein, Mordicai	*Noah and the Great Flood*
Gibbons, Gail	*Apples*
Gibbons, Gail	*Gulls...Gulls...Gulls...*
Gibbons, Gail	*Rabbits, Rabbits & More Rabbits!*
Gibbons, Gail	*Up Goes the Skyscraper*
Giblin, James Cross	*The Amazing Life of Benjamin Franklin*
Giff, Patricia Reilly	*Polka Dot Private Eyes Series*
Gilbert, Barbara Snow	*Paper Trail*
Ginsburg, Mira	*Asleep, Asleep*
Gisert, Arthur	*The Etcher's Studio*
Goble, Paul	*The Gift of the Sacred Dog*
Goble, Paul	*The Girl Who Loved Wild Horses*
Goble, Paul	*Her Seven Brothers*
Goldstein, Bobbye	*Inner Chimes*
Golenbock, Peter	*Teammates*
Gollub, Matthew	*Cool Melons—Turn to Frogs! The Life and Poems of Issa*
Goodall, John	*Shrewbettina's Birthday*

Author	Title
Graham, Jan Bransfield	Flicker Flash
Graham, Jan Bransfield	Splish, Splash
Gray, Libba Moore	My Mama Had a Dancing Heart
Greenberg, Jan and Sandra Jordan	Chuck Close, Up Close
Greenstein, Elaine	Emily and The Crows
Greenstein, Elaine	Mrs. Rose's Garden
Greenwald, Sheila	It All Began with Jane Eyre: Or, The Secret Life of Franny Dillman
Grifilconi, Ann	The Village of Round and Square Houses
Grimal, Pierre	Larousse World Mythology
Grimes, Nikki	It's Raining Laughter
Grimm, Jacob and Wilhelm	Hansel and Gretel
Grimm, Jacob and Wilhelm	Little Red Riding Hood
Grimm, Jacob and Wilhelm	Snow White
Grindley, Sally	A Flag for Grandma
Grossman, John	The Chicago Manual of Style
Guthrie, Woody	Grow Big Songs
Guthrie, Woody	This Land Is Your Land
Hague, Michael	Aesop's Fables
Hague, Kathleen	The Legend of the Veery Bird
Hague, Michael	Michael Hague's Favorite Hans Christian Andersen Fairy Tales
Hague, Michael	Mother Goose: A Collection of Classic Nursery Rhymes
Haines, Helen	Living with Books
Hale, Josepha	Mary Had a Little Lamb
Haley, Gail	The Post Office Cat
Hall, Donald	Ox-Cart Man
Hall, Donald	The Oxford Book of Children's Verses in America
Hall, Eric	Where's Spot
Halpern, Shari	Hush Little Baby
Hamilton, Virginia	The House of Dies Drear
Hamilton, Virginia	In the Beginning: Creation Stories From Around the World
Hamilton, Virginia	The People Could Fly: American Black Folktales
Hamilton, Virginia	When Birds Could Talk and Bats Could Sing: The Adventures of Bruh Sparrow, Sis Wren and Her Friends
Harley, Avis	Fly With Poetry: An ABC of Poetry
Harper, Isabelle	My Dog Rosie
Harris, Joel Chandler	Jump Again! More Adventures of Brer Rabbit
Harris, Joel Chandler	Jump on Over! The Adventures of Brer Rabbit and His Family

Author	Title
Harris, Joel Chandler	*Jump! The Adventures of Brer Rabbit*
Hastings, Selina	*Sir Gawain and the Loathly Lady*
Haugaard, Erik	*Hans Christian Andersen: The Complete Fairy Tales & Stories*
Hayes, Joe	*A Spoon for Every Bite*
Heard, Georgia	*Creatures of Earth, Sea, and Sky*
Heller, Ruth	*Color, Color, Color*
Hendershot, Judith	*In Coal Country*
Henkes, Kevin	*Lilly's Purple Plastic Purse*
Henkes, Kevin	*Owen*
Henkes, Kevin	*Sun and Spoon*
Henkes, Kevin	*Wemberly Worried*
Henry, O.	*The Gift of the Magi*
Hepworth, Cathi	*Antics!*
Herald, Diana Tixier	*Genreflecting*
Herbert Scott, Ann	*One Good Horse: A Cowpuncher's Counting Book*
Hesse, Karen	*Letters from Rifka*
Hesse, Karen	*Out of the Dust*
Hesse, Karen	*Stowaway*
Hill, Eric	*Where's Spot?*
Hinton, S. E.	*The Outsiders*
Ho, Minfong	*Hush!: A Thai Lullaby*
Hoban, Tana	*Circles, Triangles, and Squares*
Hoban, Tana	*Colors Everywhere*
Hoban, Tana	*Look! Look! Look!*
Hoban, Tana	*26 Letters and 99 Cents*
Hobbs, Will	*Downriver*
Hobbs, Will	*Far North*
Hobbs, Will	*Jason's Gold*
Hodges, Margaret,	*Gulliver in Lilliput*
Hodges, Margaret	*Saint George and the Dragon*
Hodges, Margaret	*St. Jerome and the Lion*
Hoffman, Mary	*Amazing Grace*
Holden, Robert	*The Pied Piper of Hamelin*
Holm, Jennifer L.	*Our Only May Amelia*
Holman, Felice	*Slake's Limbo*
Holman, Felice	*Wild Children*
Holt, Kimberly Willis	*My Louisiana Sky*
Holt, Kimberly Willis	*My Louisiana Sky* (book on tape)
Holt, Kimberly Willis	*When Zachary Beaver Came to Town*
Hong, Lily Toy	*Two of Everything*
Hoover, H. M.	*Orvis*
Hopkins, Lee Bennet	*My America: A Poetry Atlas of the United States*
Howard, Elizabeth	*Virgie Goes to School with Us Boys*

Author	Title
Joyce, William	*Santa Calls*
Juster, Norman	*The Phantom Tollbooth*
Juster, Norman	*A Surfeit of Similes*
Keats, Ezra Jack	*The Snowy Day*
Keith, Harold	*Rifles for Watie*
Kelley, True	*I've Got Chicken Pox*
Kellog, Steven	*Johnny Appleseed*
Kellog, Steven	*Paul Bunyan*
Kellog, Steven	*Pecos Bill*
Kellog, Steven	*Sally Ann Thunder Ann Whirlwind Crockett*
Kennedy, X. J. and Dorothy	*Knock at a Star: A Child's Introduction to Poetry*
Key, Francis Scott	*The Star Spangled Banner*
Kherdian, David	*Feathers and Tails: Animal Fables from Around the World*
Kimmel, Eric A.	*Anansi and the Moss-Covered Rock*
Kimmel, Eric A.	*Anansi and the Talking Melon*
Kimmel, Eric	*Onions and Garlic: An Old Tale*
Kimmel, Eric	*The Runaway Tortilla*
King, Dave	*My First Photography Book*
Kipfer, Barbara Ann	*21st Century Synonym and Antonym Finder*
Konigsburg, E. L.	*From the Mixed-Up Files of Mrs. Basil E. Frankweiler*
Konigsburg, E. L.	*The View from Saturday*
Kraus, Robert	*Whose Mouse are You?*
Krauss, Ruth	*The Carrot Seed*
Kroll, Stephen	*By the Dawn's Early Light: The Story of the Star-Spangled Banner*
Krull, Kathleen	*Extraordinary Women: Rulers, Rebels (And What the Neighbors Thought)*
Krull, Kathleen	*Gonna Sing My Head Off! American Folk Songs for Children*
Kunhardt, Dorothy	*Pat the Bunny*
Kurtz, Jane	*Trouble*
Lahey, Vince	*River of No Return*
Langstaff, John	*Frog Went A-Courtin'*
Langton, Jane	*The Fledgling*
Larrick, Nancy	*Cats are Cats*
Lasky, Kathryn	*She's Wearing a Dead Bird on Her Head*
Lawson, Robert	*Ben and Me*
Lawson, Robert	*Rabbit Hill*
Lear, Edward	*A Book of Nonsense*
Lear, Edward	*The Complete Book of Nonsense*
Lear, Edward	*Nonsense Songs*

Author	Title
Lowry, Lois	*Anastasia Series*
Lowry, Lois	*The Giver*
Lowry, Lois	*Looking Back: A Book of Memories*
Lowry, Lois	*Number the Stars*
Lowry, Lois	*Stay!: Keepers Story*
Lynch, Tom	*Fables from Aesop*
Lyon, George Ella	*Day at Damp Camp*
Macaulay, David	*Black and White*
Macaulay, David	*Building Big*
Macaulay, David	*Castle*
Macaulay, David	*Cathedral: The Story of Its Construction*
Macaulay, David	*The New Way Things Work*
Macaulay, David	*Pyramid*
MacDonald, Suse	*Alphabatics*
MacLachlan, Patricia	*All the Places to Love*
MacLachlan, Patricia	*Sarah Plain and Tall*
MacLachlan, Patricia	*Skylark*
Mahy, Margaret	*Aliens in the Family*
Mahy, Margaret	*The Horrendous Hullabaloo*
Mahy, Margaret	*The Seven Chinese Brothers*
Malory, Thomas	*Morte d'Arthur*
Marcellino, Fred	*Puss in Boots*
Marcus, Leonard	*A Caldecott Celebration: Six Artists Share Their Paths to the Caldecott Medal*
Marsh, Valerie	*Story Puzzles: Tales in Tangram Tradition*
Marshak, Samuel	*The Absentminded Fellow*
Marshall, James	*Goldilocks and the Three Bears*
Marshall, James	*Pocketful of Nonsense*
Martin, Ann M. and Laura Godwin	*The Doll People*
Martin, Bill	*Brown Bear, Brown Bear*
Martin, Bill and John Archambault	*Chicka Chicka Boom Boom*
Marzollo, Jean	*I Love You: A Rebus Poem*
Mattox, Cheryl	*Shake It to the One That You Love the Best: Play Songs and Lullabies from Black Musical Traditions*
McBratney, Sam	*Guess How Much I Love You*
McCaughrean, Geraldine	*The Canterbury Tales*
McCaughrean, Geraldine	*One Thousand and One Arabian Nights*
McCloskey, Robert	*Make Way for Ducklings*
McCloskey, Robert	*Time of Wonder*
McCord, David	*"Excerpts from 'Write Me Another Verse'"*
McCord, David	*One at a Time: His Collected Poems for the Young*
McCully, Emily Arnold	*Mirette on the High Wire*
McCully, Emily Arnold	*Picnic*

Author	Title
McCully, Emily Arnold	*School*
McCurdy, Michael	*The Sailor's Alphabet*
McDermott, Gerald	*Arrow to the Sun*
McDermott, Gerald	*Coyote: A Trickster Tale from the American Southwest*
McDermott, Gerald	*Daughter of the Earth: A Roman Myth*
McDermott, Gerald	*Evolution of a Graphic Concept: The Stonecutter*
McDermott, Gerald	*Raven: A Trickster Tale from the Pacific Northwest*
McDermott, Gerald	*The Stonecutter*
McDonald, Ruth	*Dr. Seuss*
McKellar, Shona	*A Child's Book of Lullabies*
McKinley, Robin	*Spindle's End*
McKissack, Patricia C.	*Dark-thirty: Southern Tales of the Supernatural*
McKissack, Patricia C.	*Flossie and the Fox*
McKissack, Patricia C.	*A Million Fish...More or Less*
McKissack, Patricia C.	*Mirandy and Brother Wind*
McMillan, Bruce	*Counting Wildflowers*
McMillan, Bruce	*Growing Colors*
McMillan, Bruce	*Jelly Beans for Sale*
McMillan, Bruce	*Night of the Pufflings*
McMillan, Bruce	*One Sun: A Book of Terse Verse*
McMillan, Bruce	*Play Day: A Book of Terse Verse*
McNaughton, Colin	*Wish You Were Here and I Wasn't: A Book of Poems and Pictures for Globe-Trotters*
Meade, Holly	*Lullabies: An Illustrated Songbook*
Meddaugh, Susan	*Cinderella's Rat*
Medearis, Angela Shelf	*Seven Spools of Thread: A Kwanzaa Story*
Melmed, Laura Krauss	*Little Oh*
Meltzer, Milton	*Ten Queens: Portrains of Women of Power*
Mercer, Mayor	*A Boy, A Dog and A Frog*
Merriam, Eve	*It Doesn't Always Have to Rhyme*
Merriam, Eve	*A Sky Full of Poems*
Milhous, Katherine	*The Egg Tree*
Minarik, Else Holmelund	*Little Bear*
Minarik, Else Holmelund	*Little Bear's Visit*
Minters, Frances	*Cinder-Elly*
Miranda, Anne	*To Market, To Market*
Mitchell, Margaree King	*Uncle Jed's Barbershop*
Mochizuki, Ken	*Passage to Freedom: The Sugihara Story*
Moerbeek, Kees	*Six Brave Explorers*
Moliere	*The Bourgeois Gentleman*
Montgomery, Lucy Maud	Anne of Green Gables Series
Moore, Clement Clark	*The Night Before Christmas or a Visit from St. Nicholas*

Author	Title
Morris, Ann	*Bread Bread Bread*
Morrow, Barbara	*Edward's Portrait*
Moss, Lloyd	*Zin! Zin! Zin! A Violin*
Murphy, Jim	*Blizzard! The Storm That Changed America*
Musgrove, Margaret	*Ashanti to Zulu: African Traditions*
Myers, Walter Dean	*Brown Angels: An Album of Pictures and Verse*
Myers, Walter Dean	*Harlem: A Poem*
Myers, Walter Dean	*Monster*
Naylor, Phyllis Reynolds	*Alice Series*
Naylor, Phyllis Reynolds	*Jade Green: A Ghost Story*
Naylor, Phyllis Reynolds	*Shiloh*
Naylor, Phyllis Reynolds	*Shiloh Series*
Neitzel, Shirley	*The Bag I'm Taking to Grandma*
Neitzel, Shirley	*The Jacket I Wear to the Party*
Neitzel, Shirley	*The Jacket I Wear in the Snow*
Neitzel, Shirley	*We're Making Breakfast for Mother*
Nikola-Lisa, W.	*The Year with Grandma Moses*
Nixon, Joan Lowery	*The Name of the Game Was Murder*
Nixon, Joan Lowery	*The Other Side of Dark*
Numeroff, Laura Joffe	*If You Give a Mouse a Cookie*
Nye, Naomi Shihab	*Salting the Ocean: 100 Poems by Young Children*
O'Dell, Scott	*Island of the Blue Dolphins*
O'Kelly, Mattie Lou	*From the Hills of Georgia: An Autobiography in Paintings*
O'Neill, Mary	*Hailstones and Halibut Bones*
Opie, Iona	*Here Comes Mother Goose*
Opie, Iona and Peter	*I Saw Esau: The School Child's Pocket Book*
Opie, Iona and Peter	*The Oxford Dictionary of Nursery Rhymes*
Opie, Iona and Peter	*The Oxford Nursery Rhyme Book*
Oppenheim, Joanne	*Have You Seen Birds?*
Ormerod, Jan	*Moonlight*
Ormerod, Jan	*Once a Mouse*
Orwell, George	*Animal Farm*
Osborne, Mary Pope	*Kate and the Beanstalk*
Oxenbury, Helen	*All Fall Down*
Oxenbury, Helen	*Clap Hands*
Oxenbury, Helen	*Playing*
Oxenbury, Helen	*Say Goodnight*
Oxenbury, Helen	*Shopping Trip*
Oxenbury, Helen	*Tickle, Tickle*
Parks, Van Dyke	*Jump*
Parks, Van Dyke	*Jump Again*

Author	Title
Polacco, Patricia	*Thunder Cake*
Politi, Leo	*Song of the Swallows*
Pomeroy, Diana	*One Potato: A Counting Book of Potato Prints*
Pomeroy, Diana	*Wildflower ABC: An Alphabet of Potato Prints*
Potter, Beatrix	*The Tale of Peter Rabbit*
Prelutsky, Jack	*A. Nonny Mouse Writes Again!*
Prelutsky, Jack	*The New Kid on the Block*
Prelutsky, Jack	*A Pizza the Size of the Sun*
Prelutsky, Jack	*The Poems of A. Nonny Mouse*
Prelutsky, Jack	*The Random House Book of Poetry for Children: A Treasury of 572 Poems for Today's Child*
Prelutsky, Jack	*The Twentieth Century Children's Poetry Treasury*
Priceman, Marjorie	*Froggie Went A-Courtin'*
Priceman, Marjorie	*Zin! Zin! Zin! A Violin*
Provensen, Alice and Martin	*The Glorious Fight: Across the Channel with Louis Bleriot, July 25, 1909*
Provensen, Alice and Martin	*A Peaceable Kingdom: The Shaker Abecedarius*
Pullman, Phillip	*The Amber Spyglass*
Pullman, Phillip	*The Golden Compass*
Pullman, Phillip	*I Was a Rat!*
Pullman, Phillip	*The Subtle Knife*
Raatma, Lucia	*How Books Are Made*
Rankin, Laura	*The Handmade Alphabet*
Raschka, Chris	*Charlie Parker Played Be Bop*
Raskin, Ellen	*Nothing Ever Happens on my Block*
Raskin, Ellen	*The Westing Game*
Rathmann, Peggy	*Good Night, Gorilla*
Rathmann, Peggy	*Officer Buckle and Gloria*
Ray, Mary Lyn	*Shaker Boy*
Reid, Barbara	*Fun with Modeling Clay*
Reid, Barbara	*Playing with Plasticine*
Reid, Barbara	*Two by Two*
Reinl, Edda	*The Little Snake*
Reinl, Edda	*The Three Little Pigs*
Rhymer, Thomas	*Tragedies of the Last Age*
Rice, James	*Prairie Night Before Christmas*
Richardson, Judith Benet	*Come to My Party*
Ringgold, Faith	*Tar Beach*
Roberts, Fulton	*Chanticleer and the Fox: A Chaucerian Tale*
Roberts, Willo	*Babysitting Is a Dangerous Job*
Robinson, Aminah Brenda Lynn	*A Street Called Home*
Roche, Hanna	*My Mom Is Magic!*

Author	Title
Rodale, J. I.	Synonym Finder
Rodgers, Mary	Freaky Friday
Rosen, Michael J.	Elijah's Angel: A Story of Chanukah and Christmas
Rosen, Michael	We're Going on a Bear Hunt
Rosenbloom, Joseph	World's Toughest Tongue Twisters
Rounds, Glen	Wash Day on Noah's Ark
Rowling, J. K.	Harry Potter and the Chamber of Secrets
Rowling, J. K.	Harry Potter and the Goblet of Fire
Rowling, J. K.	Harry Potter and the Philosopher's Stone
Rowling, J. K.	Harry Potter and the Sorcerer's Stone
Rowling, J. K.	Harry Potter Series
Rylant, Cynthia	Appalachia: Voices of Sleeping Birds
Rylant, Cynthia	Best Wishes
Rylant, Cynthia	But I'll Be Back Again
Rylant, Cynthia	Every Living Thing
Rylant, Cynthia	Henry and Mudge Series
Rylant, Cynthia	I Had Seen Castles
Rylant, Cynthia	Missing May
Rylant, Cynthia	The Relatives Came
Rylant, Cynthia	When I Was Young in the Mountains
Sabuda, Robert	Arthur and the Sword
Sabuda, Robert	The Christmas Alphabet
Sabuda, Robert	Cookie Count
Sabuda, Robert	The Twelve Days of Christmas: A Pop-up
Sabuda, Robert	The Wonderful Wizard of Oz: A Commemorative Pop-up
Sachar, Louis	Holes
Sachar, Louis	Sideways Stories from Wayside School
San Souci, Daniel	Cendrillon: A Caribbean Cinderella
San Souci, Robert D.	The Faithful Friend
San Souci, Robert D.	Short and Shivery: Thirty Chilling Tales
Sandved, Kjell	The Butterfly Alphabet
Saul, Carol P.	Barn Cat
Saul, Carol P.	The Farmer's Alphabet
Say, Allen	Grandfather's Journey
Schaefer, Lola	This Is the Sunflower
Schnur, Steven	Autumn: An Alphabet Acrostic
Schnur, Steven	Spring: An Alphabet Acrostic
Schroeder, Alan	Minty: A Story of Young Harriet Tubman
Schur, Maxine	Circlemaker
Schwartz, Alvin	And the Green Grass Grew All Around: Folk Poetry from Everyone
Schwartz, Alvin	Scary Stories to Tell in the Dark
Schwartz, David M.	G Is for Googol: A Math Alphabet Book

Author	Title
Scieszka, Jon	*The Frog Prince Continued*
Scieszka, Jon	*Squids Will Be Squids: Fresh Morals: Beastly Fables*
Scieszka, Jon	*The Stinky Cheeseman and Other Fairly Stupid Tales*
Scieszka, Jon	*The True Story of the Three Little Pigs by A. Wolf*
Scott, Sir Walter	*Ivanhoe*
Seibold, J. Otto	*Free Lunch*
Seibold, J. Otto	*Monkey Business*
Seibold, J. Otto	*Mr. Lunch Borrows a Canoe*
Seibold, J. Otto	*Mr. Lunch Takes a Plane Ride*
Seibold, J. Otto	*Penguin Dreams*
Sendak, Maurice	*Chicken Soup with Rice*
Sendak, Maurice	*In the Night Kitchen*
Sendak, Maurice	*The Nutshell Library*
Sendak, Maurice	*Outside Over There*
Sendak, Maurice	*Where the Wild Things Are*
Service, Pamela	*Stinker from Space*
Shahan, Sherry	*Frozen Stiff*
Shannon, David	*The Amazing Christmas Extravaganza*
Shannon, David	*No, David!*
Shannon, George	*Dance Away*
Sharmat, Majorie	*Nate the Great Series*
Shaw, Charles G.	*It Looked Like Spilt Milk*
Shaw, Nancy	*Sheep in a Jeep*
Shaw, Nancy	*The Sheep in a Shop*
Shaw, Nancy	Sheep on a Ship
Shelby, Anne	*Homeplace*
Shulevitz, Uri	*Dawn*
Shulevitz, Uri	*Snow*
Sidajakov, Nicolas	*Baboushka and the Three Kings*
Siegelson, Kim L.	*In the Time of the Drums*
Siebert, Diane	*Train Song*
Siegen-Smith, Nikki	*Songs for Survival: Songs and Chants from Tribal People Around the World*
Sierra, Judy	*Antarctic Antics*
Silberman, Henri	*Stone Bench in an Empty Park*
Silverstein, Shel	*A Light in the Attic*
Silverstein, Shel	*Where the Sidewalk Ends*
SimÛn, Silva	*Gathering the Sun: An Alphabet in Spanish and English*
Sìs, Peter	*Tibet: Through the Red Box*
Slate, Joseph	*The Secret Stars*
Slote, Alfred	*My Trip to Alpha I*
Small, David	*The Gardener*

Author	Title
Smith, Maggie	*Counting Our Way to Maine*
Sobol, Donald	*Encyclopedia Brown Series*
Soto, Gary	*Baseball in April*
Soto, Gary	*Chato and the Party Animals*
Soto, Gary	*Chato's Kitchen*
Soto, Gary	*Jesse*
Speare, Elizabeth	*The Witch of Blackbird Pond*
Spiegelman, Art	*Maus: A Survivor's Tale*
Spier, Peter	*Noah's Ark*
Spinelli, Jerry	*Knots in My Yo-Yo String*
Spinelli, Jerry	*Maniac Magee*
Spinelli, Jerry	*Wringer*
Spivak, Dawnine	*Grass Sandals: The Travels of Basho*
St. George, Judith	*So You Want to be President?*
Stanley, Diane	*Cleopatra*
Steig, William	*Abel's Island*
Steig, William	*CDB!*
Steig, William	*Pete's Pizza*
Steig, William	*Sylvester and the Magic Pebble*
Steptoe, John	*Mufaro's Beautiful Daughters: An African Tale*
Steptoe, John	*Stevie*
Steptoe, John	*The Story of Jumping Mouse*
Stevens, Janet	*From Pictures to Words: A Book about Making a Book*
Stevens, Janet	*The House that Jack Built*
Stevens, Janet	*Three Billy Goats Gruff*
Stevens, Janet	*Tops and Bottoms*
Stevens, Janet and Susan	*Cook-a-Doodle-Doo!*
Stevenson, Robert Louis	*A Child's Garden of Verses*
Stevenson, Robert Louis	*Treasure Island*
Stewart, Sarah	*The Gardener*
Stewart, Sarah	*The Library*
Stewig, John Warren	*The Fisherman and His Wife*
Stolley, Richard B.	*LIFE: Our Century in Pictures for Young People*
Stolz, Mary	*Storm in the Night*
Strasser, Todd	*Give a Boy a Gun*
Sutherland, Zena	*The Orchard Book of Nursery Rhymes*
Taback, Simms	*Joseph Had a Little Overcoat*
Taback, Simms	*There Was an Old Lady Who Swallowed a Fly*
Taylor, Maggie	*Pajamas*
Taylor, Mildred	*Roll of Thunder, Hear my Cry*
Taylor, Theodore	*The Cay*
Taylor, Theodore	*Timothy of the Cay*
Tejima, Keizaburo	*Fox's Dream*
Temko, Florence	*Origami Magic*

Author	Title
Terban, Marvin	*Guppies in Tuxedos*
Terban, Marvin	*Hey, Hay! A Wagonful of Funny Homonym Riddles*
Terban, Marvin	*In a Pickle and Other Funny Idioms*
Terban, Marvin	*Punching the Clock: Funny Action Idioms*
Terban, Marvin	*Scholastic Dictionary of Idioms*
Thayer, Ernest	*Casey at the Bat: A Ballad of the Republic Sung in the Year 1888*
Thomas, Joyce Carol	*Brown Honey and Broomwheat Tea*
Thomas, Joyce Carol	*You Are My Perfect Baby*
Thurber, James	*Many Moons*
Titus, Eve	*Anatole and the Cat*
Tolkien, J.R.R.	*The Lord of the Rings*
Tompert, Ann	*Grandfather Tang's Story*
Tompert, Ann	*Tangram Discovery Box*
Travers, Pamela	*Mary Poppins*
Treban, Marvin	*Too Hot to Hoot: Funny Palindrome Riddles*
Trosclair, Howard (editor)	*Cajun Night Before Christmas*
Tunnell, Michael O.	*Mailing May*
Turkle, Brinton	*Deep in the Forest*
Twain, Mark	*Tom Sawyer*
Uchida, Yoshiko	*The Dancing Kettle*
Udry, Janice May	*A Tree Is Nice*
Van Allsburg, Chris	*Bad Day at Riverbend*
Van Allsburg, Chris	*Jumanji*
Van Allsburg, Chris	*The Mysteries of Harris Burdick*
Van Allsburg, Chris	*The Polar Express*
Van Allsburg, Chris	*The Sweetest Fig*
Van Laan, Nancy	*The Big Fat Worm*
Van Laan, Nancy	*With a Whoop and a Holler: A Bushel of Lore from Way Down South*
Von Franz, Marie-Luise	*Archetypal Patterns in Fairy Tales*
Vonnegut, Kurt	*Sun Moon Star*
Vozar, David	*Yo, Hungry Wolf! A Nursery Rap*
Waber, Bernard	*Ira Sleeps Over*
Walpole, Horace	*The Castle of Otranto: A Gothic Story*
Walsh, Vivian	*Olive, the Other Reindeer*
Walter, Virginia	*Making Up Megaboy*
Ward, Cindy	*Cookie's Week*
Ward, Lynd	*The Biggest Bear*
Ward, Lynd	*The Silver Pony*
Watts, Bernadette	*Tattercoats*

Author	Title
Webb, Sophie	*My Season with Penguins: An Antarctic Journal*
Wells, Rosemary	*Dragon Shirt*
Wells, Rosemary	*Here Comes Mother Goose*
Wells, Rosemary	*Max's Breakfast*
Wells, Rosemary	*My Very First Mother Goose*
Whalen, Gloria	*Homeless Bird*
White, E. B.	*Charlotte's Web*
White, Ruth	*Belle Prater's Boy*
Whitman, Walt	*I Hear America Singing*
Wick, Walter	*A Drop of Water: A Book of Science and Wonder*
Wiesner, David	*Sector 7*
Wiesner, David	*Tuesday*
Wijngaard, Juan	*Sir Gawain and the Loathly Lady*
Wilder, Laura Ingalls	*Little House on the Prairie*
Wildsmith, Brian	*Mother Goose*
Wildsmith, Brian	*The Miller, the Boy and the Donkey*
Wilks, Mike	*The Ultimate Alphabet*
Willard, Nancy	*Pish Posh, Said Hieronymous Bosch*
Williams, Marcia	*The Adventures of Robin Hood*
Williams, Margery	*The Velveteen Rabbit*
Williams, Sherley Ann	*Working Cotton*
Williams, Suzanne	*Library Lil*
Williams, Vera B.	*"More More More" Said the Baby: 3 Love Stories*
Williams, Vera B.	*A Chair for My Mother*
Wilson, April	*April Wilson's Magpie Magic*
Wilson, Elizabeth	*Bibles and Bestiaries: A Guide to Illuminated Manuscripts*
Winick, Judd	*Pedro and Me: Friendship, Loss and What I Learned*
Winter, Jeanette	*My Name is Georgia: A Portrait*
Wisniewski, David	*Elfwyn's Saga*
Wisniewski, David	*Golem*
Wisniewski, David	*Rain Player*
Wisniewski, David	*Sundiate, Lion King of Mali*
Wisniewski, David	*The Wave of the Sea-World*
Withers, Carl	*A Rocket in My Pocket: The Rhymes and Chants of Young Americans*
Wolff, Ashley	*The Bells of London*
Wolff, Ashley	*A Year of Beasts*
Wolff, Ashley	*A Year of Birds*
Wolff, Virginia Euwer	*Bat 6*
Wood, Audrey	*Bright and Early Thursday Evening: A Tangled Tale*

Author	Title
Wood, Audrey	*Jubal's Wish*
Wood, Audrey	*The Napping House*
Worth, Valerie	*All the Small Poems and Fourteen More*
Wyeth, Sharon Dennis	*Always My Dad*
Yolen, Jane	*Ballad of the Pirate Queens*
Yolen, Jane	*The Devil's Arithmetic*
Yolen, Jane	*The Emperor and the Kite*
Yolen, Jane	*Owl Moon*
Yolen, Jane	*Sleeping Ugly*
Yolen, Jane	*Touch Magic: Fantasy, Faerie and Folklore in the Literature of Children*
Yolen, Jane	*Welcome to the Green House*
Yolen, Jane	*Welcome to the Ice House*
Yorinks, Arthur	*Hey, Al*
Young, Ed	*Lon Po Po*
Young, Ed	*Seven Blind Mice*
Young, Sue	*The Scholastic Rhyming Dictionary*
Zelinsky, Paul O.	*Rapunzel*
Zelinsky, Paul O.	*Rumpelstiltskin*
Zindel, Paul	*The Pigman*
Zolotow, Charlotte	*Mr. Rabbit and the Lovely Present*
Zolotow, Charlotte	*Say It!*

About the Authors

KATHY H. LATROBE is a professor in the School of Library and Information Studies at the University of Oklahoma where she has taught courses in library materials and services for young people since 1986. She has earned a B.A., English; an M.L.I.S.; and a Ph.D., Education. She has had over 20 years of teaching experience, including working with young people in classrooms and libraries in elementary, middle, and high schools. An active member of ALSC, YALSA, and AASL, Dr. Latrobe has served on the Newbery, the Carnegie, and the Margaret Edwards award committees as well as on the board of School Library Media Research Online.

CAROLYN S. BRODIE is associate professor in the Kent State University School of Library and Information Science. She teaches in the areas of library materials and services for children; library materials and services for young adults; and school library media centers and information sources and services for youth. She has co-directed the Virginia Hamilton Conference on Multicultural Literature for Youth with Dr. Anthony Manna since 1989. Dr. Brodie was the elected chair of the 2000 John Newbery Award Committee, and she served as a member of the 1995 John Newbery Award Committee. From 1996-1998 she served a two-year term on the Association for Library Service to Children's Notable Books Committee.

MAUREEN WHITE is an associate professor in the School Library and Information Program in the School of Education, University of Houston-Clear Lake, where she teaches children's and young adult literature. She earned her Ph.D. in library science from Texas Woman's University and was a school librarian in Texas for 16 years. Additionally, Dr. White has served on the 1996 Caldecott Award Committee, 1992 and 1998 Batchelder Award Committees, the 1998-2000 Pura

Belpré Award Committee, and 2001-2003 Notable Children's Books Committee. Children's books translated from other languages into English is her specific area of research.